Searching for Trust

Searching for Trust explores the intersection of trust, disinformation, and blockchain technology in an age of heightened institutional and epistemic mistrust. It adopts a unique archival theoretic lens to delve into how computational information processing has gradually supplanted traditional recordkeeping, putting at risk a centuries-old tradition of the "moral defense of the record" and replacing it with a dominant ethos of information-processing efficiency. The author argues that focusing on information-processing efficiency over the defense of records against manipulation and corruption (the ancient task of the recordkeeper) has contributed to a diminution of the trustworthiness of information and a rise of disinformation, with attendant destabilization of the epistemic trust fabric of societies. Readers are asked to consider the potential and the limitations of blockchains as the technological embodiment of the moral defense of the record and as a means of restoring societal trust in an age of disinformation.

VICTORIA L. LEMIEUX is Associate Professor of Archival Science at the University of British Columbia's School of Information and Founder of Blockchain@UBC, UBC's blockchain research and education cluster. Her research interests include risks to the availability of trustworthy records and how these risks impact cybersecurity, transparency, financial stability, public accountability, and human rights. The numerous awards for her contributions to the fields of archives, records management, and cybersecurity include the World Bank's Big Data Innovation Award in 2015, the 2020 Blockchain Ecosystem Leadership Award, and recognition as one of Canada's Top 20 Women in Cyber Security in 2020 by IT World.

Searching for Trust

Blockchain Technology in an Age of Disinformation

VICTORIA L. LEMIEUX
University of British Columbia

CAMBRIDGE
UNIVERSITY PRESS

CAMBRIDGE
UNIVERSITY PRESS

University Printing House, Cambridge CB2 8BS, United Kingdom

One Liberty Plaza, 20th Floor, New York, NY 10006, USA

477 Williamstown Road, Port Melbourne, VIC 3207, Australia

314–321, 3rd Floor, Plot 3, Splendor Forum, Jasola District Centre,
New Delhi – 110025, India

103 Penang Road, #05–06/07, Visioncrest Commercial, Singapore 238467

Cambridge University Press is part of the University of Cambridge.

It furthers the University's mission by disseminating knowledge in the pursuit of
education, learning, and research at the highest international levels of excellence.

www.cambridge.org
Information on this title: www.cambridge.org/9781108834872
DOI: 10.1017/9781108877350

First published 2022

A catalogue record for this publication is available from the British Library.

ISBN 978-1-108-83487-2 Hardback
ISBN 978-1-108-79244-8 Paperback

For Sasha

The theory of the future belongs to history
  —(Novalis (1772–1801), Notes for a Romantic
           Encyclopaedia)

Contents

Preface

The impetus for this book came about on May 15, 2015. I happened to be reading the news that morning as I bused into work. An article picked up from the Reuters newswire caught my eye: "Honduras to build land title registry using bitcoin technology" (Chavez-Dreyfuss, 2015). It was from that point that I fell down the rabbit hole of blockchain and distributed ledger technologies. What this article signalled to me was that blockchains were moving into the mainstream of recordkeeping. As an archival scientist – someone who studies the theory and application of recordkeeping and long-term preservation of records – this seemed like a development I should investigate further. And investigate it I did, publishing in early 2016 an article on the plans for the application of blockchain technology in Honduras (Lemieux, 2016c). Although I was skeptical about these plans, I also recognized the potential of blockchain technology to return something lost and for which many had been searching amidst the mass "datafication" of records in our current age of disinformation: epistemic trust. Blockchain's "immutability," or what recordkeepers might better recognize as intellectual and material "fixity," stands in opposition to the malleability and manipulability of information that is so often exploited in disinformation campaigns and cases of fraud.

Another impetus for writing this book arose from what I observe as the puzzling absence of archival knowledge among those involved in the design and operation of the blockchain and distributed ledger systems that purportedly seek to offer trustworthy records and recordkeeping. I have observed multidisciplinary conference after conference on blockchains and distributed ledgers call for input from computer scientists, engineers, economists, and social scientists, but not once has such a conference called for input from archival scientists. I can only surmise that this oversight is due to a lack of knowledge of archival science, perhaps understandable given the discipline's smaller scholarly "footprint" compared to these other disciplines. Thus, in this volume I aim to make an initial foray into contributing an archival perspective to the ongoing discourse on blockchain and distributed ledger technologies with an illustration of how an archival theoretic analysis of blockchain and distributed ledger systems can provide a useful lens when considering the design of such systems vis-à-vis the goal of achieving epistemic trust.

Though I began writing the book with this pragmatic and instrumental objective in mind, over the course of writing I came to see that a greater contribution from archival science to understanding blockchain and distributed ledger systems – or, rather, ecosystems – in an age of disinformation comes from the discipline's enduring presupposition that records of all types, includ-ing distributed ledgers, are deeply involved in the construction of our social worlds and, as such, offer a means to enter into and understand the life world of those responsible for records creation and keeping. From this archival vantage point, a study of blockchains and distributed ledgers – in which epistemic trust figures as a central problematic – can impart a view of our own life world in microcosm, from which we might learn something about the origins and possibilities for resolving the socio-epistemic challenges of our present times.

Given these goals, I have chosen to organize this volume into five parts. Part I comprises an introductory chapter that discusses what blockchain technology is and how the "immutability" of the distributed ledger takes shape through the interaction of social actors and technical components. Part II delves into the concept of trust, discussing the tight coupling that exists between epistemic trust and societal trust. Part III then moves on to how societal and epistemic mistrust is a defining feature of the age of disinformation. In Part IV, I focus on the topic of blockchain and distributed ledger systems as solutions to problems of epistemic mistrust. And, finally, in Part V, I explore the idea of blockchains and distributed ledgers as microcosms that provide windows into our own socio-epistemic challenges in an age of disinformation.

While primarily intended for philosophers and designers of blockchain and distributed ledger technologies who are unfamiliar with archival science theor-ies, principles, and practices, I also hope that this volume might offer archival theorists and professionals new insights as well. Specifically, I hope to provide a perspective on archival ideas that illustrates how they can inform thinking about novel blockchain and distributed ledger technologies. Very often the flow of ideas runs into archival science from other domains of discourse rather than the other way around. As I hope this volume will demonstrate, archival science can be as enriching of other domains as it is enriched by them.

For those studying the social and epistemic problems of disinformation, I hope that this volume serves to highlight the importance of a deeper exploration of records and recordkeeping systems, such as distributed ledgers, as sources of evidence supporting truth claims, as well as the potential value to be gained from using archival science theories, principles, and practices to interrogate how such sources come into existence, how they might be authenticated, protected, and preserved, and what they reveal about the challenges of our current times.

Acknowledgments

Writing a book is by and large a solitary endeavor, but it could not be done without others. I am, first, indebted to all those archival theorists whose ideas have informed the body of theory that I present, however imperfectly, in this volume, especially those involved in the InterPARES project, from whom I have drawn much inspiration over the years. I am also indebted to the many faculty, postdoctoral research fellows, and students who comprise the Blockchain@UBC community. The knowledge that we have cogenerated over the past several years has contributed to this volume in no small measure. In particular, I wish to express my sincere appreciation to University of British Columbia Adjunct Professor of Electrical and Computer Engineering Zehua Wang, postdoctoral research fellow Chang Lu, doctoral student Zac Zabawa, and, last but certainly not least, Marc-David Seidel, director of the University of British Columbia's W. Maurice Young Centre for Entrepreneurship & Venture Capital Research for each taking the time to provide valuable feedback on draft portions of this book. In addition, my thanks and appreciation go to Atefeh Mashatan, director of the Cybersecurity Research Lab at Ryerson University, Geoffrey Goodell, deputy executive director of the University College London Centre for Blockchain Technologies, and Julie McLeod, professor emerita of Records Management, Northumbria University, for reading and commenting on sections of the draft manuscript of this book. I must also express appreciation to Quinn Dupont, assistant professor at University College Dublin's School of Business, as well as James Lowry, assistant professor at the Graduate School of Library and Information Studies, Queens College, City University of New York, both of whom offered me invaluable opportunities to present and receive feedback on several core ideas from this volume as they were taking shape. I wish also to express appreciation to Primavera De Filippi for inviting me to participate in her discussion group on blockchains and trust; the insights gained from these discussions very much helped crystallize my own thinking. In all cases where I have received assistance and inspiration from others, my ideas (and any failings of those ideas) remain my own. To my erstwhile student, now editorial assistant, Jennette Chalcraft, I would like to express my thanks for many hours of work on this project and, perhaps more importantly, for holding me accountable to deliver chapters for review according to an agreed time frame. I am quite certain that without her professionalism this book would never have been completed. I also wish to thank my Cambridge University Press editor, Lauren Cowles, for her patience and the Cambridge University Press editorial team for their editorial assistance. My thanks also go to dear friends and family who encouraged me throughout the development of this book, especially my long-time friend, Lynn Coleman. Last but certainly not least, I wish to thank my daughter Sasha, who has, from time to time, had to endure my absence in body and mind as I worked on the writing of this book.

PART I

Introduction

1

What Good Is Blockchain?

The phone rang in my office. It was late summer 2017. I answered and was greeted on the other end of the line by the voice of one my colleagues in the Computer Science Department asking, "Is blockchain really a *thing*?" I have been asked this question any number of times since then, though each time it takes a slightly different form. James Mickens, a Harvard computer scientist, produced a video in 2018 entitled *Blockchains Are a Bad Idea* that is a variation on the same theme. In the video, Mickens points out that many of the features of blockchains can be provided by existing technologies. To many, blockchain technology seemingly offers nothing new, since, by and large, it presents an assemblage of preexisting theories, algorithms, and mathematics, as I will discuss in Section 1.3, and a computationally inefficient one at that (see, e.g., Truby, 2018; Li et al., 2019)![1]

Observed from a purely computational or technical (in the sense of information and communications technology) perspective, it is not easy to see what all the fuss is about when it comes to blockchains, nor why there should be such interest in them. As Mickens argues in his video, blockchain systems, such as Bitcoin, have features and capabilities that can be provided by existing systems: tamper resistance can be provided by digital signatures (discussed in

---

[1] Bitcoin mining consumes an enormous amount of electricity. According to the Bitcoin Energy Consumption Index (see, e.g., Digiconomist, 2021), a single Bitcoin transaction consumes the equivalent of the carbon footprint of 664,375 Visa transactions (299.76 $kgCO_2$) and the same amount of power as the average United States household usage over 21.63 days (631.08 kWh). De Vries (2018, p. 801) states that "The Bitcoin network can be estimated to consume at least 2.55 gigawatts of electricity currently, and potentially 7.67 gigawatts in the future," making it comparable with countries such as Ireland (3.1 gigawatts) and Austria (8.2 gigawatts) in energy consumption based on 2018 data. On this point, see also Das and Dutta (2020). Owing to the amount of energy needed to mine Bitcoin and cool the mining equipment, miners tend to gravitate their operations to places where they can obtain electricity relatively cheaply and where it is easier to keep their equipment cool (Bjarnason, 2019; Baydakova, 2021). Unscrupulous miners have also been known to steal the electricity they need (Nadeau, 2020).

3

Section 1.3) with or without blockchain, as can the ability to prove a claim or to achieve non-repudiability of a transaction (ISO, 2018a, s. 3.48); message ordering can be achieved through the use of hash pointing (discussed in Section 1.3) without resorting to blockchain; and highly available storage needs can be handled by commercial cloud storage (Mickens, 2018). Yet, as an archival scientist – someone who studies the theory of recordkeeping and the long-term preservation of authentic records – blockchain makes sense to me. Even if I doubt some of the claims I hear about it, I see it as a response to a perceived erosion of society's "fact infrastructure" in an age of disinformation and disorders of social trust. It is this perspective on blockchain technology that I will explore in this volume.

1.1 Blockchain Is Meaningless

My colleague's question about blockchain came, not unreasonably, at the peak of what has been described as the blockchain "initial coin offering hype cycle," which was ramping up to its late 2017, early 2018 crescendo. At the time, many were touting blockchain (and their own initial coin offerings, the cryptocurrency community's equivalent to initial public offerings) as a solution to all the world's problems. To illustrate the zeitgeist of the time, technology writer Alex Hern (2016) wrote a (tongue-in-cheek) piece for *The Guardian* in 2016 entitled, "Blockchain: The Answer to Life, the Universe and Everything?" that appropriately began with the sentence, "Have you heard the good news? The blockchain is here – and it's going to save everything."

Don and Alex Tapscott's 2016 book, *Blockchain Revolution: How the Technology Behind Bitcoin is Changing Money, Business, and the World*, set out a vision of how blockchain could be used to transform and change the world for the better by tracking the provenance of digital and real-world assets, banking the unbanked, and unleashing new businesses. Given the lack of real-world evidence at the time, many were (and remain) skeptical, as outlined in, for example, David Gerard's critical 2015 book *Attack of the 50 Foot Blockchain: Bitcoin, Blockchain, Ethereum & Smart Contracts*. At the same time, few really understood what the term blockchain meant. Adrianne Jeffries (2018), writing for *The Verge* in early 2018, described a blockchain Tower of Babel in which everyone was speaking their own incomprehensible blockchain language, concluding that "'Blockchain' is meaningless."

How is it that blockchains are meaningless to some, while others see their potential to transform the world? The old parable of the blind men and the elephant suggests an explanation. In this story, a group of men come across a creature they have never seen before: an elephant. Each man grabs hold of a different part of the elephant and describes it based on their own limited perception and experience. None of the men has the knowledge needed to understand the parts holistically to determine that what they are encountering is an elephant. Our attempts to make sense of blockchains are analogous when we try to provide an explanation of them without taking a holistic view.

It is for this reason that I argue we need to approach understanding blockchains not from a singular disciplinary perspective but holistically. In this volume, I will draw upon Lemieux and Feng's (2021) multidisciplinary "three-layer" model, which conceives of blockchains and distributed ledgers as *socio-informational-technical systems*. The model was "born of the need to develop an appropriate framework for the problem-centered design of blockchains, in which the problems are themselves 'wicked,' multidimensional, and multidisciplinary" (Palmer et al., 2021, pp. 591–592). It is well known that "systems designed from a single point of view have often proved to have 'blind' spots which can render them ineffective, or even dangerous. With this in mind, we aimed to design a framework which encourages holistic problem analysis and affords a common language, underpinned by a reasonably shared ontology and epistemic worldview" (Palmer et al., 2021, p. 592).

The original model was simplistic, recognizing that blockchains had social, informational (or more accurately, as I will discuss in Chapter 6, evidential), and technical dimensions. In 2019, a diverse group of blockchain scholars came together to discuss the original three-layer model, especially the interactions among the three layers. With further theoretical refinements arising from these discussions, the most recent version of the model represents blockchains as complex, dynamic systems with four interrelated sub-systems – the original three layers (the social, the informational, and the technical) and a governance sub-system – which work together to achieve trust among social actors (Lemieux and Feng, 2021).

The technical sub-system is reasonably well understood, even as there remain novel technical challenges to be overcome, being those technical components that implement blockchain and distributed ledger systems. The social sub-system – which encompasses social, political, and economic implications of these tools and platforms – though arguably less well understood, has at least been recognized as an important aspect of blockchain systems. Indeed, common use of the term blockchain "ecosystem," rather than "system," draws attention to the fact that blockchains comprise communities that are often "contentious and non-homogeneous, in which unpredictable agents can disrupt the planned flow of ecosystem participation" and in which, therefore, governance is needed (Palmer et al., 2021, p. 591). The final sub-system, the informational, focuses on the ledger itself. Paradoxically, given that a defining feature of blockchain technology is the production of an "immutable" distributed ledger that features heavily in "archival imaginaries" (Woodall and Ringel, 2020) that posit blockchain and distributed ledger technology as a cure-all for our current epistemic ailments, it is this aspect of the technology that has received the least scholarly and research attention.

Scholars who have addressed the question of the immutability of blockchain and distributed ledgers have noted that "'immutability' of blockchain records is a matter of debate, as high-profile events in the blockchain space have shown that blockchain records are changeable at will by the people who govern the blockchain system, and it currently is unclear which variations of blockchain technology actually create a record that even approaches immutability" (Walch, 2017b, p. 1). This observation highlights an important insight that is only possible from a holistic vantage point on blockchain and distributed ledger technologies – one that takes into consideration the social, informational (or evidential), and technical dimensions of the technology in equal measure. From this vantage point, blockchain immutability is best viewed not as a property of blockchain-based ledgers but as a sustained commitment that a group of individuals holds onto because they believe that the attribute is desirable, even necessary. In the remainder of this chapter, I will explore this idea more deeply.

1.2 The Social Construction of Meaning

Recognizing that it would be difficult to advance scientific discussions about blockchain technology without a stable definition of the term, in 2017, global blockchain experts became involved in an international project to develop a standard blockchain and distributed ledger vocabulary under the auspices of the International Organization for Standardization (ISO) Technical Committee on Blockchain and Distributed Ledger Technologies (TC307). This work, which involved the input of over 300 international experts from 50 countries over the span of almost three years, resulted in what has become the first ISO standard on blockchain and distributed ledger technologies, ISO 22739:2020 *Blockchain and Distributed Ledger Technologies – Vocabulary* (ISO, 2020a; Oclarino, 2020). The working group that developed the vocabulary converged on a set of interlocking definitions that capture a shared understanding of what a blockchain is and, equally importantly, what it is not.

After many months of deliberation, the ISO experts arrived at a definition of blockchain as a "distributed ledger with confirmed blocks organized in an append-only sequential chain using cryptographic links" (ISO, 2020a, s. 3.6), with a distributed ledger being defined as a "ledger that is shared across a set of [distributed ledger technology (DLT)] nodes and synchronized between the DLT nodes using a consensus mechanism" (ISO, 2020a, s. 3.22). Thus, in this volume, when I use the term distributed ledger, it encompasses the concept of a blockchain because blockchains are a type of distributed ledger. The ISO defined a ledger as an "information store that keeps records that are intended to be final, definitive and immutable" (ISO, 2020a, s. 3.43).

The idea that blockchains are a type of distributed ledger was not an uncontroversial position among ISO experts, since some held the view that the unique features of the blockchain's chained block data structure and consensus mechanism made blockchains categorically different from distributed ledgers. Despite the consensus reached by the ISO community about the meaning of blockchain, it remains true, as I have previously observed, that "different epistemic communities have formed their own ideas about what blockchain is, some with very strong political and social views around open source, sharing, and autonomy" (as quoted in Jeffries, 2018). It also remains true that legal definitions of blockchain technology continue to proliferate (see, e.g., Walch, 2017a, 2017b). As a result, it is doubtful that everyone will accept and adopt the ISO definitions. Nevertheless, these definitions can at least provide a stable foundation for discussion of blockchain and distributed ledgers for the purposes of this volume, even if they do not end the debate about the meaning of blockchain and related concepts.

It is significant that the ISO experts did not define blockchains strictly in terms of technical components, such as the networked databases that communicate and interact with one another over a network in order to implement a blockchain. ISO 22739 instead refers to these technical components as instantiating blockchain or distributed ledger technology *systems* (ISO, 2020a, s. 3.33). To attempt to understand blockchain purely in terms of the computational technologies, experts understood, is to miss the mark by focusing on the wrong abstraction layer, to use a concept from computing. In software engineering and computing, abstraction involves thinking about and representing a thing, for example, a system, at different levels of granularity or detail. Abstractions, like models, are representations that help simplify a complex world and focus the mind on important details (Butterfield et al., 2016).

In contrast to focusing on the technical system view in its definition of the term blockchain, ISO TC307 chose to focus on a *higher* level of abstraction. In ISO 22739, by recognizing blockchains as a distributed type of ledger, ISO experts connected blockchain with a long tradition of *recordkeeping*. This, in turn, connects blockchains to the theories, principles, and methods of *archival science*[2], which is the science underpinning recordkeeping. Archival science, as Thomassen (2015, p. 84) explains,

> is an academic and applied discipline that involves the scientific study of process bound information, both as product and as agent of human thoughts, emotions, and activities, in its various contexts. Its field of study encompasses personal documents, records, and archives of communities, government agencies, and other formal organizations, and archival materials in general, whether kept by archival institutions, units, or programs. It covers both the records themselves and their contexts of creation, management, and use, and their sociocultural context. Its central questions are why, how, and under what circumstances human beings create, keep, change, preserve, or destroy records, and what meanings they may individually or jointly attribute to records and to their recordkeeping and archival operations.

Thomassen (2015, p. 85) goes on to explain that archival science focuses on more than just records or archival documents to think about records or archival documents *in context*, that is, "the context of the data within a record and the contexts of creation, management, and use, as well as the socio-political, cultural, and economic contexts underlying these contexts." Although it has existed for centuries as a practical field, archival science as an academic discipline is considered relatively new, even if it has disciplinary forerunners that extend back centuries (Duranti, 1989; Thomassen, 2015). The more practical orientation of most archivists and the relative newness of contemporary archival science might account in large part for the comparative absence of archivists and archival science from discourse on blockchains.

Why should it be so important to recognize blockchains as recordkeeping systems and connect them to archival concepts? For one thing, defining blockchains in this way makes it possible to treat them as a single category. No matter how many different types of blockchains and distributed ledgers there are now in the world, or there might be in the future, they all will have one thing in common – a ledger.

Another reason is that recordkeeping and archival theories, principles, methods, practices, and professionals have been long associated with the preservation of "information created or received and maintained as evidence and as an asset by an organization in pursuit of legal obligations or in the course

---

[2] The "archive" and archives and recordkeeping research has received a great deal of attention within the academy in the past two decades. This research encompasses a diverse range of disciplinary perspectives on the "archive" and the study of archives and archivists. Such studies can be distinguished from archival science, which has its own discipline and its own unique body of theory and practices. At the same time, the cognate field of archival studies encompasses a "multiverse" of perspectives, including those from archival science and archival studies (on this point, see Duranti and Michetti, 2016; Gilliland et al., 2016).

of conducting business," that is, with records (ISO, 2020b, s.3.2.10). Evidence is here not limited to the legal sense of the term but rather is "information that could be used either by itself or in conjunction with other information, to establish *proof about an event or action* [emphasis added]" (ISO, 2020b, s. 3.2.6). In order to offer proof of an event or action, evidence must be shown to be inviolate and complete (ISO, 2020b, s. 3.26). Thus records, in order to offer evidence, must, among other things, possess the characteristics of authenticity (actually be what they purport to be),[3] reliability (complete, accurate, and able to stand for the events or actions they represent),[4] and integrity (complete and unaltered) (ISO, 2016, s. 5.2.2). It follows, then, that if we want to design blockchain and distributed ledger systems capable of creating, capturing, and preserving sources of evidence, then recordkeeping and archival theories, principles, methods, practices, and professionals offer knowledge and experience that can provide valuable guidance.

It is the promise – if not yet the reality – of being capable of producing inviolate and complete evidence – or, as expressed in the definition of a ledger in the international standard on blockchain and distributed ledger vocabulary, of being designed to produce final, definitive, and immutable records (ISO, 2020a, s. 3.43) – that sets blockchains (and other distributed ledgers) apart from other types of information systems, such as the commonly used transaction processing systems, management information systems, or office automation systems.

Indeed, in a datafied world, the capability of producing and preserving immutable evidence, as blockchains are designed to do, is a rare one. As paper records and recordkeeping have gradually fallen away to be replaced by digital records and recordkeeping, greater value has been placed on ensuring that the information created by an organization in the conduct of its business can be reassembled into new information assets that might be mined to advance organizational strategy, more often than not profit-driven, or sold to other organizations for similar purposes. As the now well-worn expression goes, "data is the new oil."[5] New business models have arisen based upon exploiting

---

[3] ISO 30300: 2020, s. 3.2.2, which reads in full "quality of a record (3.2.10) that can be proven to be what it purports to be, to have been created or sent by the agent (3.1.3) purported to have created or sent it, and to have been created or sent when purported" (ISO, 2020a).

[4] ISO 15489:2016, s. 5.2.2 describes reliable records as ones "whose contents can be trusted as a full and accurate representation of the transactions, activities or facts to which they attest" and "which can be depended upon in the course of subsequent transactions or activities." The standard goes on to note that reliable records are usually created "at the time of the event to which they relate, or by systems routinely used to conduct the transactions" (ISO, 2016). In other texts, this notion is similarly captured in the phrase "made in the usual and ordinary course of business."

[5] Clive Humby is attributed with coining the phrase "data is the new oil," but the phrase came into popular usage following a 2017 article in the *Economist* (Economist, 2017).

information as assets. To enable these new business models, what once would have been created as records in fixed form is now created and kept in a malleable and manipulable form. Datafication and the creation and storage of vast troves of information have given rise to the so-called era of Big Data and an entirely new field of endeavor – data science, the art of data manipulation and exploitation. While the ability to manipulate records by transforming them into novel forms of data has led to great innovation and scientific advances, it has also undermined the basis of societal proof about past events and actions and, in so doing, contributed to the emergence of an age of disinformation (a topic that will be discussed more fully in Chapter 4). Blockchain, a unique type of ledger, promises to restore society's evidence base. To understand how and, more importantly, why, it is helpful to reflect upon the genesis of blockchain technology.

1.3 Genesis of Blockchain

The blockchain origin story, like all good origin stories, remains somewhat shrouded in mystery. In October 2008, Satoshi Nakamoto – a pseudonym for a person or persons unknown to the present day[6] – proposed a combined digital asset, bitcoin (I will use "bitcoin" with a lower case "b" whenever I am referring to bitcoin the cryptocurrency and with an upper case "B" whenever I am referring to Bitcoin the network), and peer-to-peer payment system (the Bitcoin blockchain network) in a modest nine-page paper entitled "Bitcoin: A Peer-to-Peer Electronic Cash System" (Nakamoto, 2008a). Against the backdrop of a global financial crisis, the genesis block of the Bitcoin network was mined on January 3, 2009 and the first block thereafter was created on January 8, 2009.[7] Nakamoto (2009b) announced the release of the Bitcoin protocol software as open source the day after the first block was mined.

---

[6] Many theories exist about the real identity of Satoshi Nakamoto (see, e.g., O'Neal, 2019). Some argue that Nakamoto is the American computer scientist, legal scholar, and inventor of the concept of smart contracts Nick Szabo; others that Nakamoto was the late Hal Finney, a cypherpunk and one of the early contributors to Bitcoin's codebase; and still others posit that Nakamoto is British cryptographer Adam Back, CEO of Blockstream. Yet another possibility is Craig Wright – who has actually claimed to be Satoshi Nakamoto – an Anglo-Australian computer scientist and businessman. Rather interestingly, Wright was granted the United States copyright registrations for the original Bitcoin whitepaper and code, which he still holds (Bitcoin SV, 2019).

[7] The original block hash at Block 0 is 000000000019d6689c085ae165831e934f-f763ae46a2a6c172b3f1b60a8ce26f and the hash of Block 1 is 00000000b873e79784647a6c82962c70d228557d24a747ea4d1b8bbe878e1206. As Bitcoin is a shared and transparent ledger, readers can see this for themselves at www.blockchain.com/btc/block/000.

In this paper, the pseudonymous Nakamoto described the problem that Bitcoin was designed to solve as being one of *trust*:

> Commerce on the Internet has come to rely almost exclusively on financial institutions serving as trusted third parties to process electronic payments. While the system works well enough for most transactions, it still suffers from the inherent weaknesses of the trust based model. Completely non-reversible transactions are not really possible, since financial institutions cannot avoid mediating disputes. The cost of mediation increases transaction costs, limiting the minimum practical transaction size and cutting off the possibility for small casual transactions, and there is a broader cost in the loss of ability to make non-reversible payments for non-reversible services. With the possibility of reversal, the need for trust spreads. Merchants must be wary of their customers, hassling them for more information than they would otherwise need. A certain percentage of fraud is accepted as unavoidable. These costs and payment uncertainties can be avoided in person by using physical currency, but no mechanism exists to make payments over a communications channel without a trusted party.
>
> *(Nakamoto, 2008a, p. 1)*

Bitcoin solved the problem of trust by introducing a mechanism for making financial transactions computationally impractical to reverse, that is, by solving "the double spending problem," which is discussed further below. It achieved this by "using a peer-to-peer distributed timestamp server to generate computational proof of the chronological order of transactions" – the blockchain – which would be secure "as long as honest nodes collectively control more CPU power than any cooperating group of attacker nodes" (Nakamoto, 2008a, p.1). As such, the blockchain to which Bitcoin gave birth relied on the capabilities of two fundamental technological primitives: cryptography and distributed systems.

Cryptography is a centuries old "discipline that embodies the principles, means, and methods for the transformation of data in order to hide their semantic content, prevent their unauthorized use, or prevent their undetected modification" (ISO, 2020a, s. 3.17).[8] Public-key cryptography, upon which Bitcoin relies, is a type of cryptography in which there is a public key – that, just as the name implies, is made public – and a corresponding private key that must always be kept secret. For encryption, the public key is used for encryption and the private key for decryption; for digital signatures, the keys' roles are reversed (ISO, 2020a, s. 3.62 and 3.65). A digital signature, which relies upon public-key cryptography, is data that when appended to a digital object, such as a document, allows someone to verify its authenticity and integrity. (ISO,

---

[8] On the history of cryptography, see Dooley (2018).

2020a, s. 3.21). In the Nakamoto paper, bitcoin – the cryptocurrency – was described as a chain of digital signatures (Nakamoto, 2008a, p. 2).

All this might have been quite ordinary, save for the fact that most digital signature schemes rely upon a third-party trust anchor – a certificate authority (CA) – which issues digital certificates to certify who owns a public key. This allows trusting parties to rely upon signatures or on assertions made about the private key that corresponds to the certified public key. In Bitcoin, on the other hand, public and private key pairs are created without reliance upon an external CA (Narayanan et al., 2016).[9] As a result, reliance upon traditional CAs to generate key pairs is not necessary with blockchain technology, which may even be a defense against malevolent CAs.

The use of digital signatures is an important aspect of how the Bitcoin network works. To prevent forgery of digitally signed content, an input message is converted into a hash, which is comprised of a 256-bit string, produced when a hash function algorithm is applied to an input message. The input message can be of any size. For example, in theory you could take the entirety of the Bodleian Library or the Library of Congress, if they were completely digitized, and reduce them to a 256-bit hash. For each bitcoin transaction, the hash consists of a hash value of the concatenation of the following fields: version number, transaction inputs, transaction outputs, and lock time. To improve Bitcoin's robustness, an update of the Bitcoin protocol called SegWit was introduced on August 24, 2017, in block number 481824. It includes another two fields called flag and witnesses (see Chapter 8 for more on the SegWit update). Once the input message is hashed, it is nearly impossible to regenerate it from the hash output. In other words, you cannot reverse the hash function to reproduce the Bodleian Library, the Library of Congress, or a bitcoin transaction from its hash, or at least it is currently considered computationally impossible to do so. Hashing, therefore, is a one-way function, not a two-way function as in the case of encryption (and its counterpart, decryption).

The fact that it is not easy to guess or reproduce the content of the original input message from its hash is helpful for maintaining integrity because the hash helps detect any changes to the input message. A change in the input message will produce a different hash output, signalling that the original message could have been tampered with.

As Nakamoto notes in his paper, however, digitally signing transactions alone would not prevent someone from double spending a coin or transferring

---

[9] Bitcoin uses the Elliptic Curve Digital Signature Algorithm to do this (see Narayanan et al., 2016, pp. 17–19).

it a second time. To solve this problem without relying on a trusted third party, additional features need to be designed into the system. Bitcoin achieved this through establishing a *transparent ledger* visible to all participants on the network: "transactions must be publicly announced" with "a system for participants to agree on a single history of the order in which they were received" (Nakamoto, 2008a, p. 2).

The process of establishing a shared ledger begins with each participant on the Bitcoin distributed network digitally signing transactions that propagate to other participants across the network in a "gossip-like way" (Narayanan et al., 2016; Greenspan, 2017). The Bitcoin network, a network of indeterminate size (Narayanan et al., 2016, p. 69),[10] runs on the Transmission Control Protocol (TCP) network protocol and has a random topology, meaning that each participating node communicates randomly with other participating nodes. There is no hierarchy among the participating nodes; each one can come and go as it pleases from the network without any permission (Narayanan et al., 2016, p. 66). This is why Bitcoin is called a "permissionless" distributed ledger. Each participant verifies that every new transaction it receives complies with Bitcoin's rules, and checks and validates the transaction, including checking for any conflicts with previous transactions (Narayanan et al., 2016).[11] Once a transaction is verified, it enters the participant's list of provisional unconfirmed transactions (the "memory pool") and is forwarded on to other participants on the network. Transactions that fail verification enter the participant's "orphan pool.".

At this point, provisional unconfirmed transactions still need to be confirmed. Confirmation begins when the "Merkle root" of a tree of hashes of provisional sets of unconfirmed transactions are grouped together into blocks (see Figure 1.1). Each block is limited to a megabyte, or about 1 million bytes, in size. If each transaction is about 250 bytes, then each block can hold a maximum of about 4,000 transactions (Narayanan et al., 2016, p. 72). However, as transaction sizes can vary significantly, this can only be considered a very rough estimate. Each block also has a header that includes, among other data, a hash of the block transaction data (i.e., the Merkle root, or a hash of all previous transaction hashes of the transactions to be incorporated into a specific block, as shown in Figure 1.1), a timestamp, and a hash link to

---

[10] Narayanan et al. (2016, p. 69) note that "it is difficult to measure how big the [Bitcoin] network is, since it is dynamic and has no central authority."

[11] Narayanan et al. (2016, p. 68) explain that "Nodes run the script for each previous output being redeemed and ensure that the scripts return true. Second, they check that the outputs being redeemed haven't already been spent. Third, they won't relay an already-seen transaction … Fourth, by default, nodes only accept and relay standard scripts based on a small whitelist of scripts."

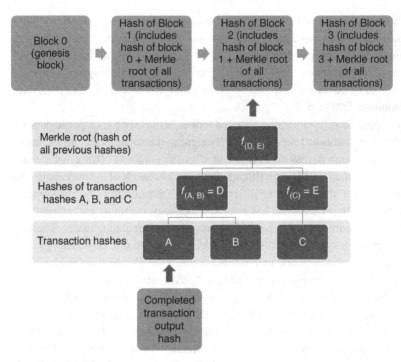

Figure 1.1 Bitcoin as a chain of hashes

the block that precedes it in order to create an append-only, sequential chain that forms a blockchain (Nakamoto, 2008a, p. 2). This assures that the correct order of transactions is recorded in the ledger and cannot be altered without detection.

To create a transparent and shared ledger on which all participants can agree without resorting to reliance upon a third-party arbiter of the truth requires another novel feature of the Bitcoin network: a mechanism for achieving consensus among network participants on the validity of blocks. To achieve consensus, Bitcoin network participants can choose to work on solving a computational puzzle called Proof-of-Work (PoW) that generates a block hash output that is below a certain difficulty target, typically represented as a hash beginning with the correct number of zeros (19 at the time of writing) when added to a nonce (a random or pseudo-random number) (Nakamoto, 2008a, p. 3; Narayanan et al., 2016, pp. 64–66). Puzzle solvers, called miners, must use central processing unit (CPU) power to find the unknown value. It is computationally very hard to solve the puzzle, so miners are rewarded for their effort with a certain number of new coins (the block reward) in order to incentivize them to expend costly CPU power to maintain the network. Block rewards also help to keep miners honest, on the assumption that it is more profitable for them to expend CPU energy on honestly maintaining the network than subverting the source of their income generation and the basis of their wealth (Nakamoto, 2008a, p. 4).

Mined blocks are then propagated out to other participants across the network. The client software that each participant runs is programmed to validate the blocks it receives first. Once validation is complete, participants update their copies of the ledger, at which time the transactions within the new block are considered confirmed by that participant (Narayanan et al., 2016, p. 68).[12] Once confirmed, any transactions in the participant's memory pool or orphan pool that conflict with those in the new block are then discarded. The confirmation process continues until each participant in the network has completed it. As ideally configured, each network participant is under separate control and independently confirms the validity of blocks. This approach to creating a transparent and shared ledger on which all participants can agree has come to be known as "Nakamoto consensus" (ISO, 2021).

Nakamoto consensus solved a well-known and long-standing problem in distributed computing: the "Byzantine Generals problem." This is a problem that was first theorized by the mathematicians Leslie Lamport, Robert Shostak, and Marshall Pease. In their paper (Lamport et al., 1982), they explain the problem of achieving consensus among peers in an open distributed network when it is unknown which peers might be trusted. To illustrate the problem, they used the metaphor of Byzantine generals on the verge of attacking an enemy city during a siege. The generals are located in different areas surrounding the city and can only communicate via messengers in order to coordinate their attack. However, it is highly probable, or even certain, that there are traitors among the messengers or that the messages of honest messengers have been corrupted. The problem, therefore, lies in the ability to effectively coordinate an attack when it is unknown if messages or messengers have been interfered with. Nakamoto's consensus mechanism solves the problem for Bitcoin by requiring participants to rely upon and add only to the longest chain. Chains containing confirmed updates always grow the fastest and are the longest, since participants producing these updates have solved the PoW puzzle first (Finney, 2008). This helps protect the integrity of the network since,

---

[12] Narayanan et al. (2016, p. 68) explain, "Validating a block is more complex than validating transactions. In addition to validating the header and making sure that the hash value is in the acceptable range, nodes must validate every transaction included in the block. Finally a node will forward a block only if it builds on the longest branch, based on its perspective of what the blockchain ... looks like."

as explained by Nakamoto, "If a majority of CPU power is controlled by honest nodes, the honest chain will grow the fastest and outpace any competing chains. To modify a past block, an attacker would have to *redo the proof-of-work of the block and all blocks after it and then catch up with and surpass the work of the honest nodes* [emphasis added]" (Nakamoto, 2008a, p. 3). In this way, the Bitcoin network remains trustworthy even if some network participants send incorrect or harmful information.

1.4 Bitcoin Antecedents

Bitcoin's assemblage of cryptography, distributed networking, transparent ledger, and Nakamoto consensus to incentivize honesty in network participants (i.e., to achieve "trustless trust" [Werbach, 2019], or trust without a central intermediary) was, and remains, novel. It did, however, create a challenge relating to privacy and tracking. To explain, in traditional cash-based systems, ledgers keep track of transactions in third-party recordkeeping systems. For example, when we purchase a cup of coffee with cash, no one asks for our signature, digital or otherwise, though the vendor or their representative (e.g., a cashier) may record the transaction using a cash register and generate a receipt for it. After our purchase, the transaction cannot easily be traced back to us. When we pay with a bank card, on the other hand, we are often required to digitally sign for the transaction by typing in a PIN. In this case, the transactions are easily tracked, are recorded by our bank or third-party payment processor, and can be traced back to us. As a result, we give away a great amount of personal information about our spending habits. Bitcoin, which was designed to cut out these third-party middlemen, aims at affording the digital world the same privacy that comes with using traditional, non-digital cash.

To do this, bitcoin keeps public keys pseudonymous;[13] that is, transacting parties are only identified by their bitcoin address, not by name, and may change their address for each successive transaction (indeed, this is considered good practice), so that it is difficult to link the address to a specific individual. It is in this sense that bitcoin manages to combine the seemingly oppositional

---

[13] The Nakamoto (2008a, p. 6) paper actually uses the word anonymous; however, even that paper acknowledges that the method is not completely anonymizing, observing, "Some linking is still unavoidable with multi-input transactions, which necessarily reveal that their inputs were owned by the same owner. The risk is that if the owner of a key is revealed, linking could reveal other transactions that belonged to the same owner." An array of techniques has emerged, aimed at obfuscating the origins of cryptocurrency transactions (cryptocurrency tumblers) and has even given rise to entirely new privacy-preserving blockchains (e.g., Monero). For a further discussion of this, see chapter 6, "Bitcoin and Anonymity," in Narayanan et al. (2016).

properties of transparency and privacy. Note, however, that privacy in the context of bitcoin relates to the identity of individuals originating bitcoin transactions and not to the records of those transactions captured on the blockchain (i.e., ledger records). These remain open for all to see, including any data embedded into those transactions unless the embedded data are purposefully encrypted to preserve confidentiality.

The pseudonymity of bitcoin transactions has the advantage of protecting individuals' financial privacy. At the same time, it can shield from detection those who are using bitcoin for nefarious purposes. This has made the bitcoin cryptocurrency popular with hackers, money launderers, and tax evaders and given bitcoin some of its bad reputation. Proponents of bitcoin argue that traditional "hard" cash can be used for the same purposes, yet there's no denying that the digital nature of bitcoin makes it an attractive form of currency for hackers. New methods of tracking and tracing bitcoin transactions, and of identifying their originators, have emerged. These methods have also been countered by new privacy-preserving techniques adopted for use by alternative cryptocurrencies (e.g., Monero)[14] or cryptocurrency services (e.g., "mixers" or "tumblers" such as the Wasabi wallet).[15]

Although it may seem as though bitcoin sprang "full grown from the head of Zeus," this was not the case. As Clark (2016, p. ix) writes, there was actually a "long road to Bitcoin." One of the first steps along the road, according to Clark, was a company called CyberCash that implemented a protocol called SET, designed to avoid the need for e-commerce customers to send their payment details to merchants or enrol with an intermediary payment processor. Unfortunately, CyberCash did not survive, largely due to user experience problems (Clark, 2016, p. xiii). Another antecedent to bitcoin came from David Chaum's DigiCash company, which was based upon his proposal for e-cash involving cryptographic "blind signatures" aimed at preventing people from spending units of digital currency twice (the "double spending" problem) (Clark, 2016, pp. xiv–xv). Clark argues that the patents Chaum took out on his invention spurred others to invent their own open-source version of e-cash, for example, MagicMoney and Lucre (Clark, 2016, p. xvii).

"Netcash" was the first to propose the idea of minting digital cash through solving a cryptographic puzzle, leveraging cryptographic hash functions similar to the idea of Bitcoin's mining. The idea was first proposed in 1992 by cryptographers Cynthia Dwark and Moni Naor as a potential way to reduce email spam, and a similar idea was discovered independently, according to Clark, by Adam Back in 1997, which Back called Hashcash (Nakamoto

[14] See www.getmonero.org. [15] See https://wasabiwallet.io.

[2008a, p. 3] references Back in his Bitcoin paper). In 1991, Stuart Haber and Scott Stornetta proposed, for the first time, the idea for secure timestamping of documents in which clients send documents to a timestamping service and the service signs the document together with a timestamp and a hashpointer to the previous document (Clark, 2016, pp. xx–xxi). B-money and Bitgold (which was proposed by Nick Szabo in 1998, though he did not publicize it until 2005) are both cited as earlier solutions that combined the use of computational puzzles with timestamping to secure transaction records in a ledger (Clark, 2016, pp. xxii–xxiii).

1.5 Blockchain and Immutability

From the original Nakamoto paper and its antecedents emerge the basic characterization of blockchains in intricate and delicate balance: a decentralized ledger, the entries of which are tamper-evident, agreed among all participants, transparent, and of pseudonymous origin. Working together, these characteristics generate arguably the most significant and controversial property of blockchains, *immutability*. Immutability, in the context of block-chain and distributed ledger technology, can be understood as the "property wherein ledger records cannot be modified or removed once added to a distributed ledger" (ISO, 2020a, s. 3.24).

Immutability, however, is better characterized as an emergent property of blockchains and other distributed ledgers. C. D. Broad (1925, as cited in O'Connor, 2020) explains emergentism as,

> the characteristic properties of the whole R(A, B, C) (where R marks their structural arrangement) [that] cannot, even in theory, be deduced from the most complete knowledge of the properties of A, B, and C in isolation or in other wholes which are not of the form R(A, B, C).

That is to say, the structural property of immutability in blockchains cannot be predicted from knowledge of any one of the individual properties of block-chains (e.g., tamper evidentiality, decentralization, transparency, or pseudo-nymity). Each of these properties must be present, and work in harmony with the others, to produce ledger immutability.

To explain, it would not be possible to achieve tamper evidentiality or resistance without the existence of a transparent ledger, which renders visible any alterations in original input data that might occur. Similarly, if the ledger were to be maintained by a single controlling interest, there would be nothing to prevent that controlling interest from altering ledger records if it were to choose to do so, even if digital signing of transaction records and blocks makes alterations evident. Once control of the ledger is decentralized, however, no single controlling interest can unilaterally alter it because a majority of participants must first agree on the alteration. In the Bitcoin network, this only becomes possible when participants who collectively control more than 50 percent of the CPU effort it takes to confirm blocks agree to change the ledger.

The more decentralized the participants in the network – in the sense of being free from the power and control of one another – the more censorship resistant is the ledger, that is, the more likely it is that an incomplete or altered copy of the ledger held by one of the participants would be rejected. This characteristic also contributes to immutability because it prevents a single controlling interest, or consortium of interests, from exercising control over the ledger in order to rewrite the ledger history. Altering or deleting records written to the ledger requires the agreement of the majority of all the participants on the network to that action, which is very difficult to gain (Daian, 2016), or the destruction of all of the hard disks of all of the participants on the network, which would be nearly impossible if participants are truly decentralized. It is precisely the difficulty of doing this that contributes to a blockchain system's immutability.

Finally, pseudonymity, while protecting privacy, also serves to prevent collusion among network participants since, if participants cannot identify one another, it is more difficult for them to form cartels or fall under one another's control.

Should any of these underlying properties be absent, or altered, ledger immutability may be affected. For instance, so called "51 percent attacks" – when a Bitcoin network participant or group of participants gains more than 50 percent of the hashing power on the network to form a controlling interest – can lead to alterations in the ledger. In this case, those with the controlling interest will have sufficient CPU energy to modify a past block by recomputing the PoW of all blocks to catch up with and surpass the work of the honest nodes (Eyal and Sirer, 2014). In essence, this gives the controlling interest the power to roll back history.

A 51 percent attack is not outside the realm of the possible, given that the formation of mining pools – groups of miners that form consortiums to lower the reward variance for participating miners – create a risk of CPU power concentration on the network. Narayanan et al. (2016, p. 128) noted that, as of 2015, nearly all miners were mining through pools, and in June 2014, one of those mining pools – GHash.IO – actually gained more than 50 percent of the network's CPU power; this led to a backlash against the mining pool. While the community of miners generally agreed to avoid becoming too large, some speculated that the true concentration of mining power may not be visible given that miners can participate in many mining pools simultaneously, which tends to obfuscate their true size (Narayanan, 2016, p. 130). Indeed, a number of mining pools still represent an outsized amount of the network's CPU power (see Figure 1.2).

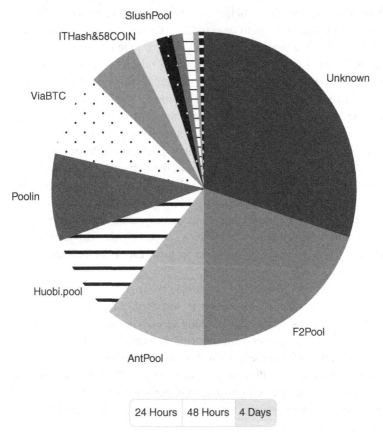

Figure 1.2 An estimation of hashrate distribution among the largest mining pools as of December 27, 2020

Note: The source of Figure 1.2 (www.blockchain.com/pools) includes the following caveat: "This graph shows the market share of the most popular bitcoin mining pools. It should only be used as a rough estimate and for various reasons will not be 100 percent accurate. A large portion of blocks are grouped into the "Unknown" category. This does not mean an attack on the network, it simply means it has not been possible to determine the origin."

In addition, quantum computing has been identified as an existential threat to the immutability of blockchains, since it allows for the possibility of breaking the cryptography upon which the immutability of the blockchain partially depends (Fernández-Caramès and Fraga-Lamas, 2020). New, quantum-capable computers threaten both the digital signature cryptography and the hash functions used to secure blockchains. This has spurred recent efforts aimed at redesigning blockchains to create what are variously called post-quantum, quantum-proof, quantum-safe, or quantum-resistant cryptosystems (Fernández-Caramès and Fraga-Lamas, 2020; Mashatan and Turetken, 2020; Mashatan and Heinztman, 2021).

In a 2017 paper, legal scholar Angela Walch, commenting on a new law in a state of Arizona (USA) statute[16] that gave recognition to signatures secured through a blockchain as "immutable and auditable and provid[ing] an uncensored truth," drew attention to the problematic nature of the concept of immutability in blockchains (Walch, 2017a). One of the high-profile events to which Walch refers is the DAO exploit of 2016, which involved the Ethereum blockchain.

Programmer Vitalik Buterin originally conceived of Ethereum in 2013. Development was crowdfunded in 2014, and the network went live on July 30, 2015.[17] In its original form, Ethereum bore many similarities to Bitcoin, but a key difference was that it incorporated a virtual machine that could execute Turing-complete scripts and run decentralized programs, called smart contracts. The DAO exploit – DAO standing for decentralized autonomous organization – involved a smart contract, which encoded rules for the operation of the DAO, within which there was written a fatal flaw: it allowed a poorly written function that permitted the repeated withdrawal of DAO funds, rather than the single withdrawal allegedly intended by the contract's author. An attacker was able to exploit this flaw to siphon off Ether (Ethereum's native cryptocurrency) worth an estimated USD 50–70 million (Daian, 2016; Tapscott and Tapscott, 2016; Butijn et al., 2020). All this would have been fine as far as the immutability of blockchain goes, but it was certainly not okay with those whose funds had been misdirected into the attacker's account.

How to handle this obviously unintended situation sparked a fierce debate in the Ethereum community. Some, including Buterin, proposed an update to Ethereum's software that would allow for the recovery of the Ether (Daian, 2016; Butijn et al., 2020). Those who maintained a commitment to immutability – that is, to the idea that "code is law" and that the blockchain should not be

---

[16] Act of Sept. 21, 2006, ch. 26, ARIZ. REV. STAT. ANN. § 44–7003 (2006) (amended by 2017 Ariz. Sess. Laws 2417). https://legiscan.com/AZ/text/HB2417/id/1528949
[17] See https://ethereum.org/en/history.

subject to human interference – stood firmly against this notion. In the end, a majority (about 89 percent) of Ethereum network participants "voted" for the solution supported by Buterin by updating to the new version of Ethereum. Opponents of this approach did not update to the new version, leading to a split in the ledger (a "hard fork," which occurs when blocks generated using a new version of a blockchain protocol are not accepted by those operating an older version [ISO, 2020a, s. 3.38]). Essentially, by majority rule, those who updated to the new version of Ethereum agreed to "interfere" in the operation of the ledger in order to restore DAO funds, while those who did not agree to this interference continued to add to and accept only the original version of Ethereum, which became known as "Ethereum Classic."

As Gideon Greenspan (2017) points out, supporters of Ethereum Classic paid a hefty price for their commitment to immutability: Ethereum Classic is worth a fraction of the price of Ethereum. Although the DAO exploit highlights that the property of blockchain immutability is conditional, it also shows that alteration is not easy. In the DAO example, alteration involved debate among the entire Ethereum community, required a majority of participants on the network to agree to the change, and ultimately caused a division in the Ethereum network. A realistic way to view immutability in the context of blockchains is expressed by Greenspan "there is no such thing as perfect immutability. The real question is: What are the conditions under which a particular blockchain can and cannot be changed? And do those conditions match the problem we're trying to solve?" (Greenspan, 2017).

Threats to immutability may be dismissed as being possible (even increasingly likely) but outside the expected normal operations of blockchain networks. However, even normal blockchain and distributed ledger operations may deliver less-than-immutable ledgers; indeed, it might even be considered desirable for them to do so under certain conditions. Debate surrounding the EU's General Data Protection Regulation (GDPR) and the "right to be forgotten" – which requires the erasure of personally identifiable information from data stores under certain conditions – best illustrates this point, though these regulations are not the only legal requirements for erasure or alteration of information.[18] GDPR establishes data protection as a fundamental right of all EU citizens (Finck, 2018; Hofman et al., 2019). Article 17 of the GDPR makes provision for a "right to be forgotten," or the right to erasure, stating that

---

[18] The US Fair Credit Reporting Act also requires deletion of personal information, for example. Under this law, consumer reporting agencies must correct or delete inaccurate, incomplete, or unverifiable information, typically within 30 days. The US Federal Trade Commission has estimated that 40 million Americans have inaccuracies in their credit reports under the current system.

[a] data subject shall have the right to obtain the erasure of personal data concerning him or her without undue delay and the controller shall have the obligation to erase personal data without undue delay where [one of the legislative grounds] applies.

(European Parliament and the Council of European Union, 2016, Article 17,
Section 1)

The right to erasure is not absolute; indeed, it is only required when one of several principles specified in the regulations applies. For instance, a data controller may deny a request for erasure if there is a legal reason to retain the data, or if there is an "archival purpose" for retention of the data, such as to meet public interest, scientific, or historical research purposes. As Hofman et al. (2019) observe, the right to erasure may well apply to blockchains where the ledger contains personal information and the legislated limitations do not apply.

In order to circumvent the apparent incompatibility between the immutability of blockchains and the right to erasure, a number of solutions have been proposed (Hofman et al., 2019), among these being the somewhat infamous and much derided "editable" blockchain. This was an idea proposed by Accenture in 2016. In a *Coindesk* post on the subject, David Treat argued that immutable blockchains would slow adoption of the technology:

For those who only believe in the permissionless mode of blockchain solutions, there is no need to discuss alternatives. But as industries explore new uses for blockchain beyond cryptocurrency and permissionless systems, there will be situations when that same immutability could make it difficult for the technology to advance.

(Treat, 2016)

Treat was referring to the rise of private and permissioned distributed ledgers, or distributed ledgers that are accessible only to a limited number of participants and that require authorization to participate or to perform a specific activity (ISO, 2020a, s. 3.57–3.61). Such distributed ledger variants had arisen in response to government and private organizations' desire to retain control over their technology and platforms, which the large permissionless blockchains and distributed ledgers – such as Bitcoin and Ethereum, in which participants operated independently (even if only theoretically) and without special authorization – do not allow.

The need to comply with regulatory requirements, such as GDPR, was one driver of organizations' preference for permissioned over permissionless blockchains. In the context of permissionless blockchains, Treat noted a number of problems that likely could only be solved by incorporating the capability to edit blockchains. For example, if records can only ever be added to the chain, ledger size and storage costs will continue to grow. Those in favor of blockchain editability also argued that it should be possible to delete illegal content, such as child pornography, or to correct mistakes created by human error or intent, such as the DAO. Finally, the need to comply with regulatory requirements to remove or redact data makes it necessary to be able to edit a blockchain. These issues led Accenture, for whom Treat worked, to conclude that

> On one side of the debate are those who argue that immutability is precisely what makes the blockchain such a significant innovation. On the other side are pragmatists who increasingly see where and how in enterprise environments immutability may prohibit adoption due to human error, mischief and privacy laws.
>
> *(Accenture, 2016, p. 3)*

Accenture's solution was to introduce a new variation of the "chameleon" hash function to enable blockchain editing, allowing the creation of a "virtual padlock" linking two blocks. Deleting or altering a block would involve unlocking the padlock with a private key (called a "trapdoor"), which unchains the blocks and allows insertion of a new or altered block in place of the old one without breaking the integrity of the entire blockchain (Accenture, 2016, p. 7).

Accenture (2016, p. 7) acknowledged that the solution was designed for permissioned systems, wherein there is a designated administrator responsible for managing the system, and rules, procedures, and roles are defined in advance, unlike in Bitcoin. Accenture further noted that redaction should only be available in exceptional circumstances, such as the correction of typos and factual errors, or to bring the data into compliance with the requirements of changed legislation.

Opponents of the approach immediately called out the potential for financial fraud (Kelly, 2016). As Kelly (2016) wrote in a critical *Coindesk* commentary, "The moment you allow someone to change the record you begin to erode trust. While the change may be for the most benign reasons, like human error, it invariably opens the door to the erosion of trust." Commenting on financial market manipulation, Kelly went on to observe that it was "the ability to change the permanent record that enabled Bernie Madoff to commit the largest fraud in financial history" and that "[a] blockchain is a great way to keep a record that you don't ever want changed – this is the heart and soul of a trustless system – it is a feature, not a flaw" (Kelly, 2016).

1.6 Concluding Thoughts

Given the conditionality of blockchain immutability, whether intentional or not, it is inadvisable to view it in essentialist terms as a fixed and stable blockchain property. Rather, blockchain immutability is as much socially constructed as technically implemented and is best viewed as a sustained commitment that a group of individuals holds onto because they believe that the attribute is desirable and necessary. This commitment has been affirmed by experts from countries around the globe participating in the development of international standards on blockchain and distributed ledger technology, even though they acknowledge that immutability is a design goal of blockchain and distributed ledgers, not something that can be absolutely guaranteed (ISO, 2020a). Why should so many individuals have come to see the property of immutability as desirable or necessary, despite its limitations? Nakamoto's original paper provides the answer: *trust*. It is to the question of trust that we now turn in the next chapter.

PART II

Trust

2

Trust and Its Discontents

2.1 A Problem of Trust

On October 31, 2008, Satoshi Nakamoto sent an unpretentious post to the Cryptography Mailing List: "I've been working on a new electronic cash system that's fully peer-to-peer, with no trusted third party" (Nakamoto, 2008b). He had been working on the project for about a year and half by then (Nakamoto, 2008c). Over the next several months, Nakamoto exchanged messages on the Cryptography Mailing List,[1] the Peer-to-Peer Foundation Forum (the P2P Forum), and in private emails. The problem of trust and its discontents ran as through lines in these communications against the background of an ongoing global financial crisis that had engendered widespread distrust in the 1 percent – the wealthy elite – among the 99 percent, the rest of humanity. Typifying this theme was a post to the P2P Forum not long after the creation of Bitcoin's genesis block on January 3, 2009, and Nakamoto's announcement of the launch of bitcoin on the Cryptography Mailing List on January 9, 2009 (Nakamoto, 2009a). The post, dated February 11, 2009, read:

> I've developed a new open source P2P e-cash system called Bitcoin. It's completely decentralized, with no central server or trusted parties, because everything is based on crypto proof instead of trust ... The root problem with conventional currency is all the trust that's required to make it work. The central bank must be trusted not to debase the currency, but the history of fiat currencies is full of breaches of that trust. Banks must be trusted to hold our money and transfer it electronically, but they lend it out in waves of credit bubbles with barely a fraction in reserve. We have to trust them with our

---

[1] A "successor" list to the distributed, unmoderated "Cypherpunks" list to which many had previously belonged. The connection between early Bitcoin developers and the Cypherpunk movement has been well covered (see Golumbia, 2016; Popper, 2016a; Bandyopadhyay, 2018; Brunton, 2019; Dupont, 2019) so will not be repeated in this volume, but readers will likely find these publications both informative and entertaining.

privacy, trust them not to let identity thieves drain our accounts. Their massive overhead costs make micropayments impossible.

A generation ago, multi-user time-sharing computer systems had a similar problem . . . Then strong encryption became available to the masses, and trust was no longer required. Data could be secured in a way that was physically impossible for others to access, no matter for what reason, no matter how good the excuse, no matter what.

It's time we had the same thing for money. With e-currency based on cryptographic proof, without the need to trust a third party middleman, money can be secure and transactions effortless.

(Nakamoto, 2009b)

2.2 What Good Is Trust?

Nakamoto's post to the P2P Forum and his original Bitcoin paper (Nakamoto, 2008a) point to some of the costs he associated with poorly functioning intermediary trust mechanisms: reversible payments for nonreversible services; the cost to settle disputes; the need for trust spreads; over-collection of information; and unavoidable fraud (Nakamoto, 2008a, p. 1). In the 1970s, the Nobel Prize– winning economist Kenneth Arrow had made similar observations. Arrow (1972) viewed lack of mutual trust as representing a distinct loss to economic systems which require it for the success of collective undertakings. "Virtually every commercial transaction," he wrote, "has within itself an element of trust, certainly any transaction conducted over a period of time. It can be plausibly argued that much of the economic backwardness in the world can be explained by the lack of mutual confidence" (Arrow, 1972, p. 357). Perceived trustworthiness – the basis of trust, Arrow posits – lowers monitoring and transaction costs. Financial transactions do not occur easily absent trust: contract monitoring can be ineffective, sanctioning for contractual breaches can be difficult, and transaction costs can increase, all of which undermine the foundations of financial exchange and production.

Beyond the financial system, trust in government is said to be an important foundation for legitimacy and sustainability of political systems and is essential for social cohesion and wellbeing, as it affects a government's ability to govern and enables it to act without having to resort to coercion (OECD, 2013, p. 21). Fukuyama (1995, p. 7) writes that "a nation's well-being, as well as its ability to compete, is conditioned by a single, pervasive cultural characteristic: the level of trust inherent in the society." Putnam (2000) writes about trust as "social capital," suggesting that its existence creates the conditions for social cohesion, and, in a similar vein, Pettit (1995) views trust as necessary to flourishing civil societies. More broadly, Locke (1689, as cited in Laslett, 1988, p. 359) argues that the existence of trust is the most fundamental requirement for the formation of societies. Trust makes collective undertakings possible, for without trust individuals would be unsure whether, if they engage in an action that benefits others, their action will be reciprocated – put another way, trust enables cooperative behavior (Gambetta, 1988). Trust, writes Hardin (2002, p. 173), "enables us to cooperate for mutual benefit."

The German social theorist Niklas Luhmann (1979) argues that trust serves as a mechanism for making complexity manageable. In doing so, argues Luhmann, trust enables coordinated and cooperative action that would not have been possible, or at least would be very improbable, without it (Luhmann, 1979). Others have pointed to its value in promoting adaptive organizational forms, such as network relations, and rapid formulation of ad hoc work groups (Meyerson et al., 1996).

Objections can, and have, been raised to the idea that trust is universally a "good thing" for society (see Hardin, 2002, pp. 81–84). History, after all, is rife with examples showing that trust in political leaders without the means of determining their trustworthiness has led to the most egregious of human tragedies. Nevertheless, many writers agree that a certain level of trust is essential to the coordination and cooperation necessary in a complex society at every level of its operation.

2.3 A Crisis of Trust

If trust is necessary to the economic, political, and social coordination and cooperation underpinning society, then it is surely problematic that we currently seem to be in the midst of a crisis of trust. Though some scholars are skeptical about claims that there is a global crisis of trust (see, e.g., Hardin, 2002; Henderson and Churi, 2019; O'Neill, 2020), there is a growing body of literature and evidence concerned with declining trust. One frequently cited indicator is the Edelman "Trust Barometer" annual global study, which has measured global attitudes to trust for the past 20 years.

In 2016, an Edelman trust survey found that in two-thirds of 28 countries surveyed, the average level of trust in institutions such as government, business, the media, and NGOs was below 50 percent, an all-time low in the survey's 17-year history (Edelman, 2016, p. 2). In 2017, Edelman observed a global "implosion of trust," reporting that, across 43 countries surveyed, CEO credibility was at its lowest point ever; trust in media fell and was at an all-time low in 17 countries; and trust in government dropped in 14 countries, being the least trusted institution in half of the countries surveyed (Edelman, 2017). In the introductory overview for its 2020 survey, Edelman reported that,

> People today grant their trust based on two distinct attributes: competence (delivering on promises) and ethical behavior (doing the right thing and working to improve society). This year's Trust Barometer reveals that none of the four institutions [government, business, NGOs, and media] is seen as both competent and ethical. Business ranks highest in competence, holding a massive 54-point edge over government as an institution that is good at what it does (64 percent vs. 10 percent). NGOs lead on ethical behavior over government (a 31-point gap) and business (a 25-point gap). Government and media are perceived as both incompetent and unethical.
>
> *(Edelman, 2020)*

Declining voter turnout in liberal democracies is also cited as evidence of a growing decline in trust – with the United States, the United Kingdom, and France recording drops in voter participation of about 30 percentage points over the last 50 years (Harsin, 2019) – as is the proliferation and rise of political parties expressing alienation from mainstream liberal democratic policies, including the Rassemblement National in France, the UK Independence Party, Germany's AFD (Alternative for Germany), and, in the United States, the insurgent democratic socialist challenge by Bernie Sanders (Harsin, 2019) and "Trumpism." Social-political movements such as *les Indignados* in Spain, Occupy in the United States, and *Nuit Debout* in France (Harsin, 2019) – as well as, more recently, QAnon – are also said to be indicators of lower levels of trust in governments and their policies (Harsin, 2019).

The literature identifies a wide variety of explanations and contributory factors for declining trust in governments, including the impact of media and technology, economic health, and socio-political causes. Edwards (2015) finds that declining trust in government often arises from factors over which the government has no control. He provides several examples of external events that have reduced public trust, including the global financial crisis (also the backdrop to the rise of bitcoin). The election of a new government, on the other hand, can increase public trust: following the 2014 election in India, trust rose by 30 percentage points (Edelman, 2015, p. 4; Edwards, 2015). Longer-term economic and socio-political factors may also affect public trust, including trends such as declines in deference to authority or in social capital (Van de Walle et al., 2008, pp. 8–9). Globalization and related technological, political, and economic changes also alter state–society relations; for example, a rise in individualism may make it more difficult for governments to meet each citizen's needs (Heintzman, 2007, p. 2; Sullivan, 2015). Changing expectations of citizens in relation to their governments and their political representatives may also affect levels of trust (Warren, 2006, p. 7; Blind, 2007). Rapid implementation of new technologies may depress trust and lead to concerns about the pace of change (Edelman, 2015). This notion may also be linked to a focus on the media as a driver of growing distrust (e.g., the priming theory [Hetherington and Rudolph, 2008]). According to Edwards (2015), the nature and causes of declining political trust can be expected to vary to a significant degree with the country and cultural context, and there remains much uncertainty about the relative strength of these causes, the importance of different factors in different contexts, how they might interrelate, and whether these relationships are causal or merely correlative.

Several researchers emphasize economic factors as contributing to a decline in public trust. Mansbridge (1997) and Newton and Norris (2000) associate periods of poor economic performance and citizens' perception that the government is incapable of dealing with current fiscal and financial challenges with lower levels of trust. The political economy literature points to higher levels of trust in wealthier areas and, conversely, lower levels of trust in poorer areas (Leigh, 2006), but Edelman's 2020 survey of trust finds the opposite. Fiorina (1978) and MacKuen et al. (1992) suggest that people place more trust in governments that can bring about economic growth, create jobs, provide access to education, and deliver services in an easy and transparent manner. Nye (1997) argues that citizens' negative evaluation of the national economy and their negative perceptions of their governments' ability to respond to economic challenges engender even more distrust in the age of globalization. Competitive pressures and economic dislocations of globalization, growing economic inequality, and increasing numbers of marginalized people in both the developed and the developing world have fuelled a loss of political trust in governments' capability and willingness to act in a timely and adequate manner, according to Alesina and Wacziarg (2000). Hetherington (2005) also discusses the fact that, in the American political landscape, citizens trust governments less when the state spends highly on redistributive programs.

In contrast to economic arguments for declining trust, some of the literature concerned with trust in government emphasizes socio-political causes. The literature also makes a distinction between factors that relate to a government's performance (or what it achieves) and those that relate more to how a government goes about meeting its citizens' needs (Arizti et al., 2010; Cheema, 2010; Bannister and Connolly, 2011; OECD, 2013; Edwards, 2015). A World Bank publication, for example, differentiates between *what* a government does and *how* it does it, identifying two public management levers affecting public trust: *performance* and *accountability* (Arizti et al., 2010, p. 203). According to the World Bank, accountability matters more than performance for trust in Organisation for Economic Co-operation and Development (OECD) countries, but in Latin America it is possible that performance could have a bigger impact (Arizti et al., 2010, p. 203). The same publication also notes that improvement in performance in some services matters more than in others (Arizti et al., 2010, p. 203). Cheema (2010) finds that in developing countries "weak systems ... of democratic governance, as well as inadequate access to services and economic opportunities, tend to erode trust in government" whereas "in the developed countries ... citizens have greater access to information and higher levels of education and thus demand more transparency" (see, e.g., Arizti et al., 2010, p. 208; OECD, 2013, p. 34; Edwards, 2015). Similar to the findings of the World Bank, the OECD, in focusing on what governments can influence, finds that it is "not only the *what* of public policies that matters, but also the *how*, the *for whom*, and the *with whom* [emphasis in the original text]" (OECD, 2013, p. 28). Consequently, not only the final results of policy but also the processes used to attain them are important for both citizens and business to trust government (OECD, 2013, p. 28).

Blind (2007, pp. 11–12) emphasizes the important impact of corruption on declining trust, and Espinal et al. (2006) maintain that security and corruption are much more important for trust in government in the developing world than in industrialized countries. Nevertheless, political performance on issues of security and corruption are associated with increasing trust (Lipset and Schneider, 1983; Turner and Martz, 1997; Mishler and Rose, 2001). Job (2005) finds that if individuals perceive corruption in politics, then their trust in local institutions is adversely affected. Since trust in local government institutions is the strongest predictor of trust in remote political institutions, such as the national congress and/or the presidency or similar leadership role, corruption becomes an important indirect determinant of overall political trust.

Another factor influencing trust is the quality of leadership in the political and public service arenas (Blind, 2007; Popovski, 2010; OECD, 2013). Some researchers have conducted studies showing that lower levels of government are more trusted (e.g., Berman, 1997). Similarly, the more contact citizens have with government officials, the higher the level of trust (e.g., local health workers may be trusted more than national politicians) (see, e.g., Arizti et al., 2010; OECD, 2013; Edwards, 2015). Theiss-Morse and Hibbing (2005) suggest that citizens mistrust when they perceive politicians to be more interested in their own interests than in the interests of their citizens.

With so many problems related to trust – as exemplified by the above survey of the literature on trust in government – and such apparently high levels of distrust, it is a wonder that society has not already collapsed. Claims that societies need high levels of trust to function are evidently false, since even with purported declining and low levels of trust, liberal democratic societies continue to soldier on. This may simply be because there are ways besides relying on trust to achieve the cooperation and coordination that societies need. For example, social norms and institutions, such as the law, exist in large part to overcome the absence of trust (Hardin, 2002, p. 173). In doing so, they can deliver the "trustless trust" (Werbach, 2019) also said to be offered by Bitcoin.

The difficulty of pinpointing a single or group of fixed factors contributing to a decline in trust suggests that trust is deeply embedded and intertwined with the constitution and functioning of the socio-informational-technical ecosystems in which we exist – it is difficult to understand a decline in trust in traditional media, for example, without also understanding the rise of social media platforms and how they configure our epistemic orientation to the world and our social "realities" (about which I will have much more to say in Chapter 4). To fully understand this point and lay the foundation for the following chapters, however, requires a deeper foray into the meaning of trust.

2.4 What Is Trust?

We tend to rely on trust every day and, clearly, we miss it when it is gone. But do we really understand what it means? The sociologist Diego Gambetta (1988) has referred to trust as an elusive notion and Edwards (2015, p. 2) notes that the concept of trust is "vague, slippery, subjective, mutual, multidimensional, multi-disciplinary and complex." A review of literature on the subject of trust reveals why: conceptualizations vary according to the actors involved, the nature of their relationships, the types of behaviors expected of trustees, and the context of the situation. Conceptualizations of trust also vary based on whether the writer is exploring the subject of trust conceptually or empirically, and according to disciplinary perspective (e.g., psychology, sociology, economics, or philosophy). Additionally, in empirical work, the concept of trust may appear as an independent variable (cause), a dependent variable (effect), or an interaction variable (a moderating condition for a causal relationship) (Rousseau et al., 1998, p. 396).

Theorists and researchers (and thus the scholarly literature on trust) lack agreement on the nature of trust: whether trust is a static binary proposition or something more dynamic and scalar; whether someone or something can be both trusted and distrusted at the same time; whether trust involves actions and emotions; whether trust is mere reliance; whether it is a form of belief; whether we can consciously decide to trust; and whether trust has a moral dimension (Rousseau et al., 1998, pp. 395–396). These, and a myriad of differing viewpoints

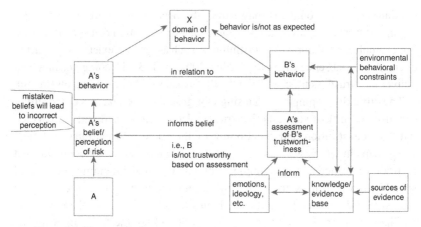

Figure 2.1 The model of trust

on trust, naturally lead to quite a variety of definitions and conceptualizations of the term.

In this discussion, I intend to focus on not only the trust that people experience in individual-level day-to-day interactions but also the trust that people place in institutions and laws that govern their individual interactions, as depicted in Figure 2.1. This dual vantage point, which I will call *societal trust*, is necessary because that is how trust is embodied in blockchain systems (as I discuss in Chapter 3).[2]

Trust between Individuals

One widely relied-upon understanding of trust is Hardin's (2002) notion of trust as "encapsulated interest." As such, it makes for a good jumping-off point into a deeper exploration of various debates about the meaning of trust, including the notion of societal trust on which I focus in this volume. A key feature of Hardin's conceptualization of trust is that it is relational. Despite diverse conceptualizations of trust, scholars tend to agree on one point: trust involves a relationship between a person doing the trusting (the trusting party, or trustor) and the person or thing being trusted (the trusted party, or trustee) (Castaldo et al., 2010).

---

[2] My conceptualization of societal trust is different from, and can be compared with, McDowell's (2002, p. 52) notion of "social trust," which they define as "trust of a moral and social sort rather than an epistemic sort." McDowell therefore makes a sharp distinction between social trust and epistemic trust, whereas I argue that trust is always epistemic in nature, even as it conditions the relations between social actors.

Many accounts of the relational nature of trust consider it to be a two-part relationship, that is, a relationship between a trustor and a trustee. Hardin (2002), on the other hand, takes the position that trust is a three-part relationship that exists when a trustor trusts a trustee with respect to a specific domain of activity (i.e., A trusts B with respect to X).[3] He is therefore critical of generalized notions of trust without a contextual foundation, claiming that they are simply founded on poorly worded empirical questions (Hardin, 2002, p. 61). Generalized trust, or the predisposition to trust, does, however, figure prominently in discussions and empirical studies of trust in society (see, e.g., McKnight et al., 2011), so needs to be accounted for when considering the notion of societal trust in this volume, a point to which I return below.

In Hardin's encapsulated interest view of trust, trust is only in play when the trusting party is motivated by a belief that their interests are included in the trustee's "utility function" (or what the trustee values), such that the trustee values what the trustor desires because the trustee wants to maintain good relations with the trusting party, or wants to maintain a reputation for being trustworthy in the network of relations in which the trustor–trustee relation is embedded. Other writers on the subject of trust also identify the trusted party's motivations as essential to the notion of trust but attribute such motivations variously to moral integrity on the part of the trusted person (McLeod, 2002); to holding the trusted person to a moral obligation (Nickel, 2007); or to recognition of the fact that the trustor depends on the trustee as a reason to perform (Jones, 1996; Faulkner, 2007a). For Hardin, then, if there is no motivation for an ongoing relationship, then there is no trust in operation (Hardin, 2002, p. 3). The motivation for this ongoing relationship arises from the trusted party's belief that they have an interest – that is, the encapsulated interest – in fulfilling the trust placed in them by the trustee to maintain and continue the relationship with respect to a certain domain of activity. In other words, says Hardin, "I trust you because I think it is in your interest to take my interests in the relevant matter seriously in the following sense: You value the continuation of our relationship, and you therefore have your own interests in taking my interests into account" (Hardin, 2002, p. 1). That incentive may be positive in nature (such as the benefits received from the continuing relationship) or it may be negative (in the form of sanctions such as the ending of a relationship from which the trusted party benefits or, more indirectly, some form of social censure or diminution of reputation) (Hardin, 2002, p. 14).

---

[3] According to Nickel et al. (2010), this three-part formulation of trust can be traced back to the work of philosopher H. J. N. Horsburgh (see, e.g., Horsburgh, 1961).

To illustrate, I might believe that a public health official that I know personally has my interests at heart when ordering me to stay home during a pandemic. This is not only due to my judgement of the reputation of the public health official's good character or honesty – though this does figure into the formation of my belief – but also because the public health official's interests are grounded in the institutions of science and government, which I also trust. This points to the fact that it is possible to trust "institutions" and "systems" as complex networks of relationships, a topic that I discuss further below and to which I return in the next chapter in my discussion of trust in blockchain and distributed ledger technologies. For the purposes of this discussion, however, the important aspect of my trust in these mechanisms is that I believe them to incentivize the public health official (in whom I am also placing my trust) to take my interests into consideration. Specifically, I understand that these institutions have power over the actions of the public official, which constrains their actions and compels them to form public health policy based on reliable research results and in the public interest, which I assess as encompassing my own interests. The power to constrain or compel the actions of the public health official derives, in part, from the network of relations that forms the social institution of science, which includes mechanisms to guard against scientific fraud (such as processes of peer review, reproducibility of research, and censure of irresponsible or dishonest behavior). Here, actions are further constrained by the institutional rules of government. All these mechanisms contribute to incentivizing the public health official – who is a scientist and a government official – to behave in a trustworthy manner, which is to say, to rely upon honest and scientifically rigorous research in formulating policy in the public interest. This example illustrates that trust, as Origgi (2020) has argued, is also a social property that is mutually constructed by the perceiver (trustor), the perceived (trustee), and the social context.

The above conceptualization of trust – in which external regulating factors assure alignment of the trustee's interests with those of the trustor – seems to leave the door open to a situation in which a trusting party knows that the trustee will act in their interests only because they really have no choice other than to do so (unless the trustee decides to behave against their own interests). Can this really be construed as a trusting relationship? Hardin argues that this situation is one of mere compliance since the trusted party is only concerned with their own interests and not those of the trusting party. To qualify as trust, in the encapsulated interest sense, the trusted party must have a reason to consider it in their best interest to behave in a manner that aligns with the interests of the trusting party. This may not be possible when there is no way for the trusted party to ascertain the interests of the trustor, as in the case of collective trust (see the discussion below). Nevertheless, it is still possible to believe that the trusted party is considering the trustor's interests and how well aligned they are with their own interests, even in the most extreme case of a gun being held to the trusted party's head forcing them to act in the trustor's interest.

A more compelling reason why this scenario might not rise to the level of trust is that the trusting party does not incur any risk or vulnerability in respect to the behavior of the trusted party. Trust, argues Hinchman (2005, p. 578), "is a species of willed dependence, where the dependence is under appropriate guidance of a counterfactual sensitivity to evidence of untrustworthiness in the trusted." In the case of a gun being held to the head of the trusted party, the trustor can know with almost complete certainty that the trusted party is unlikely to risk their life to behave in a manner that is against the trustor's interest (on this point, see Nissenbaum, 2001; De Filippi et al., 2020). This allows for the notion of the trustless trust that is said to characterize blockchains, which I discuss in detail in the next chapter, in the sense that the system creates the conditions that are said to eliminate risk and vulnerability for the trustor. Suffice to say for now that it is a sort of quasi-trust, for the trustor is not required to completely trust the trustee – due to some constraining factor governing the trustee's behavior – but nor might trust be completely absent from the relationship if there is still some residual vulnerability or risk on the part of the trustor.

The above explanation points to another key dimension of Hardin's notion of trust, which is that trust is cognitive in nature.[4] Hardin views trust as cognitive in the sense of being grounded in consideration of evidence, which links it to the class of concepts associated with *epistemology*, such as knowledge. The evidence-based grounds for trust form the basis of the trustor's expectation or belief that the party to be trusted will behave in the interests of the trustor (Hardin, 2002, p. 7). Critics of this "doxastic" view of trust[5] – that is, views of trust that invoke the notion of belief, like Hardin's – often point to the fact that one *cannot decide* to believe something – one either believes it or not – but one *can decide* to place trust in someone or something. So, if trust involves belief, one should not be able to decide to trust either.

Hardin agrees that it is impossible to choose to trust; the grounds for trust either exist or do not exist in the eyes of the trustor. He elaborates, "We can

---

[4] Many philosophers and social theorists have considered the extent to which trust involves cognitive deliberation or, rather, behavior, including Arrow (1974, p. 26); Luhmann (1979, p. 24); Held (1984, p. 45); Baier (1986, p. 244); Dunn (1988, p. 73); Becker (1996); Origgi (2004); and Nguyen (in press).

[5] On the question of whether trust involves belief, see also Hieronymi (2008) and Keren (2014).

choose to put ourselves in a position to come to know something, but we cannot look at the evidence then decide to know" (Hardin, 2002, p. 58). Once the trustor has sufficient grounds to conclude that the trustee is trustworthy and can therefore be trusted, choice then enters into matters of trust in that the trustor might choose to act on the basis of that trust if the situation calls for it. It is, however, entirely possible to trust another party without acting upon that trust. The choice then is not *whether* to trust, but whether to *act* upon that trust. On the other hand, trusting can be said to involve acting when applied to the trustee if we accept Hardin's proposition that trust is a three-part relation involving A's trust of B in relation to a domain of activity, X. It is thus more accurate to characterize the trustee's side of the trust relationship as behavioral, rather than relating to action; that said, the trustor might be trusting the trustee *not* to do something as much as trusting them to act (e.g., "I trust you not to drink and drive").

As soon as the trustor decides to behave in a manner consistent with their trust – that is, to rely upon the trustee to behave as expected – they open themself up to risk (Luhmann, 2000). Now, risk is another rather tricky and complex concept, variously defined in the literature, but which for the purposes of this volume I will define as a deviation from expected outcome, with a probability of negative or positive ramifications for the trustor (ISO, 2018b). Indeed, Williamson (1993) observed that the terms trust and risk were often used interchangeably. Without the possibility of risk, there is no trusting relationship, only mere expectation (Hardin, 2002, p. 3). Risk arises because trust involves some uncertainty on the part of the trustor about whether the party to be trusted is, in fact, trustworthy. This uncertainty is caused by information asymmetry favoring the trustee, that is, the party to be trusted knows more about their motivations and how they are likely to act than does the person doing the trusting. Due to this information asymmetry, the trusting party makes themself vulnerable on some level to another party, since there is always a chance that the trustee might take advantage of the trustor and behave in an unexpected manner that causes harm or loss (Castaldo et al., 2010).

Assessment of the trustee's trustworthiness requires that the trustor – in forming the belief that will motivate the decision to behave according to their trust – use available information to determine the probability that the trustee will behave as expected. Hinchman (2005, p. 578), however, argues that trust does not require actively assessing if the trusted party is trustworthy: "it is enough merely to be (and, counterfactually, have been) disposed to notice and respond appropriately to evidence of untrustworthiness should there be (or have been) any." Both types of assessment (i.e., of trustworthiness or of untrustworthiness) are possible in the formation of trusting beliefs, depending on the situation. In some cases, trustors might be more inclined to assess evidence of untrustworthiness (e.g., when the trustee is known to the trustor or fulfils a social role that is generally considered to be filled by those who are trustworthy), while in other cases, the trustor might seek out evidence of trustworthiness (e.g., when the trustee is unknown to the trustor, or where the stakes of trusting are high for the trustor).

Such assessment also requires that the trustor consider the personal consequences of any deviation from expectations in the behavior of the trustee (Rousseau et al., 1998). It is at least partially on the basis of the trustor's risk-based consideration of evidence of the (un)trustworthiness of the trustee that the trustor develops a justified true belief that they can trust the trustee, a trust which may precede some action on the part of the trustor (Castaldo et al., 2010). Assessing the (un)trustworthiness of trustees is difficult. Evidence may be missing, partial, or unreliable. In cases when the trusting party has no previous knowledge of the party to be trusted, the information asymmetry between trustor and trustee might be quite large. Over time and with iterative interactions, the trustor might come to gather more information about the trustee's behavior, contributing to a trusting party's belief that a party to be trusted has an incentive to act in alignment with a trustee's interests or to an opposite belief (i.e., mistrust). The trustor's knowledge of the trusted party's trustworthiness might also increase when there are, as Hardin calls them, "thick relationships," such as when the trustee operates within a small community where other social actors are able to gather and share information with the trusting party (Hardin, 2002, pp. 21–22). Even if evidence of the trustee's past behavior is available, however, there is no guarantee that it will predict the trustee's future behavior. Consequently, there is always some level of risk involved in trusting.

Setting aside the question of whether assessments follow from an *a priori* "credulous" or "unquestioning" attitude (Hinchman, 2005; Faulkner, 2007a; Nguyen, in press) that shifts only when sufficient grounds exist of the untrustworthiness of a trusted party or, in contrast, precede the placing of trust in another, describing trust in terms of the evidence-based assessment of the degree of trustworthiness of the trustee, and the fact that the trustee might deviate from expected behavior thereby putting the trustor at risk, suggests that trust is purely cognitive and rational. This proposition is open to debate. Trusting beliefs tend to resist conflicting evidence (Baker, 1987; Jones, 1996; Lahno, 2001, 2020; Faulkner, 2007b). Lahno (2020, p. 156) argues that a theory of trust as an emotional attitude easily explains this characteristic, which seems to conflict with the idea that trust is purely based on rational assessment of evidence, observing that

> Trust is a biased mechanism for the transformation of information into belief: it
> works as a filter which hides certain information from the attention of a trustor, it
> suggests certain favorable interpretation strategies and it guides the mind in
> integrating new pieces of information into a consistent positive outlook onto the
> interaction with the trusted partner. The same considerations show why trust, once
> destroyed, is so hard to recover.

While seemingly at odds with a cognitive "rational choice" notion of trust, the idea that trusting might be non-deliberative, even unconscious and affective, is really not at odds with it at all. In his 2011 book *Thinking Fast and Slow*, Daniel Kahneman explains that risk assessment is not an entirely rational process. Instead, it involves an interplay between "System 1 thinking," a legacy of our evolutionary past, which is fast, automatic, and subject to unconscious bias, and "System 2 thinking," which is slow, deliberative, and thoughtful. System 1 thinking saves time and cognitive resources. In a similar vein, Nguyen argues that a default unquestioning attitude – which is to say, trust – spares the trustor's limited cognitive capacity (Nguyen, in press). Any belief formation involves both types of thinking, which can account for the introduction of non-rational, affective, and unconscious thought in the operation of trust, as per the interplay illustrated in Figure 2.1 and further discussed in Chapter 4.

The belief that it is good, reasonable, or safe to trust, then, is based on the trustor's assessment (not necessarily consciously calculative) of their own interests in a matter, the trustee's interests and likely behavior in relation to the trustor's interests (i.e., whether they are aligned), the trustee's trustworthiness (i.e., whether the trustor perceives that the trustee is likely to behave as expected, that is, in the interests of the trustor), and the trustor's perception of the impact if the trustee does not behave as expected (see Figure 2.1 for a representation of this "model of trust").

Assessment of how likely the trustee is to behave in the trustor's interests can be determined by several factors, as already discussed, such as the trustor's knowledge of the trustee's past behavior or knowledge of the trustee's reputation (Dasgupta, 1988). In addition, belief formation might involve knowledge that the trustor possesses about the costs that the trustee may incur if they act in an untrustworthy manner. For example, if the trustor observes that the trustee will be subject to stiff penalties if they act against the interests of the trustor, the trustor might be more likely to form the belief that the trustee can be trusted (Williamson, 1993; Morgan and Hunt, 1994). The trustor uses this knowledge to determine whether it is safe to place trust in the trustee. This is, again, why some theorists refer to trust as an epistemic concept, that is, because it relates to knowledge the trustor has about the trustee and how that knowledge is formed into a belief.

Belief formation in the context of trust does not only involve the trustor's knowledge of the trustee but also depends upon the trustor's own state of mind. This state may be influenced by the trustor's underlying propensity to trust (McKnight et al., 2011), how general societal or organizational cultures influence the trustor's predilection to trust (Williamson, 1993), the difficulty of the decision problem, the cognitive limitations of the trustor's mind, the time available to make the decision (i.e., bounded rationality), human cognitive biases, the trustor's emotions, the trustor's political ideology,[6] and the trustor's values (which accounts for what many observe as a moral dimension to trust)[7] (Kahneman, 2011; Baumgaertner et al., 2018; Van der Linden, 2020). Thus, there are many filters through which information about the trustee must pass in the process of a trustor forming a belief that it is good, safe, or reasonable to trust, or, conversely, mistrust. Once a decision is reached to trust or not to trust, then further active gathering of information often ceases, with the trustor adopting an unquestioning mind, integrating the trusted person or object into their own cognitive and behavioral "trust" boundary (Nguyen, in press). This process might account for why trusting beliefs sometimes are resistant to counterfactual information (Baker, 1987), since doing so requires the effort of recommencing active questioning and alienating the trusted party from within the trustor's cognitive and functional "sphere" (Nguyen, in press).

A final important point on the subject of interpersonal trust is the distinction between trust and trustworthiness, terms that are frequently conflated according to Hardin (2002, chapter 2). Trust is usually taken to be an attitude held by the trustor, while trustworthiness is a quality perceived by the trustor to inhere in the object of trust (Nickel et al., 2010). Hardin argues that, though trust and trustworthiness are distinct, declarations of "I believe I can trust you" and "I believe you are trustworthy" are equivalent in the sense that trust occurs when the trusting party believes the trustee to be trustworthy (Hardin, 2002, p. 10). Indeed, Hardin contends that behaving on the basis of trust – for example, on

---

[6] A study conducted by Baumgaertner et al. (2018), building on the prior work of Rabinowitz et al. (2016), looked at whether individuals were likely to choose vaccination. The researchers found that ideology has a direct effect on vaccine attitudes and that it predicts an indicator capturing trust in government and medical experts, which helps to explain individual-level variation in attitudes about vaccination. In other words, individuals participating in the COVID-19 protests, many of whom were "anti-vaxxers," tended already to have low levels of trust in public health officials, which was, in turn, influenced by underlying conservative ideological propensities. Though the work of these researchers focused on the United States, similar commentary about Canadian protestors confirms these results (Van der Linden, 2020).

[7] That is to say, the behavior of the trustee is judged according to the moral standards of the trustor. If the trustee's behavior is found not to adhere to what is expected (which will be conditioned by what the trustor believes to be moral, among other things such as emotions), the trustor will not only perceive the trustee as being untrustworthy but might also feel a sense of moral indignation at the behavior.

moral grounds – without ascertaining trustworthiness is foolhardy and likely to end badly. Consequently, consideration of the trustworthiness of a trustee is a very important aspect of any trusting relationship.

Though there is a connection between trust and trustworthiness then, it is not a deterministic or causal one. Trust is better viewed as one possible outcome, but not the only one, of the trustworthiness of a party to be trusted, since it is possible that entirely trustworthy parties might still not be trusted. Furthermore, a party might be trustworthy not because the trustor's interests are encapsulated in those of the trustee, as in Hardin's notion of trust, but because of some other incentive, such as a requirement to follow the law (Hardin, 2002, p. 29), or even by general disposition of the trustor. Moreover, it is possible for entirely untrustworthy parties to be trusted (as anyone who has ever had their trust betrayed will know). Thus, trust is not equivalent to, nor necessarily caused by, trustworthiness, nor is trustworthiness equivalent to or caused by trust.

Trust in "Systems" of Government

In the example I gave above of my placing trust in a public health official, I noted that my trust in this official was also contingent upon trust that I was placing in the "institutions" of science and government. Here, I am referring to institutions in the sociological sense, that is, as *a system for organizing stand-ardized patterns of social behavior* (Parsons, 1954).[8] Current concerns (discussed above) about trust in government and public authorities – what may be called political trust – calls for some exploration of this notion.

In political philosophy, trust is often described as a voluntary transfer of power to those who govern, "a transfer that cannot be justified simply in terms of coercion or of rational argument" (Origgi, 2004, p. 2). Blind (2007) subdivides political trust into (1) macro-level, or organizational, trust and (2) micro-level, or individual, trust based on the object to which trust or mistrust is directed. Political trust at the micro-level or individual level of trust, Blind says (2007, p. 4), happens when trust is directed toward individual political leaders. Individual political trust involves a person-oriented perspective

---

[8] To elaborate on the idea of institutions as systems, "the essential aspect of social structure lies in a system of patterned expectations defining the proper behavior of persons playing certain roles, enforced both by the incumbents' own positive motives for conformity and by the sanctions of others. Such systems of patterned expectations, seen in the perspective of their place in a total social system and sufficiently thoroughly established in action to be taken for granted as legitimate, are conveniently called 'institutions'. The fundamental, structurally stable element of social systems then, which, according to the present argument, must play a crucial role in their theoretical analysis, is their structure of institutional patterns defining the roles of their constituent actors" (Parsons 1954, p. 231).

whereby citizens become trustful or distrustful of government "because of their approval or disapproval of certain political leaders." Macro-level or organizational trust, on the other hand, refers to an issue-oriented perspective whereby citizens become trustful or distrustful of government "because they are satisfied or dissatisfied with policy alternatives" (Blind, 2007, p. 4). The focal organization in macro-level trust can be a national or local government, a specific agency, or an arm of government such as the judiciary, police, parliament, political parties, or the public service (Edwards, 2015). Blind further sub-divides organizational trust into diffuse (or system-based) trust and institution-based trust: "Diffuse political trust refers to citizens' evaluation of the performance of the overall political system and the regime. Specific political trust, on the other hand, is directed toward certain political institutions, such as the Congress or the local police force" (Blind, 2007, p. 4). This form of trust differs from the interpersonal type of trust and speaks to a more impersonal, or institutional, form that is prevalent in complex societies (Lahno, 2001).

Hardin (2002, p. 151) argues that institutional trust is not analogous to notions of trust between individuals, except allowing for elected officials' mutual trust with their constituents and other cases when the interactions are at the personal level, which would seem to rule out Blind's notion of macro-level political trust. Hardin (2002, p. 153) notes that, though the concept of trust as encapsulated interest can in principle be generalized to institutions, in practice it might be difficult to apply because two conditions must first be met.

First, in the encapsulated interest model of trust, trust develops over successive iterative interactions, which may not occur between a citizen and their government. Hardin (2002, p. 153), however, admits that it is possible for citizens to make *inferences* about government or public authorities' reliability from available information, and, arguably, this is what we do in most cases where information about a party to be trusted is scarce.

Second, the knowledge that citizens need to determine the interests of trustees and for trustees to determine the interests of citizens may not be readily obtainable. Mechanisms that promote open government and the free flow of information about government actions – such as access to information laws, open government, and a free press – help to solve this fundamental epistemic problem (Lemieux and Trapnell, 2016). However, as I will discuss in subsequent chapters, such methods can introduce their own problems, related to the trustworthiness of information, that impede the proper functioning of trust-based societal relations.

Even if some resolution to these two fundamental challenges to the applicability of the encapsulated interest model of institutional trust can be found,

Hardin (2002, p. 155) also questions whether citizen trust in government is necessary at all, since governments with low levels of reported citizen trust still obviously manage to operate. What is more important, according to Hardin, is institutional *trustworthiness*. "Whatever might be the importance of citizens' trust for the functioning of government, *it is surely more important that government be trustworthy than it is trusted* [emphasis in the original text]," writes Hardin (2002, p. 152).

Without providing a comprehensive survey of the literature on defining political trust, there are several examples that emphasize assessments of government trustworthiness,[9] though they vary significantly on the question of *which* characteristics citizens might use to determine whether a government is trustworthy. Hetherington (2005) offers a definition that focuses on the degree to which government is producing results consistent with citizens' expectation of outcomes, while Blind (2007, p. 4) argues that political trust "happens when citizens appraise the government and its institutions, policy-making in general and/or the individual political leaders as promise-keeping, efficient, fair and honest." In contrast, a definition offered by the World Bank says that political trust involves an assessment by citizens of a government's entitlement to enforce its decisions, laws, and regulations, as well as the probability that it will deliver on its obligations (Arizti et al., 2010, p. 52). Another definition, offered by the United Nations, brings in notions of legitimacy and the public interest: "Public trust is rooted in citizens' perceptions of the legitimacy of government action, for example, in the ability of officials to manage public resources effectively and more generally to act in the public interest" (Prasajo, 2015, p. 3). Miller and Listhaug (1984) conjecture that it is not only the "what" of trustworthiness that is important to citizens but the "how," defining political trust as "judgment of the citizenry that the system and the political incumbents are responsive, and will do what is right even in the absence of constant scrutiny." Finally, Edwards (2015, p. 161) writes that, in the public sector context of engaging with citizens, trust is inferred to follow from interpersonal and interorganizational behaviors where the expectations of each party are clear, and confidence exists that what is committed to will be delivered. Thus, epistemic assessments of trustworthiness form a key aspect of notions of political trust, as well as interpersonal trust, and trust in government without assessing government trustworthiness – or what might be called "blind trust" – is likely to end in disappointment or worse (on this point, see O'Neill, 2020).

---

[9] Fukuyama (1995) differs from these definitions in that his conceptualization of political trust encompasses a moral element – a sense of shared moral community, both political and social, with an agreement on what values a society ought to pursue.

For the purpose of the questions that I explore in this volume, whether the trustworthiness of governments or public authorities leads to trust or mere compliance is important, because of its potential to affect the trusting relationship between transacting individuals. As noted above, governments frequently establish the institutional rules of the game that incentivize or constrain interactions between individuals. An example of the former is when governments set out regulations that limit individual freedoms to ensure public health, as they have done in many countries during the COVID-19 pandemic. Such mechanisms that regulate relationships can encourage trustees to be more reliable and tend to enhance cooperation and reduce the risks associated with trusting others (Barber, 1983, p. 170; Coleman, 1990, p. 114; Hardin, 2002, p. 46). If government or public authorities are not seen to be trustworthy (e.g., when public officials are perceived as not following the rules themselves or as instituting policies that, while purportedly aiming at protecting public health, seem merely to be aimed at increasing government powers) the basis for trust is diminished, or even reliance on governments to faithfully fulfil their missions. In such cases, individual citizens may protest the institutional rules that governments or public authorities lay out or enforce (voice), or they may even reject government institutional rules of the game outright (exit),[10] which might lead to the formation of subversive political movements.

At other times, trust is transitive. Governments may act as trust intermediaries to provide guarantees of trustworthiness in interactions between individuals. An example of this is when governments issue licences to restaurants to signal that a restaurant is safe to eat in. If the issuing government agency is seen as being untrustworthy, then citizens will also not trust or have confidence that the restaurant is safe.

Thus, governments and public authorities perform important functions vis-à-vis trusting relationships within society, and the degree of perceived trustworthiness of governments – whether considered as a unity or in relation to specific individual agencies, arms of governments, or to individual public officials – matters.

2.5 Conclusion

In this chapter, we have considered the problem and nature of trust in both an interpersonal and an institutional (collective) form, asserting that trust involves

---

[10] I refer here to the theory of exit, voice, and loyalty articulated by Hirschman (1978). The theory presents a choice that consumers face when encountering deteriorating quality of goods: either exit (leave the market) or voice (protest/complain). Hirschman's ideas have been applied in a wide range of fields, including political science.

a three-part relationship between a trustor, a trustee, and some domain of behavior wherein the trustee's behavior is perceived to encapsulate the interests of the trusting party. We have also understood trust as epistemic in nature since it involves the acquisition of knowledge about a trustee on the part of the trustor and the formation of a justified true belief as the basis of a choice about whether to act on the basis of trust or not. Further, we have said that trust always involves some level of risk on the part of the trusting party.

Equipped with a clearer notion of trust in its interpersonal and institutional forms, it is now possible to consider the relationship between trust and block-chains. Given trust's many discontents, as discussed in this chapter, it is certainly possible to understand why Satoshi Nakamoto sought to disintermediate third-party trust middlemen – an approach that has been called "trustless trust." It is down this rabbit hole that we will go in the next chapter.

3

From "Trustless Trust" to "The Great Chain of Certainty"

In the digital age, technology has become another important consideration in relation to trust. Science fiction films from *2001: A Space Odyssey* to *Ex Machina* illustrate how questions of human trust in computer technology have entered into our social consciousness. In the 2014 science fiction film *Ex Machina*, for example, a computer programmer, Caleb, wins a contest to spend a week at the private estate of his company's CEO, an inventor of novel technology. Caleb's time at the estate takes a dark turn when he discovers that he is a participant in a Turing test devised to reveal the capabilities of the CEO's latest invention – a humanoid robot named Ava. Ava, it transpires, is more intelligent and manipulative than imagined and (spoiler alert) she soon betrays the trust of both her creator and Caleb.

While Hardin's (2002) encapsulated interest model of trust – which I explored in Chapter 2 – certainly seems to apply to Caleb's relationship with Ava, can it provide a foundation for thinking more broadly about trust and blockchain and distributed ledger technology? Hardin does not specifically address the question of trust in technology. Indeed, Hardin's work, and much of the literature on trust, concerns trust between people or institutions, not trust in technology. Some might even question whether it is possible to trust technology or to say that it is trustworthy, at least in the same sense that we use the notion of trust and trustworthiness when speaking of social relations. Yet, there can be no question that technology plays an increasingly important role in human trusting relationships. Exploring the nature of trust in technology, leading into a discussion of trust in blockchains and other distributed ledgers, is what we will turn to next.

3.1 Trust and Technology

One field that has looked closely at the issue of trust in technology is management information systems (MIS). The particular context of much of the MIS literature on trust concerns users' interactions with e-commerce systems, such as the ubiquitous Amazon or eBay. Beatty et al. (2011, p. 2), in a survey of the literature on trust and information systems, note that the relationship between the customer and the retailer in an e-commerce environment involves trust, since users "must entrust their personal information to an organization they know only from images displayed on a computer screen." For most research in the MIS field, trust in e-commerce situations is conceived of as a relationship between the vendor of an e-commerce website – such as Amazon – and a user, rather than as between sellers and buyers in transactions mediated by a particular platform – as in the case of bitcoin – or between the platform and the user (McKnight et al., 2002; Beatty et al., 2011). This formulation sidesteps the question of whether trust and trustworthiness are concepts that can be applied to such technological artifacts themselves, as might be necessary to answer the questions surrounding trust in blockchain and distributed ledger technology.

Some philosophers (Nickel et al., 2010; Ess, 2020) object to the idea that a technical system – perhaps excepting the robot Ava – can fulfil a trust placed in it, since it lacks an awareness of being a self – distinct from others – and of its affective states, both of which would be needed to be able to reflect upon the trustor's interests and the trustee's own choices about how to behave in relation to a trustor's expectations. Hardin's encapsulated interest conceptualization of trust requires that the trustee have interests of their own, which a technical artifact might not possess in the same way as a human. "Since all of these qualities are normally possessed only by humans," write Nickel et al. (2010, p. 432), "it would make sense to conclude that technology can never be genuinely trustworthy; it can only be reliable." That is, a computer system can only ever be said to be performing as it is intended to function "under given conditions of use for a specified period of time or number of cycles" (ISO, 2017, s. 315).

To circumvent this issue, McKnight et al. (2011, p. 3), focusing on the relationship of trust between users and non-intelligent technical artifacts, argue for a more relaxed notion of trust: "Our position is that trust situations arise when one has to make oneself vulnerable by relying on another person or object, regardless of the trust object's will or volition," they write. Similarly, Nguyen (in press) argues that the concept of trust can be applied to non-agentic objects as much as agentic persons, since trust manifests when the trustor holds an unquestioning attitude toward the trusted person or object. This formulation, however, does not appear to provide a path to applying an encapsulated interest notion of trust and trustworthiness to non-intelligent technological artifacts.

A number of writers (Winner, 1978, 1985; Latour, 1992; Latour and Venn, 2002; Nickel et al., 2010), however, allow for derived notions of trust and trustworthiness in the case of socio-technical systems that do point the way to application of the encapsulated interest model through the notion of a socio-technical system. The concept of a socio-technical system – a social system operating on a technical base – is widely accepted nowadays and encompasses the notion of what some researchers characterize as a "social machine" (Smart and Shadbolt, 2015). From this perspective, the system – a concept originating in von Bertalanffy's (1950, 1968) general systems theory – is constituted by both a social system and a technical system. Socio-technical systems are a way of thinking about systems that integrates what social scientists typically think about – that is, people and social institutions – with what software engineers and computer scientists think about – that is, devices and software. These different aspects of focus can be characterized as different abstraction layers – that is, the social and the technical abstraction layers – constituting the system as a whole but also recognizing an interdependency between the social and the technical dimensions of systems. Each abstraction layer may involve focusing on specific aspects of a system as the primary objects of analysis. In the case of the computer scientist, the focus is easily understood as the devices and software constituting an information system. In the case of the social scientist, the focus might take the form of system users or socially negotiated protocols by which humans interacting with the system agree to interact.

The characterization of systems as socio-technical also recognizes that the social and technical dimensions of a system – the human and the technical – not only function interdependently but are also cogenerative, or co-creative, of one another. Cogeneration recognizes that human agents (i.e., core developers) create the blockchain technical protocols that govern how a blockchain system operates, which in turn affects the interaction of human network participants (e.g., those using bitcoin as digital cash) and the ledger that their interactions inscribe. Over time, the collective behaviors of network participants may lead to changes in the technical protocols (e.g., the need for a block size increase seen with Bitcoin Cash) that alter the interactions of human network participants; that is, some participants adopt a revised protocol while others reject it. This, in turn, affects the technical system; for example, it might result in the creation of a hard fork (see Chapter 8 for further discussion of this dynamic). It is in this sense that it is possible to argue that blockchains can be ascribed agentic behavior that allows for the attribution of motivations that derive from the aggregate intentionality of human participants as interdependent and co-generative "components" of a system.

Nickel et al. (2010) caution that this allows only for a "thin" notion of trust and trustworthiness, in the sense of not requiring agentic behavior on the part of the trustee, that therefore does not straightforwardly translate the application of an encapsulated interest model to technological artifacts. That might very well be true if we were discussing a mere technical artifact in considering blockchain and distributed ledger technology. However, as I have previously discussed (see Section 1.1), blockchains and distributed ledgers are more than technical artifacts. They are socio-informational-technical "ecosystems" in which patterned expectations of behavior are defined and embodied, along the lines of "social machines." Trust is therefore an inherent part of how they operate, whether we are referring to how core developers bring blockchain and distributed ledger protocols into being or to the interactions that take place between network participants as they transact with one another and co-create a distributed ledger.

3.2 Blockchains, Trust, and Trustworthiness

In the following sections, I aim to add clarity to the understanding of trust and trustworthiness in relation to blockchains and distributed ledger technologies by arguing that there are (at least) three distinct but interrelated forms of trust applicable to them (see Figure 3.1). First, there is the notion of the user's perception of trust in blockchain systems or applications – I call this "user trust," which encompasses the usability of blockchain and distributed ledger systems – a growing area of research – and user perceptions of the trustworthiness of blockchains and distributed ledgers based on who the users of the technology are (or are imagined to be) and what they use it for (or are imagined to use it for). Then, there is the widely discussed notion of "trustless trust," which is trust in the "mathematics" of the consensus mechanisms of blockchain and distributed ledger systems and is where most of the prior research and writing on trust and blockchain technology has been concentrated. Finally, there is what I will call "ledger trust," which focuses on trust in the ledger as a source of evidence. This form of blockchain trust is often subsumed within the concept of trustless trust and has received much less attention in blockchain research and writing; however, I argue, it is really at the heart of what enables trust in the context of blockchains and distributed ledgers.

User Trust

The cryptography, distributed networking, and consensus mechanisms that drive the operation of blockchain and many other distributed ledger networks are obscure to most people. Knowledge of the trustworthiness of a given distributed ledger is mediated for most users – if they have direct experience with these technologies – by their interaction with a ledger's user interface and

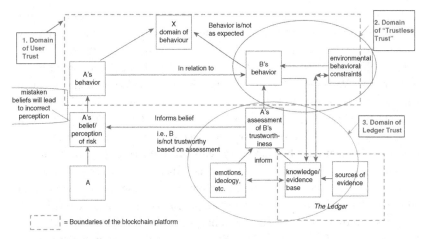

Figure 3.1 Three types of trust in blockchains and distributed ledger platforms
Note: This figure builds upon the model of trust presented in Chapter 2, in which
I discussed the idea of trust being a relationship between A (a trusting party) and B (a
trusted party), with respect to X (some domain). The blockchain or distributed ledger
platform encompasses the evidence base, the ledger, upon which A will base their
assessment of B's trustworthiness. The three types of trust are also represented in this
model. User trust (Domain 1) concerns how the platform is perceived by users to
mediate the interaction of A and B. Trustless trust (Domain 2) pertains to the
constraints and incentives on B's behavior (the incentive mechanisms of blockchains),
while ledger trust (Domain 3) is trust in the ledger as providing the evidence A needs to
assess B's trustworthiness. A assesses B's trustworthiness to determine whether it is
justified in order to form a belief that B can be trusted. In order to make this
assessment, A draws upon evidence – to the extent that it is available – of B's past
behavior to draw inferences about whether B is likely to behave as expected, evidence
of B's interests, and knowledge of the factors – such as laws or norms – that might
constrain or incentivize B's behavior. This builds upon the previous model (see
Figure 2.1) to overlay the boundary of the (public permissionless) blockchain platform,
which A and B use to interact. It also includes some aspects of the constraints or
incentives governing B's behavior (some remain outside the system even in public
permissionless blockchains).

their experience with using the system or, if they lack direct experience, by
what they learn from others about the use (or imagined uses)[1] of these technologies. In other words, they maintain a surface view of the blockchain and
distributed ledger system in which, for the most part, the ledger is viewed as
a "black box" that delivers services (Wand and Weber, 1995).

It is well recognized that blockchain and distributed ledger systems face
a usability challenge, usability referring to "the degree to which something is fit

---

[1] On the importance of also considering imagined uses of technologies, see Müller and Tworek
(2016).

and able to be used" (Lexico, 2021). There are, for example, issues relating to how to back up wallets or what people should do if they lose their private key (Swan, 2015; Voskobojnikov et al., 2020). Users generally have become used to being able to seek help from a third party (e.g., an IT help desk) in the event of problems. With many blockchain and distributed ledger systems, no such help exists, which poses a challenge for users who lack sufficient understanding of the technology to help themselves. Eskandari et al. (2015) suggest, based on a cognitive walkthrough for various bitcoin key management systems, that the metaphors being used in blockchain systems can often be unclear for end users, leading them to make dangerous errors. Even experienced users report that they have lost their private keys or wallet passwords.[2] These findings have been confirmed by Voskobojnikov et al. (2020, p. 13), who state that "Users ha[ve] dangerous knowledge gaps and misconceptions when it [comes] to the key building blocks of cryptocurrencies. Some users [do] not know the difference between public and private keys, and one incorrectly believed that they had access to their private key while using an exchange." In addition, a recent technology acceptance study by Shrestha and Vassileva (2019), involving the usability of a prototype blockchain interface, found that both the quality and user enjoyment of the system influence users' intentions to adopt blockchain-based systems. Blockchain application programming interfaces (APIs) also are often not user-friendly and do not follow the current standards for usable APIs, with much scope for improvement in their design (Swan, 2015; Gao et al., 2016; Filippova et al., 2019; Kumar and Kumar, 2020; Voskobojnikov et al., 2020). While most of the research on the usability of blockchains is Bitcoin-centric (Gao et al., 2016; Krombholz et al., 2016; Sas and Khairuddin, 2017) – and Voskobojnikov et al. (2020) point to some variance according to users' level of expertise, application area, and the type of crypto-asset – there still can be no question that blockchain usability is a widespread and largely unresolved issue.

These usability issues affect users' willingness to trust blockchain and distributed ledger technology sufficiently to adopt it for use. As the MIS literature suggests, trusting parties will form beliefs about the trustworthiness of a given system based, in part, upon knowledge of a number of attributes of a system (e.g., good interface design or how helpful the user perceives the system to be [see McKnight et al., 2011, pp. 12–17]) from which the trustor might also make inferences about the trustworthiness of parties on the other side of a transaction (McKnight et al., 2011). Gao et al.

---

[2] Stories abound of even people who are technically savvy losing their private keys or bitcoin wallet passwords (see, e.g., Murray, 2021; Goodyear, 2021).

(2016) find that those with limited knowledge turn away from using a system (e.g., the Bitcoin network) due to lack of understanding and perceived usefulness. When trusting parties lack knowledge of blockchain and distributed ledger systems or when information is misleading or confusing, trusting parties are likely to perceive the risks of transacting as too high and thus are likely to avoid using that type of system to transact (see Figure 3.1, Domain 1).

It is also important to recognize that trust in the designers, sponsors, or users of blockchain systems will affect perceptions of the trustworthiness of blockchains as a category of thing, which, in turn, influences perceptions of the trustworthiness of specific instances (i.e., specific blockchain platforms or networks [C. Lu et al., 2020]). Voskobojnikov et al. (2020) note that lack of understanding skews users' perceptions of the risks of using blockchain systems, including user-cited concerns about the potential for governments to trace cryptocurrency transactions back to them or that trading in cryptocurrency could affect their reputational standing within their social group. Concerns about reputational damage likely arise from bitcoin's perceived popularity among hackers and money launderers, periodic warnings against bitcoin as an investment, and a history of cryptocurrency scams (see, e.g., Phillips and Wilder, 2020 and Alex Hern as interviewed in Humphreys, 2021). The bottom line is that perceptions of the users and uses of distributed ledger systems – especially blockchains – and users' general lack of understanding of how such systems operate often contribute more to distrust than to trust in blockchain and distributed ledger systems as a general category. Trust in blockchains and distributed ledgers as a category is critical to adoption of the technology, however. As Nissenbaum (2001, p. 636) observes, "People shy away from territories they distrust ... consumers balk because they are fearful that they will be cheated [or] defrauded, ... businesses stay away fearing costly losses from such actions as failure to pay, repudiation of their commitments, and so on."

While user trust provides an important perspective on trust in blockchains and distributed ledger technologies, especially as it relates to adoption of such technologies, it does not capture the notion of trust that Satoshi Nakamoto had in mind in developing Bitcoin. For an understanding of this type of trust, we must turn to another concept: "trustless trust."

Trustless Trust

In considering trustless trust, we make a critical shift from observer-relative perceptions of the trustworthiness of blockchain and distributed ledger technologies based on usability or what a user perceives and comes to believe about uses of the technology to a perspective focused on the "deep structure" (Wand and Weber, 1995)[3] of the technology and how the creators of block-chains and distributed ledger systems seek to address problems of trust among human social actors. Here, it is important to note, we strip away any moral judgements about those social actors; in other words, trustless trust is as apt to apply to social actors that operate well within the bounds of what a given society considers socially acceptable (e.g., participants in a supply chain aiming to assure food security) as to those who operate outside of the norms of society (e.g., money launderers). That is to say, "Trust between partners in crime increases the chances of criminal success, and social solidarity among oppressive communities strengthens their efficacy" (Nissenbaum, 2001, p. 642) as much as it does between partners operating according to the mores of society.

As discussed in Chapter 1, public, permissionless blockchains aim to address problems of societal trust – trust between social actors – trustlessly, that is, to offer trustless trust. The term trustless trust, an apparent oxymoron, was coined by the American entrepreneur Reid Hoffman in a 2014 post he wrote on why he was investing in the company Blockstream,[4] a Bitcoin and blockchain com-pany. In his post, Hoffman (2014) writes,

> Bitcoin is often characterized in the media as a volatile virtual commodity that can optimize speculation even more efficiently than gold, securitized subprime mortgages, or tulips. That's not how I think about it. . . . The blockchain creates the possibility of trustless trust. Parties no longer need to know or trust each other to participate in exchanges of value with absolute assurance and no intermediaries. So the blockchain greatly reduces the need for third-party payments processors and the fees they charge. It eliminates the possibility of credit card fraud. It creates new possibilities for micro-payments. (You can send someone a fraction of a bitcoin, with transaction fees so disruptively low [recall that he was writing in 2014], that the Wall Street Journal or New York Times could effectively charge a penny to read a single article. AMC could charge a quarter to watch the latest episode of The Walking Dead commercial-free.) The blockchain makes all kinds of cross-border commerce easier, especially when it involves places where there aren't credit card networks or robust banking systems.

---

[3] Wand and Weber (1995, p. 206) explain the deep structure of technology as "manifest[ing] the meaning of the real-world system the information system is intended to model. Hence, following linguistic traditions . . . we call it the deep structure of the information system. For example, the rules embodied in an accounting system that indicate how transactions are to be posted to ledgers reflect deep-structure characteristics. These rules indicate how the wealth of certain organiza-tions and individuals in the real world alters as contracts in an economy are exchanged and executed."

[4] See Blockstream.com.

Hoffman's expression took root and "trustless trust" is now widely used to describe trust in the context of blockchains (see Werbach, 2019), even if the implication that the need for trust will disappear turns out to be mistaken.

From the perspective of those with absolute faith in technology – the "techno-fundamentalists" – the unique features and capabilities of blockchains might appear to eliminate the need for trust (cf. Walch, 2015, citing Vaidhyanathan, 2012). Exemplifying this view is a quote from the *New York Times*, attributed to Tyler Winklevoss, in 2013 on a decision to invest in Bitcoin: "We have elected to put our money and faith in a mathematical framework that is free of politics and human error," he states (Popper and Lattman, 2013). And Szabo (2017) writes that blockchains seek to replace "trust in the secret and arbitrarily mutable activities of a private computation" with "verifiable confidence in the behavior of a generally immutable public computation." Like Szabo, De Filippi et al. (2020) argue that blockchain's use of cryptography, mathematics, and game theoretical incentives makes it a "confidence machine," not a machine of trust, because participants (most of the time) face no risk. With trustless trust, blockchain system users can interact with untrusted parties without suffering a loss due to the failure of external third-party trust intermediaries. And, as Antonopoulos (2014) says, public, permissionless blockchains involve a "shift from trusting people to trusting math." Thus, trust in third-party intermediaries backed by trust in the law, or *lex juris*, is replaced by trust in the blockchain, backed by a consensus algorithm, or *lex cryptographia*, said to reduce the risk of transacting even among parties who lack the knowledge to trust one another. Any materialized risk, such as the DAO exploit of 2016, is accounted for not as a failure of trust but rather as a mere technical glitch or anomaly associated with the operation of the system.

In contrast to this view, many writers have commented upon how blockchains such as Bitcoin merely shift the locus of risk, and trust, rather than eliminating it completely (Walch, 2015; Bratspies, 2018; De Filippi et al., 2020). Walch (2015, pp. 888–889) argues that Bitcoin is subject to human politics as much as any other human endeavor; she writes,

witness the debates over its future in the Bitcoin message boards, the important role the core developers play in determining its future, and the potential conflicts of interests raised by the core developers' sources of income. Witness the power struggle ongoing between the grownup, moneyed interests coming into the Bitcoin ecosystem through venture capital investments, and the early adopters who were or are interested in Bitcoin as a cool computer project or a realization of the dreams of Austrian economics. Bitcoin is inescapably a people project, and, like all such projects, is flawed in certain ways.

Similarly, Bratspies (2018) finds that there are layers of trust – and risk – embedded in blockchain-based cryptocurrencies, citing the fact that most cryptocurrencies are much more centralized than advertised and end up requiring interacting parties to place their trust in individual nodes; that blockchains such as Bitcoin, which rely upon mining, depend upon the honesty of the miners (which is certainly not guaranteed); that blockchains are subject to the whims of their core developers and to the vagaries of coding errors; that cryptocurrency wallets and exchanges are subject to hacks and thefts; and that initial coin offerings mostly involve scammers. De Filippi et al. (2020), despite describing blockchains as confidence machines, also point to the fact that trust is necessary whenever anyone transacts using a public, permissionless blockchain such as Bitcoin: trust in wallets and cryptocurrency exchanges, in core developers, and in miners and mining pools. From this we might conclude that blockchains are no more to be trusted as a reliable investment or store of value than tulip bulbs should have been in the seventeenth century.[5] It is this seemingly contradictory way in which blockchains – at least the public, permissionless ones – offer trust but might not quite be trustworthy that resolves to the notion of trustless trust. This has serious implications: if unquestioningly relied upon, the implied presumption of trustless trust (i.e., that trust is no longer necessary) leaves participants vulnerable to breaches of a trust that they did not even realize they had placed in the blockchain and distributed ledger systems that they are using to transact.

Though some may strongly assert otherwise, public, permissionless blockchains' form of trustless trust creates the conditions for trust between interacting parties in much the same way as government institutions establishing laws and regulations do – and should thus create incentives and institutionalized rules of the game that serve to align or constrain the interests of a trustee with those of the party doing the trusting (see Figure 3.1). Recall, as we discussed in Chapter 2, that trust involves a three-part relationship between a trustor, a trustee, and some domain of behavior wherein the trustee's behavior encapsulates the interests of the trusting party. Trust always involves some level of risk of harm to the trusting party, but also recall that norms and laws can be used to incentivize or constrain the trustee's behavior to reduce the risk of harm, as in the example of the public health official. This idea connects to Seligman's

[5] JP Morgan CEO Jamie Dimon has famously been quoted as saying about Bitcoin: "It's worse than tulip bulbs. It won't end well. Someone is going to get killed." (Imbert, 2017). Dimon was referring to the tulip bulb market bubble that occurred in the Netherlands during the early to mid-1600s, when speculation drove the value of tulip bulbs to ridiculous heights: the rarest tulip bulbs traded for as much as six times the average person's annual salary. By the end of 1637, prices began to fall and many people who had purchased bulbs on credit had to sell their bulbs at disastrously discounted prices and declare bankruptcy.

concept of trust in systems as trust in a set of institutions (Seligman, 1997). In this same way, a public, permissionless blockchain's unique features and mode of operating reduce the trustor's risk of relying on the trustee, since the trustor trusts the system to shape the behavior of the trustee in a way that encapsulates the trustor's interests (see Figure 3.1, Domain 1). In this sense, so-called trustless trust is not so much trustless as a form of trust that, in theory, shifts risk-reducing strategies from human institutions (e.g., governments and the law) to a combination of algorithms and noninstitutional actors. Equally though, without a proper understanding of how trustless trust mechanisms work, users of blockchain and distributed ledger systems could end up taking on risks they do not even realize they are accepting.

What makes blockchain-based trustless trust different from previous forms of trust is how this mechanism works. Many of the rules that constrain the behavior of the trustee do not exist outside of the system. For example, in public, permissionless blockchains, there is no external third-party guarantor of the trustworthiness of an interacting party.[6] There is no government regulator promulgating and enforcing laws and regulations, nor any financial intermediary – such as a bank – guaranteeing either the value of bitcoins or that they have not been double spent by their sender. Indeed, Bitcoin seeks to disintermediate such external trust mediators, thereby circumventing traditional institutional logics and modalities of trust (or confidence) production, regulation, and control – the *rule of law* – to reconfigure them in the Bitcoin network using very different logics and modalities – the rule of code or *lex cryptographia* (Seligman, 1997; Swan, 2015; De Filippi and Wright, 2018; Lemieux, 2019; Yeung, 2019; Bodó, 2020). In this way, governance by law is replaced with a form of "technologically encoded authority" (Aneesh, 2002, p. 1).

At the technical level of abstraction, there is also no external third-party certificate authority vouching for the digital signatures that form an essential component of the way in which bitcoins are sent and received, nor in how the Bitcoin network functions to generate consensus about the state of the shared ledger. Instead, the Bitcoin network incorporates endogenous mechanisms to prevent double spending. Principally, as discussed in Chapter 1, Bitcoin uses cryptographic chaining together of hashes of transactions and the Proof-of-Work (PoW) consensus mechanism to either constrain or incentivize the behavior of participants on the network so that their interests align. In the operation of PoW, for example, all participants, in theory, have an equal chance to discover

---

[6] The sociologist Anthony Giddens states that such guarantees are achieved by (or mediated through) symbolic tokens or expert systems. The former refers to "media of interchange which can be 'passed around' without regard to the specific characteristics of individuals or groups that handle them at any particular juncture" (Giddens, 1990, p. 22, as cited in Bodó, 2020).

blocks and mine them to receive a reward. As their wealth accumulates, the PoW mechanism is designed to align the incentives of network participants: it is considered much more valuable to participants to be able to continue to mine blocks, even taking into consideration the investments that they must make in mining capacity, as a means of preserving and increasing their wealth than it is to cheat. Similarly, at the scale of transactions, a decentralized and transparent ledger encourages honesty by rendering any tampering evident and by discarding any transactions that are inconsistent with the history of the longest chain. As Nakamoto (2008a, p. 1) writes in the original Bitcoin paper, this achieves "an electronic payment system based on cryptographic proof instead of trust, allowing any two willing parties to transact directly with each other without the need for a trusted third party" or, in other words, trustless trust. In this way, though it might not be possible for an individual to trust a pseudonymous user of the Bitcoin network with whom they are interacting because they lack knowledge of the other user's trustworthiness, it might be possible for them to trust the blockchain technology to create the conditions needed to justifiably believe that it is reasonably safe to interact with even an untrusted counterparty about whom nothing is known – similar to jumping into a taxi and trusting the taxi driver to take you to your destination because you know that laws and regulations constrain the taxi driver's behavior.

The concept of trustless trust only truly applies to public, permissionless blockchains – such as Bitcoin and Ethereum – and not to private, permissioned blockchains or other types of distributed ledgers. The trust models are quite different in private, permissioned distributed ledgers (Wüst and Gervais, 2018). In these types of systems, a single controlling interest or a consortium of controlling interests takes the role of trust guarantor: first, by identifying and authorizing participating parties to use the system and, second, by setting out the rules for participation, often in legal contracts that provide parties with recourse to the courts should the behavior of one party in a transaction prove to be less than trustworthy. For this reason, trustless trust cannot fully encapsulate how trust is embodied in all types of blockchains and distributed ledgers. For a more encompassing notion of trust, we must turn to what all such systems have in common: a ledger.

Ledger Trust (Epistemic Trust)

The third form of blockchain trust is trust in the ledger as a source of "final, definitive and immutable" evidence of truth claims. This form of trust, like trustless trust, is concerned with the deep structure (Wand and Weber, 1995) of a distributed ledger system; however, unlike trustless trust, it applies to all types of distributed ledger system, since, by definition, they all incorporate a ledger. Ledger trust is often conflated with or subsumed within the other forms of trust discussed above and has received relatively little separate attention in the literature. Given blockchain's origins in parallel with the cryptocurrency bit-coin, it is hardly surprising that discussions of trust and blockchains have been dominated by, and embedded within, notions of the market-based economics that underpin the concept of trustless trust and blockchains as digital cash, crypto-assets, or payment platforms.

It was not until several years after the Bitcoin codebase was released that commentators began to see real potential for Bitcoin's shared ledger beyond its application as a form of digital cash and economic exchange, giving rise to what has come to be known as Blockchain 2.0 (Bheemaiah, 2015). Developers were already experimenting with this possibility on the Bitcoin network in its early days, however, as evidenced by the number of what former lead main-tainer of Bitcoin's codebase Gavin Andresen is reported to have referred to as "bizarre hacks" to embed content into the Bitcoin blockchain and debates about block bloat (Bradbury, 2013).[7] Colored Coins, which aimed to extend Bitcoin's use into new domains, was one of these methods. A whitepaper on the approach describes a variety of applications that could use Colored Coins to represent physical assets, such as buying and selling of houses or cars (Rosenfeld, 2012).

Shortly after the release of the whitepaper, Ubitquity – a Bitcoin-based real estate transaction platform – piloted the use of Colored Coins and bitcoin to support land sales in Brazil (Lemieux, 2017a). But many of the methods used for embedding data increased the amount of storage required to maintain the ledger because data had to be entered into the Unspent Transaction Output (UTXO) dataset in order to be recorded.[8] To address the growing problem of block bloat, a 2013 update to the Bitcoin core protocol introduced a new method of embed-ding data that did not require that the data be entered into the UTXO dataset, instead, it used the new OP_RETURN transaction parameter. This helped drive forward Blockchain 2.0 use cases. The rise of Ethereum in 2013–14 as a new blockchain platform incorporating the capability to encode smart contracts – "computer program[s] stored on a DLT system wherein the outcome of any execution of the program is recorded on the distributed ledger" (ISO, 2020a, s. 3.72) – also heightened awareness and experimentation with use cases for blockchains beyond cryptocurrencies and payments. With the rise of Blockchain 2.0, the importance of the ledger as an anchor for trust came into sharper focus.

---

[7] See Sward et al. (2018) for a description of the various methods being used.

[8] UTXO is used to efficiently verify new generated transactions. Bitcoin makes use of the UTXO dataset to keep track of output transactions that have not yet been spent and thus can be used as inputs to new transactions (see Narayanan et al., 2016).

Observers of these developments, such as the *Economist*, began to take note, recognizing the potential of the underlying ledger to meet the need for "a trustworthy record, something vital for transactions of every sort" (Economist, 2015b). In a piece that clearly distinguished between three things that had, up to that point, been "muddled up" (and arguably still are) – bitcoin currency, the underlying blockchain ledger, and blockchains in general – the *Economist* exuberantly stated,

> The blockchain is an even more potent technology [than bitcoin the currency] . . . [it could] make cheap, tamper-proof public databases – land registries, say, (Honduras and Greece are interested); or registers of the ownership of luxury goods or works of art. Documents can be notarised by embedding information about them into a public blockchain – and you will no longer need a notary to vouch for them. Financial-services firms are contemplating using blockchains as a record of who owns what instead of having a series of internal ledgers. A trusted private ledger removes the need for reconciling each transaction with a counterparty, it is fast and it minimises errors. . . . The notion of shared public ledgers may not sound revolutionary or sexy. Neither did double-entry book-keeping or joint-stock companies. Yet, like them, the blockchain is an apparently mundane process that has the potential to transform how people and businesses co-operate.
>
> *(Economist, 2015b, p. 13)*

In the same issue of the magazine, the *Economist* also described the blockchain ledger as "the great chain of being sure about things" (Economist, 2015a).

Echoing and amplifying this theme, Paul Vigna and Michael Casey's 2018 book, *The Truth Machine: The Blockchain and the Future of Everything*, describes the transformative power of the blockchain accounting ledger. In a 2018 article in *Newsweek*, Casey is quoted as summing it up this way, "The entire global system of record keeping is going to go through a 5,000-years paradigm shift ... We've tracked and checked records, and records are the foundational layer of economic exchange systems, they go right back to Sumerian tablets. We had centralized versions of that for 5,000 years. Now, we're doing a decentralized thing that is a game changer." (Piore, 2018).

What these authors recognized and highlighted is that records and record-keeping *provide epistemic grounds for trust that has enabled human social coordination and cooperation over centuries*. In their research on recordkeeping and human evolution, Basu and Waymire (2006, p. 204) theorize that systematized keeping of "memory of past dealings (i.e., records) promotes greater cooperation because it helps actors identify trustworthy partners."[9] It is, therefore, a "culturally evolved institution that enables complex economic

---

[9] According to Cosmides and Tooby (1992), the evolved human brain allows for better communication and assessment of trustworthiness.

interaction." Systematic recordkeeping enables the formation of a "collective memory," that is, institutionalized social memory that exists outside an individual human mind and which "is a necessary condition for the emergence of extended economic cooperation" (Basu and Waymire, 2006, p. 201; see also Basu et al., 2009).[10] Basu and Waymire write (2006, p. 202),

> The basic recordkeeping function embodied in the modern journal entry lies at the core of all accounting systems. Internal controls and verification by auditors transform transactional records into "hard" information that later makes it "difficult for people to disagree" (Ijiri 1975, 36). The hard transactional record institutionalizes memory of past exchanges and enables third-party verification of prior events and obligations to resolve ex post disputes. Institutionalized memory via immutable, verifiable records of past exchange, combined with norms of honesty embodied in law and other exchange-supporting institutions, are needed to sustain the trust that enables complex economic cooperation between strangers over time. Opportunities for exchange, in turn, promote the extensive division of labor as well as the larger, more complex societies that are the primary causes of modern wealth generation (Smith 1776, Book I, Chaps. 1 and 2). Indeed, the "paper trail" generated by economic exchange is ubiquitous in modern advanced economies.[11]

Basu, Waymire, and others were able to empirically demonstrate that a rise in the number and complexity of reciprocal exchanges in a society yields a concomitant rise in formal recordkeeping due to the need to supplement the limitations that human memory experiences in keeping track of the past behavior of many interacting parties (Basu and Waymire, 2006; Basu et al., 2009). They also found that recordkeeping, communications technologies, and law co-evolve in larger complex societies, exhibiting a two-way causality in which core recordkeeping technology enables complex cooperative agreements and those agreements give rise to new forms of recordkeeping (Basu and Waymire, 2006), which is an idea also supported by Latour (1986) and

[10] As Basu and Waymire (2006, p. 204) explain, "As the scale and complexity of exchange transactions grows, at some point even the most developed brain becomes overwhelmed. Accounting records are abstract physical representations of past exchange and cooperative endeavor, and they act as backup and/or primary memory for economic agents engaged in large-scale complex exchange. By expanding memory capacity far beyond the biological constraints of the human brain, accounting records vastly increased the scale and scope of human cooperation. Combined with language, law, and other coordination-supporting institutions, hard transactional records helped human civilizations to emerge."

[11] Basu and Waymire (2006, p. 209) go on to say, "Sustaining complex cooperation between people who are initially complete strangers in a large social network requires new institutions to store and disseminate information about each person's past cooperative behavior. We hypothesize that verifiable recordkeeping is an institution that is necessary (but not sufficient) for the emergence of large-scale human cooperation in less compact groups. We believe the importance of this cannot be overstated – without institutions that store and disseminate reliable information about a person's honesty and trustworthiness, extensive market exchange and a complex division of labor would not evolve."

Manoff (2004).[12] While recordkeeping is not the only modality of collective memory formation – for example, many Indigenous cultures have evolved formalized storytelling – it remains an important one across many societies.

In such societies, the ledger – which emerges from the interaction of transacting parties – provides the epistemic foundation for assessment of the trustworthiness of parties to be trusted (see Figure 3.1, Domain 3). Trust in the ledger, therefore, operates quite differently to the trustless trust discussed above. Rather than relying upon trust in the mechanisms of the system (aka trustless trust) – sometimes rather blindly as it turns out – ledger trust is more empowering in that it provides trusting parties with the evidence needed to assess the trustworthiness of trustees. While that assessment relies upon the evidence that a ledger provides, the ledger does not assume control over the assessment. Assessment remains the purview of human assessors, who will have certain capabilities that fully automated systems do not yet possess. For example, they can exercise moral judgement, which might be advantageous when fairness demands that evidence of previous transgressions be "forgotten" when more recent evidence indicates that a previously untrustworthy actor is now "reformed."

As discussed in Chapter 2, trustworthy evidence is needed for a trusting party to form a justified true belief about the degree to which it is safe to trust a party on the other side of a transaction. When evidence about trustworthiness is missing or incomplete, an assessment cannot be made, and a trustor's belief about the degree of trust that can be placed in a trustee will be nonexistent to very low. Memory is essential to the formation of trust. Trust, as Hardin (2002) says, is iterative, and knowledge of the trustworthiness of the party to be trusted builds over time. Individual human memory is limited, however; we can recall the past actions of only a relatively small group of individuals with whom we interact personally. Large, complex societies, on the other hand, require that we can access a "collective memory" about a much larger number of parties with whom we need to interact. Moreover, complex societies require us to interact with parties about whom

---

[12] The institutional economists North and Thomas (1973; see also North, 1990) provide analyses of how economic institutions evolved to capture gains from trade and the division of labor, in which accounting recordkeeping played an important role. De Soto (2000) also argues that a well-functioning property rights system requires that ownership be recorded when someone invests resources to develop or to improve an asset and that the ability to demonstrate legal title through recordkeeping has allowed many individuals to build capital to increase their wealth. Basu and Waymire (2006, p. 212) contend that "recordkeeping and accounting co-evolve with the scale of exchange, complexity in the division of labor, and changes in law and other economic institutions that sustain cooperation. Economists have long understood that market and legal institutions co-evolve spontaneously over extended periods, even in the absence of explicit planning."

we know nothing, which precludes relying on direct knowledge of the other party and our own limited memories (Origgi, 2019).

Records, then, both as cultural institutions – as Basu and Waymire (2006) describe them – and as distinct material forms of communications and cognition-expanding technologies extend the limited capabilities of our memories into the social realm and fix socially agreed "facts" in forms that enable those facts to transcend space and time. The ability to transcend the limitations of human memory, to transcend space and time so that trusting parties can accumulate knowledge about the trustworthiness of parties in which they might place trust, is what records – and distributed ledgers – provide. In this way, records give us the capability to learn about the past in order to assess and mitigate the riskiness of any interaction with another party. In a property transaction, for example, how do we know that the other party is an honest dealer and is not selling us something that is really owned by someone else? Records provide assurance. How can we prove to the other party that we have the funds to purchase the property? Again, records provide proof of the claim. Beyond this value, however, records create a collective cultural memory that instantiates and binds a society together (Berger and Luckmann, 1966; Searle, 1985; Martinez-Ávila and Zandonade, 2020).

Here it is important for us to recall, however, that the totalizing inscription made possible by blockchain and distributed ledgers in relation to transactions between interacting parties (cf. self-sovereign identity-based blockchain and distributed ledger systems, discussed in Chapter 7) means that there also arises the possibility of a distinct threat to personal privacy. Nakamoto dealt with this in the design of Bitcoin by introducing pseudonymized transactions (originally thought to be anonymized); however, the limitations in his design have been revealed through successful efforts to track and link the originators of Bitcoin transactions to natural persons (Naqvi, 2018). In the context of law enforcement, this might be viewed as a feature, not a flaw; but in the context of human rights and freedom of expression, it could equally be viewed as quite the opposite. The challenge is that decisions on such matters rely upon standards of judgement, which, in turn, depend upon whose standards are applied, as I will discuss further in Chapter 4.

This observation further reminds us that records embed power and authority, which is significant for the operation of trust. Both knowledge of the rules and knowledge of trustees' behavior in respect of those rules inform the assessments that trusting parties make in the formation of their beliefs about the risk of interacting with other parties. If trusting parties know that a powerful authority has laid down the rules of interaction and can enforce those rules, they are likely to believe that it is much safer for them to undertake an otherwise risky transaction – assuming they trust the rule-making authority, that is. Traditionally, records have conveyed the power of their issuing authorities – a nation state, for example – to establish and enforce the rules of interaction within a society. In blockchains and some distributed ledgers, power and authority are algorithmically encoded into the ledger. They are *endogenous*; that is, they are achieved via the operation of the rule of code, rather than emanating from the laws of an external government or other authority – authorities that, nowadays, are often perceived to be less trustworthy. Proponents of blockchains argue that the algorithmic nature of the ledger's "rules of the game" free blockchains from the human self-interest and manipulation that afflict traditional institutions. From our previous discussion of trustless trust, and as will be discussed further in Chapter 8, we know that this is not entirely the case. Nevertheless, like all records, the blockchain ledger instantiates and represents institutionalized rules of the game – algorithmic "code as law," for example – that provide the epistemic foundation of trust by means of guaranteeing a trustworthy (in theory) collective memory of past transactions and incentivizing and constraining the behavior of interacting parties.

The genius of records and their importance to the functioning and evolution of society is something we do not often stop to contemplate; records are often missing or invisible as objects of analysis when considering information and its processing. Take for example, the conceptual modelling of information systems. Often such models focus upon business processes, not records (see e.g., Raj and Owen, 2003; Object Management Group, 2020). Latour (1986) describes records and other representations of human cognition as part of the "everyday techne" that constitutes and constructs human social relations. They are "immutable mobiles" (Latour, 1986) – a representation that both fixes and makes mobile what otherwise would be impossible to transport, like a map represents the land and allows us to carry the land with us, metaphorically speaking. The very ordinariness, or "taken for grantedness" (Basu and Waymire, 2006; Ling, 2012), of such materialized representations render them, for the most part, invisible or not worthy of our analytic gaze – that is, until something goes wrong with them, as in the case of the "robo-signing" fiasco of the global financial crisis, the manipulation of land records in Honduras, or, as we will come to in Chapter 6, the manipulation of sources of evidence in disinformation campaigns. The tendency to overlook this socio-technically materialized evidential layer of abstraction is dangerous, however. It can leave individuals vulnerable to breaches of trust and render entire ecosystems more fragile. To rely on records to anchor the sophisticated assessment of the grounds for trust that underpins complex human social and economic relations requires that the records themselves be trustworthy. When these sources of evidence are untrustworthy, a trusting party might form an incorrect or faulty belief about the other party's trustworthiness, resulting in "misplaced trust" (i.e., either trust is given when it is undeserved or it is not given when it is deserved). Thus, studying blockchains and other types of distributed ledgers not only as socio-technical systems but as *socio-informational (evidential) technical* systems (Lemieux and Feng, 2021), in which the ledger as the epistemic foundation of societal trust emerges as a first order object of analysis, is critically important.

Keeping records in a manner that protects their trustworthiness is not a new problem. Even the ancient Sumerians faced it, as Basu and Waymire (2006, p. 214) observe, and devised ways to address it:

> Shortly before 3200 BC, tokens began to be sealed inside hollow clay balls ("bullae") that protected against fraud by imprinting "signatures" of the transacting parties and witnesses (via seals) on the envelope's exterior ... The bullae were then baked, making the records permanent and difficult to alter. The bullae are "hard," as defined by Ijiri (1975, 36), in that transactional data are recorded so that ex post it "will be difficult for people to disagree." Over the next 200 years, the tokens also began to be impressed on the bullae exteriors, the hollow bullae gave way to solid tablets, and the token impressions were replaced first by pictographs (proto-Cuneiform) and finally Cuneiform writing.

Fast-forward several millennia and we now have new blockchain-based forms of securing records through tokenization and affixing signatures that bear a remarkable similarity to the techniques of the ancient Sumerians. Over the centuries, recordkeepers have devised numerous ingenious ways to protect and ascertain the trustworthiness of records as their forms have evolved from clay tablets to paper (see, e.g., Duranti, 1998; Yeo, 2013; Lemieux, 2019), a task that the former British Deputy Keeper of the Public Record Office Sir Hilary Jenkinson (about whom I will have more to say in Chapter 6) referred to as the "moral defense" of the archives (Jenkinson, 1937).[13] The digital age has brought new challenges, however (see, e.g., Duranti and Rogers, 2012; Yeo, 2013; Stančić, 2020). Novel forms of record creation and storage – such as internet-based applications and cloud computing infrastructure – have in many cases rendered obsolete the familiar techniques of systematic recordkeeping designed to protect the trustworthiness of records. Moreover, computerized information processing in the "Big Data Era" is largely designed to efficiently

---

[13] For more on the moral defense of archives, see Jenkinson (1922) and MacNeil (2013). Also, this argument builds upon arguments I first advanced in a World Bank World Development Report background paper (Lemieux, 2016a).

manipulate data, not protect the integrity of records (Saha and Srivastava, 2014). This focus on efficiency and manipulability over the protection of records (the ancient task of the recordkeeper) has contributed to a diminution of the records' perceived trustworthiness and a rise of disinformation (Berti-Équille and Borge-Holthoefer, 2015; Berti-Equille and Ba, 2016) with attendant destabilization of the trust fabric of societies.

The rise of digital technology is not the only cause of the decline in the perceived trustworthiness of records. In the past, the trustworthiness of records was seen to be guaranteed by the trustworthiness of the authorities who created them: public officials, for example, and public recordkeepers – the archivists – who preserved records and managed the institutions in which records were kept (Duranti, 1996; Yeo, 2013; Lemieux, 2019). Recent fluctuations in trust in government and in authorities of all kinds, including professional authority, has contributed to declining trust in the authoritativeness of records: neither records' issuing authorities nor recordkeepers are accorded the same degree of trust they once were (Yeo, 2013). In the past, professional recordkeepers such as archivists, and the special repositories where records were kept, were largely seen to be acting in the public interest, to be trusted (Duranti, 1996; Lemieux, 2019). Declining societal trust has opened to question whose interests recordkeepers actually serve.

Some of the issues that have arisen around the trustworthiness of records in the digital age have, however, come about as a result of the disintermediation of professional recordkeepers (Yeo, 2013). During the global financial crisis, for example, it proved to be impossible to determine who actually owned the properties that underpinned the mortgage-backed securities that had triggered the crisis. The problem was a new digital service, the Mortgage Electronic Registration System, that had been introduced to supplant the supposedly inefficient recordkeeping of the county clerk's offices in the United States with a new, more efficient computerized system. It failed spectacularly, instead introducing short-cuts, such as "robo-signing," that affected the trustworthiness of the records (Dalesio, 2012; Lemieux, 2012, pp. 1–13).

What is so transformative about blockchain ledgers, according to their proponents, is that they provide verifiable facts, the kind of trustworthy sources of evidence needed to assess the trustworthiness of interacting parties as a foundation for trust, and that they are designed to do so (largely) endogenously, that is, without relying on an external human or social trust anchor – instead, they use math. Early developers of Blockchain 2.0 projects realized the potential of blockchains to address problems created by untrustworthy records – and untrustworthy recordkeepers. The president of Factom, a project that early on saw this potential and sought to capitalize on it in a land registry project in Honduras, commented at the time that

> Factom creates permanent records that can't be changed later. In a Factom world, there's no more robo-signing scandals [referring to US mortgage foreclosures during the financial crisis]. In a Factom world, there are no more missing voting records. In a Factom world, you know where every dollar of government money was spent. Basically, the whole world is made up of record keeping, and as a consumer, you're at the mercy of the fragmented systems that run these records ... The dream of many is to extend the honesty inherent to an immutable ledger validated by math to chaotic, real-world interactions. By allowing the construction of unbounded ledgers backed by the blockchain.
>
> *(Higgins, 2014)*

Of course, honesty is not an inherent property of distributed ledger–based recordkeeping any more than it is with traditional forms of recordkeeping (on this point, see Lemieux, 2016c). However, with growing interest in the unique affordances of the blockchain's great chain of certainty, a variety of applications of blockchain ledgers began to proliferate: tracking provenance, establishing the true origins and authenticity of blood diamonds, helping displaced refugees re-establish their identities, giving artists greater control over their artistic creations. All these projects recognized and sought to leverage the power of the immutable blockchain ledger as a trustworthy source of facts. The problems that the Blockchain 2.0 projects sought to address were, therefore, primarily epistemological in nature; that is, they involved issues of trust in sources of evidence. The idea of a trustworthy source of proof was and remains compelling in a world in which society's evidence base is seen to be rapidly unravelling and in need of salvation. The problem, as we will come to in Chapter 7, is that the developers of these projects understood computers, not records, and computational information processing, not recordkeeping. Thus, in many cases, their solutions promised trustworthy records but were not designed to deliver them. Nevertheless, the goal remains a noble one: to restore the trustworthiness of records that is necessary as a basis for societal trusting relationships and the complex and large-scale societal transactions those relationships engender.

3.3 Concluding Thoughts

If, as I argued in the previous chapter, trust is – at least in part – an epistemological concept, requiring evidence of the trustworthiness of parties to be trusted, then it is logical to ask where that evidence comes from. One source of evidence is records, which, as discussed above, constitute an important communications and collective memory formation technology that when combined with systematized and culturally institutionalized recordkeeping, externalizes and reifies human memory and extends it through space and time, providing a foundation for trust – but only, of course, if records and recordkeeping can be trusted. A particular type of record is the ledger, which has a long history of use in the recording of all sorts of human transactions, especially financial ones. Distributed ledgers – which include blockchains – theoretically contribute to the formation of grounds for trust through affording a new form of recordkeeping that is said to assure trustworthy records as sources of evidence relating to transacting parties. Such trustworthy evidence is sorely lacking in an age of disinformation, a topic to which I now turn to deepen an understanding of the appeal and promise of blockchains and distributed ledgers in epistemically troubled times.

PART III

Disinformation

4

Mistrust and the Rise of Disinformation

Between 2014 and 2016, I lived in Washington, DC in a neighborhood known as North Cleveland Park. On weekends, I would often cycle or walk through this lovely area to the nearby Rock Creek Park. On those days, I often passed by a place called Comet Ping Pong, a popular pizzeria on Connecticut Avenue, next to my favorite lunch spot (Little Red Fox) and bookstore (Politics and Prose). In the midst of this tony Washington, DC neighborhood, Comet Ping Pong was as innocuous a place as could be imagined.

Not so according to some, however. On December 4, 2016 – an otherwise peaceful Sunday afternoon – Edgar Maddison Welch, a 28-year-old man from Salisbury, North Carolina, entered Comet Ping Pong and fired three shots from an AR-15 style rifle inside the restaurant (Hsu, 2017). What drove this man to take such extreme measures? According to Welch, he was compelled to "personally investigate" rumors of a child sex trafficking ring he believed was somehow connected with Hillary Clinton and allegedly operating out of tunnels (nonexistent, as it turned out) beneath the restaurant. To those living in the neighborhood and frequenting Comet Ping Pong and nearby businesses, Welch's accusations were as puzzling as his actions were disturbing.

Yet more bizarre was that Welch was not alone in believing that a child sex trafficking ring was operating from the nonexistent basement of Comet Ping Pong. In plea papers, Welch acknowledged that he had become agitated by reports and videos he had read online about the supposed sex ring (Hsu, 2017). "Pizzagate," as this conspiracy theory came to be known, was circulating widely on the Internet in online forums such as 4Chan, 8Chan, and Reddit, and apparently was believed by a good number of individuals beyond just Edgar Maddison Welch (Wendling, 2016).

According to some, Pizzagate was triggered in October 2016, just before the 2016 United States presidential election, when FBI Director James B. Comey reopened the investigation of presidential candidate Hillary Clinton's use of a private email server during the time she served as secretary of state. Comey's decision rested upon the discovery of new emails belonging to former New York Congressman Anthony Weiner, the estranged husband of top Clinton aide Huma Abedin (Fisher et al., 2016). On October 30, 2020, someone tweeting under the handle @DavidGoldbergNY cited rumors that the new emails "point to a paedophilia ring and @HillaryClinton is at the center." The rumor was retweeted more than 6,000 times (Wendling, 2016; Zhang and Clark, 2018). The connection between the alleged Clinton sex ring and Comet Ping Pong apparently came in early November, with a WikiLeaks release of emails from Clinton's campaign chairman, John Podesta, in which James Alefantis, the owner of Comet Ping Pong, was associated with Democratic Party fundraisers (Wendling, 2016). On November 4, 2016, the host of a far-right talk show suggested on his popular YouTube program *InfoWars* that Hillary Clinton was involved in a child sex ring and that Podesta indulged in satanic rituals. By December 6, this video had been viewed more than 427,000 times (Wendling, 2016).[1] The Pizzagate story was further enlivened on the Internet when it became connected with child abuse scandals in Turkey, using the English hashtag "#Pizzagate" to make the connection (Sozeri, 2020).

Figure 4.1 Comet Ping Pong (pictured) was at the center of a disinformation campaign connecting it to a fictitious child sex ring
("Comet Ping Pong in Northwest Washington, D.C." by Farragutful, licenced under CC-BY-SA-4.0)

---

[1] The video has since been removed from YouTube.

4.1 Societal Trust and Information in the Age of Disinformation

As Fisher et al. (2016) put it, "Welch did not shoot anyone in the disturbance on Connecticut Avenue NW, but he delivered a troubling message about the shattering of trust in a troubled time." Sadly, Pizzagate is just one example of the many ways in which disinformation both is emblematic of and has been contributing to an undermining of societal trust. As trust has an epistemic dimension to it, the ability to trust the information we need to assess the trustworthiness of social actors in which we might need to place trust (here, I use the term in its more relaxed sense, following McKnight et al. [2011]) is critical to the formation of trusting relations, as I argued in Chapter 2. How do we develop justified true beliefs about whom or what to trust without trustworthy information? It is certainly very difficult and can contribute to many social disorders: public health might be affected as individuals do not know whether they can place their trust in the advice of scientists; disaster communication might fail when individuals do not know if reports are real or fake; and liberal democracies might come under threat when information about the integrity of an electoral process is doubted. Examples of the havoc caused by disinformation abound, from its impact on the "Brexit" referendum in the United Kingdom (Pogue, 2017) to its role in the troubled 2016 and 2020 United States presidential elections (Silverman, 2016; Pennycook and Rand, 2021) or the way it has fomented public mistrust of the COVID-19 vaccine (Enders et al., 2020). According to Lazer et al. (2017, p. 5), "such situations can enable discriminatory and inflammatory ideas to enter public discourse and be treated as fact. Once embedded, such ideas can in turn be used to create scapegoats, to normalize prejudices, to harden us-versus-them mentalities and even, in extreme cases, to catalyze and justify violence." In the age of disinformation, the societal stakes are high.

How is it that we live in an age of "information abundance" but that we trust the information that surrounds us less and less; or, when we do place our trust in it, we are frequently dismayed to find that our trust has been misplaced and the information cannot be trusted at all? Commenting upon our current condition, Soviet-born British journalist, author, and TV producer Peter Pomerantsev (2019) writes,

> More information was supposed to mean more freedom to stand up to the powerful, but has also given the powerful new ways to crush and silence dissent. More information was supposed to mean a more informed debate, but we seem less capable of deliberation than ever. More information was supposed to mean mutual understanding across borders, but it has also made possible new and more subtle forms of subversion. We live in a world in which the means of manipulation have

gone forth and multiplied, a world of dark ads, psy-ops, hacks, bots, soft facts, deep fakes, fake news, Putin, trolls, and Trump.

What Pomerantsev describes – and what I and many others characterize as "the age of disinformation" (see, e.g., Rubbi, 2018; Froehlich, 2020) – manifests many intertwined epistemological problems. The nature of these problems is the subject of this and the subsequent chapter.

4.2 The Many Faces of Disinformation

Although I use the term disinformation in this volume, there are many other labels that have been assigned to this and similar types of problematic communications: "fake news," "misinformation," "yellow journalism," "junk news," "false information," "false news," "pseudo-news," "hoax news," "propaganda," "advertorial," "mal-information," "alternative fact," and "post-truth" – which was even the 2016 Oxford English Dictionary Word of the Year (Oxford University Press, 2016) – to name just a few.

In a recent survey of fake news and related concepts, Wang (2020) notes that the meaning of fake news is still ambiguous and the boundary between the definition of fake news and other relative concepts is blurred (see Table 4.1). As Kapantai et al. (2020, p. 6) observe, "Each study introduces ad hoc definitions, leading to conflicts or overlaps," nor is there agreement as to what scientific label should be given to such communications. For example, Derakhshan and Wardle (2017, p. 6) note that,

> researchers like Claire Wardle, Ethan Zuckerman, danah boyd, and Caroline Jack and journalists like the Washington Post's Margaret Sullivan have argued, the term "fake news" is woefully inadequate to describe the complex phenomena of mis- and dis-information ... [with Zuckerman stating that it is] "a vague and ambiguous term that spans everything from false balance (actual news that doesn't deserve our attention), propaganda (weaponized speech designed to support one party over another), and *disinformatzya* (information designed to sow doubt and increase mistrust in institutions)."

This situation, according to Lazer et al. (2018), is impeding a scientific approach to answering questions such as, "How common is fake news?" and "What is its impact on individuals?"

Wang's (2020) survey reveals that studies of "information disorders" are on the march, with a steep rise in the number of publications referring to various forms of problematic communications post-2016 (following the US general election). As noted by Wang (2020, p. 162),

Table 4.1 *Example definitions of common types of problematic communications*

Term	Definition
Fake news	A message that contains wrong or false information but does not report the incorrectness of the information
News satire	A type of parody, usually with ironic humor, presented in the form of an ordinary news report
Yellow journalism	Shocking or "clickbait" headlines, exaggerating facts or rumors to catch audience attention
Junk news	News content that is considered as useless as trash; includes propaganda and ideologically extreme, hyper-partisan, or conspiratorial political news and information that is massively disseminated
Pseudo-news	News that reports a nonexistent story
Hoax news	News that contains humorous or malicious deceptions
Propaganda news	A paid report containing propaganda messages that is disguised as a news report but does not disclose the source, the funding provider, or the motivation
Advertorial	An advertisement that is presented in the format of a news report
False information	Incorrect information
Fake information	Incorrect information
Misinformation	Incorrect and misleading information
Disinformation	Deliberately and covertly spread false information intended to influence public opinion
Mal-information	Information used to hurt others
Alternative fact	A misstatement of a fact
Post-truth	Consideration of a statement as truth because of a political standpoint; a political concept of the disappearance of shared objective standards for truth, wherein a message is considered as truth although that message is considered false based on scientific inquiries

Note: Adapted from Wang, 2020, particularly table 1, p.152.

Among the 390 papers published during the period of 2000 to 2019 that contained fake news in paper titles, abstracts, and keyword lists, 379 (97.2%) were published in 2017, 2018 and 2019. Among the 170 papers with fake news in the paper titles published during the period 2000 to 2019, 166 (97.6%) were published in 2017, 2018 and 2019. Thus, it can be concluded that fake news is a new term frequently used after 2017.

Wang's observations are supported by Google Trends,[2] which indicates that the terms "disinformation" and "misinformation" have roughly tracked one

---

[2] Google Trends (www.google.com/trends) is a search trends feature that uses normalized samples of Google search data to provide insights into how frequently a given term is entered into

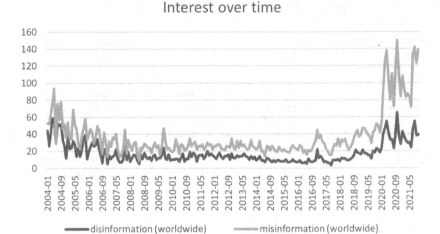

Figure 4.2 The terms "disinformation" and "misinformation" roughly track one
another in respect of usage in Google searches in the period 2004 to January 2021.
Note the spikes in 2004 and in more recent times
(Data source: Google Trends www.google.com/trends)

another in worldwide popularity from 2004 to January 2021 (see Figure 4.2).
Fake news, however, saw a sharp uptick in 2016 and has now become the
category leader (see Figure 4.3).

The term fake news first occurred in America in relation to video news
releases produced by public relations firms that were then broadcast by
television news as if they were content produced by journalists (Rampton,
2005, cited in Harsin, 2018b). Fake news, however, is a term that has more
recently taken on a wider meaning to encompass content that "includes
core false statements (things that did not happen, that do not even exist),
and therefore are sometimes wrongly referred to as lies" (Harsin, 2018b).
Lazer et al. (2018, p. 1094) chose to define "fake news" as "fabricated
information that mimics news media content in form but not in organizational process or intent," in part because politicization of the term serves to
draw attention to an important subject worthy of more scientific enquiry.

Wang (2020) notes that "misinformation" has been the most frequently used
term in the past 20 years but that most of the papers over this period had no
colocation with the concept of fake news, while Lazer et al. (2018, p. 1094)

Google's search engine relative to the site's total search volume over a given period of time
(see https://support.google.com/trends for more information).

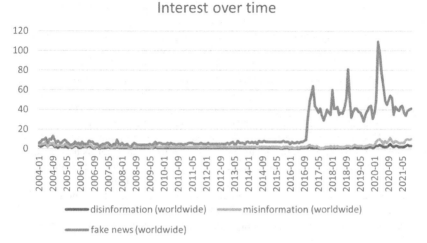

Figure 4.3 The term "fake news" has overtaken the terms "disinformation" and "misinformation" in respect of its usage in Google searches since 2015 (Data source: Google Trends, January 2021, www.google.com/trends)

identify the rise of "fake news" as emblematic of "long-standing institutional bulwarks against misinformation in the internet age."

"Disinformation," on the other hand, notes Wang (2020, p. 161), is a term gaining increasing use though it is still less used than "misinformation." Disinformation is defined by UNESCO's handbook on journalism, fake news, and disinformation (Directorate-General for Communication Networks, Content and Technology, 2018, p. 5), as "all forms of false, inaccurate, or misleading information designed, presented and promoted to intentionally cause public harm or for profit." In this context, public harm refers to attempts to confuse or manipulate people, to ignite passions for ill effect and to exploit polarization, to cast doubt on legitimate reporting and other public interest information, and to profit by doing so. Disinformation, then, comes in many forms, all characterized by a deliberate agenda to mislead through the spreading of false or inaccurate information.

This terminological muddle signifies an increasingly complex information ecosystem characterized by "disordered" epistemological dynamics. (Wardle and Derakhshan, 2017; Lazer et al., 2018; Wardle, 2018). As communication, media, and culture scholar Jayson Harsin (2018b, p. 2) writes,

> the post-trust information ecosystem is characterized by constant discursive obsession with and accusations of dishonesty, especially lying, and by the public anxiety and distrust it generates. It lies in the frequency and volume of the

increasing amounts of labor to produce and attempt to debunk or clarify inaccurate or deceptive statements, the proliferation of "fact-checking" and rumor or hoax debunking organizations, usually individual businesses or wings of news organizations; it lies in the market for them, too (Graves & Cherubini, 2016). It lies in numerous international surveys measuring distrust (of multiple institutions and actors). It lies in a culture saturated with artifice and promotionalism. It lies in the material impact of false or intentionally misleading claims and the emotionalized public opinion they generate, from demands to and then release of a president's full birth certificate, to rumors of a candidate's child sex slavery ring in a Washington, DC, pizza parlor, resulting in armed confrontation. It lies in the documentation of politics and business built around the deception of artificial intelligence (bots), whose armies present the mirage of popularity or of supporters who sear their targets with brands of repugnance and chimerical flaws. It also lies in the industry of political consulting (now heavily informed by cognitive science and big data analytics, corresponding to emotionally pin-pointed, demographically microtargeted influence strategies and practices).

In the age of disinformation, nothing is certain until, of course, a great chain of certainty – the blockchain – rides to the rescue, as we will discuss in Chapter 6.

4.3 A Short Overview of the Long History of Disinformation

In fairness to the current era, deliberately misleading information is not something new. In fact, it has a long and storied past, from wartime propaganda to advertising and public relations (Harsin, 2018b). Posetti and Matthews (2018, p. 1) trace the use of disinformation to sow ignorance back to ancient Rome, in fact:

> Octavian waged a propaganda campaign against Antony that was designed to smear his reputation. This took the form of "short, sharp slogans written upon coins in the style of archaic Tweets." [quoting Kaminska, 2017] These slogans painted Antony as a womaniser and a drunk, implying he had become Cleopatra's puppet, having been corrupted by his affair with her. Octavian became Augustus, the first Roman Emperor and "fake news had allowed Octavian to hack the republican system once and for all." [again, quoting Kaminska, 2017]

In the sixth century, the Byzantine historian Procopius's "Secret History" sought to destroy the reputation of his patron, the Emperor Justinian, by passing off as true stories that Justinian could make his own head disappear (Korte, 2005).

During the American Revolution, Benjamin Franklin sought to sway British public opinion to his case for reparations by printing a fake newspaper supplement (Liberman, 2017). In 1890, the *New York Journal* and the

New York World described an explosion of the USS Maine off the coast of Cuba as a deliberate act of Spanish aggression to boost the circulation of their newspapers. Propaganda was also used by the British Army in the Boer War to popularize a stereotype of "the Boer" that would sway British public opinion to support an unpopular conflict (Posetti and Matthews, 2018, citing Kent, 2013). Similarly, propaganda was used in World War I for recruitment and to "demonize" German soldiers and it is also well-documented that the Nazi regime used propaganda to incite violence and hatred against Jews and justify genocide (Posetti and Matthews, 2018). The journalist Ian Cobain (2016) recounts decades-long campaigns by British intelligence employing disinformation.

Relatedly, deception and false claims have been frequent tactics in advertising at least since the days when "snake oil" was touted as a cure-all, with more recent examples including cigarette advertising (Witkowski, 1991). As Proctor and Schiebinger (2008, p. 18) recount,

> The tobacco industry early on recognized health concerns as market impediments, which is why L & M Filters were offered as "just what the doctor ordered," Camels were said to be smoked by "more doctors," and so forth. The industry was barred from making such claims in the 1950s and moved to more subtle inducements, associating smoking with youth, vigor, and beauty, and later freedom, risk, and rebellion. For a time in the 1980s, when health infringements centered around secondhand smoke, we were told that smoking was a form of free speech.

Political satire, as opposed to propaganda, has been more often used by those outside the halls of power, usually to criticize and provoke change. Examples include the British satirical puppet show *Spitting Image* (ITV News, 2014) and the American television programs *The Daily Show* (which billed itself as "the most trusted name in fake news" [Williams, 2018]) and *Saturday Night Live!* (Posetti and Matthews, 2018). *The Daily Show* rose to prominence in the United States following the reelection of George W. Bush in 2004 – which accounts for the sharp spike in searches using the keywords disinformation, misinformation, and fake news in 2004 (see Figure 4.2 above). During this same period, *The Onion*, a satirical newspaper and online news site, also became popular with critics of the George W. Bush presidency (Williams, 2018). Importantly, as Williams (2018) notes, "this was also the last era before the internet and social media splintered American news consumption habits, meaning there was still a recognizable institutional news voice that made sense to parody," and, it might be added, a recognizable American social epistemic consensus.

4.4 What's New(s)? Causes of Disinformation

Given the long history of disinformation, what is so different now that the current age should be demarcated as an age of disinformation? To answer this question, it is helpful to draw upon social epistemology, which is "the study of the influence of social mechanisms and social institutions in the production, diffusion, and legitimization of knowledge" (Origgi, 2019, p. 78; see also Fallis, 2006; Hardwig, 1991).

Most of what we know nowadays about the world is not directly obtained through experience. Rather, it is by means of the testimony of others[3] – whether that testimony is received orally (e.g., from a lecture we are listening to) or from what has been written down (e.g., in a social media post). Further, their testimony might be based upon the testimony of others as well, so that any knowledge we come to have passes through an extended chain of knowledge transmission operating within a complex ecosystem of knowledge production. Testimonial knowledge formation involves a sender transmitting some knowledge to a receiver by some means. The speaker provides testimony using a declarative, which advances a proposition that the hearer must decide whether to believe (van Elswyk, 2019). Social epistemology widely endorses the notion that, for knowledge to be transmitted, there must be *sufficiency* and *necessity* of transmitted knowledge.

Sufficiency is the idea that when a person believes another's testimony about some fact (e.g., it's raining outside), if the sender knows that fact, then the recipient comes to know and accept it too. Relatedly, *necessity* is the idea that if a person believes another's testimony about some fact but the sender does not know that fact in the first place, then there is no way that the recipient can come to know that fact simply by believing the sender. Depending on the circumstances – and assuming the sender and the recipient are both rational – then if the testimony is intelligible to the recipient, the recipient has reason to believe that a giver of testimony is competent and sincere in the giving of that testimony and it is consistent with the recipient's other beliefs (i.e., there exist no grounds to doubt the testimony) – or at least if there is no reason to doubt that the giver of the testimony is competently and sincerely expressing their own justifiable true beliefs – then there will be sufficient and necessary grounds for belief. So far so good – message received.

If only knowledge transmission were that straightforward in our current times. Unfortunately, there are all sorts of circumstances that can confound the passing on of knowledge through testimony that can provide a recipient

---

[3] I define testimony as "Personal or documentary attestation in support of a fact or statement" (Oxford University Press, 2021e).

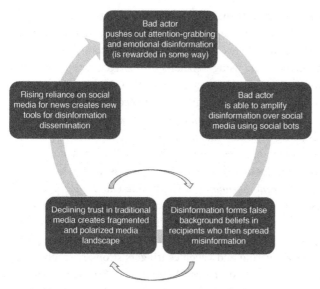

Figure 4.4 Our epistemic ecosystems often form "not so positive" disinformation feedback loops

with justifiable grounds for believing that something is true when it is not, or vice versa. In epistemology, many such circumstances are described in a range of cases labeled "Gettier problems."[4] When this is combined with the institutional, technological, and political changes to processes of knowledge transmission that have taken place over the past several decades, we have the makings of the range and scale of epistemological dysfunctions that demarcate the current age of disinformation (see Figure 4.4).[5]

Firstly, we know that, in the age of disinformation, there exist any number of "bad actors" who aim to pass along unsubstantiated or patently false claims with mal-intent. What we do not necessarily know, however, are the intentions of a given actor. In other words, discerning the "good" from the "bad" actors is a key challenge. Bad actors are typically motivated by the desire for political or economic gain, or both. The spread of disinformation often begins when a bad

---

[4] The label "Gettier problem" derives from the work of the American philosopher Edmund Gettier, who challenged the long-held justified true belief (JTB) account of knowledge. The JTB account holds that knowledge is equivalent to justified true belief; if all three conditions (justification, truth, and belief) are met for a given claim, then we have knowledge of that claim. Gettier gave counterexamples showing how individuals can have a justified true belief regarding a claim but still fail to know it because the reasons for the belief, while justified, turn out to be false (see Gettier, 1963; Hazlett, 2015).

[5] I say current age of disinformation, since this is not the first age of disinformation that humanity has experienced (see Chapter 7), and it likely won't be the last.

actor creates a message to cause harm, such as the online Pizzagate messages accusing Hillary Clinton of child sex trafficking (Wardle and Derakhshan, 2017). Next, that bad actor pushes the message out to communities that might be interested in it, often using "social bots" – automated accounts impersonating humans (Wardle and Derakhshan, 2017). Varol et al. (2017) report that between 9 and 15 percent of active Twitter accounts are bots.[6] Here, we have the first and most obvious problem – our knowledge-formation transmission chain is being flooded with bad messages.

Many of these messages are designed to "hot wire" human cognition. Columbia Law School professor Tim Wu (2017) writes in his book *The Attention Merchants: The Epic Scramble to Get Inside Our Heads* about an industry whose business model revolves around selling the attention they capture – our attention – in exchange for the "free" content they produce. Information on divisive issues such as immigration, climate change, religion, and, more recently, mask-wearing and vaccines triggers strong reactions, and more money-generating clicks and shares (Mourão and Robertson, 2019). Moreover, the performative nature of social media platforms encourages individuals to share posts, even ones containing false claims, with their followers to generate engagement and attract new followers (Carter, 2016).

Bad or complicit actors sending bad messages over social media platforms do not alone account for the current epistemological dysfunctions, however. Social epistemology recognizes cases when the giver of testimony – the sender of a message – may have a false background belief that could just as easily lead to the transmission of false information that they believe to be true.[7] This example represents just the type of scenario we currently see a great deal in the passing on of misinformation. Those who transmit misinformation are not necessarily bad actors; they might simply have a false, or self-interested,

---

[6] Unfortunately, as Lazer et al. (2018, p. 1095) note, "Bot detection will always be a cat-and-mouse game in which a large, but unknown, number of humanlike bots may go undetected. Any success at detection, in turn, will inspire future countermeasures by bot producers. Identification of bots will therefore be a major ongoing research challenge."

[7] An example used to illustrate this point, given by Dretske (1982), is that of a wine drinker, Alice, who knows that Medocs are a type of Bordeaux wine, but also mistakenly believes that Chiantis are from the Bordeaux region. After attending a dinner party, at which she drinks a Medoc, she tells her friend Bob that she drank a Bordeaux. Alice's testimony is true, but she may just as easily have meant that she drank a Chianti (making her claim false), which is why some argue (e.g., Dretske, 1982) that it is not possible to gain knowledge from Alice's testimony. In another variant on this theme – the "almost a liar" variant (Lackey, 2006, 2008) – Alice makes a true claim (e.g., it's raining outside) but would easily make an untrue claim (e.g., it is sunny outside) if it were in her interest to do so, or she might tell Bob that it is raining (a true claim) even if she lacked direct knowledge (e.g., by looking outside) and was only relying on the Farmer's Almanac or upon the testimony of others who might tell her it is sunny simply because they know that is what she would prefer to hear. In all these cases, Alice's testimony is unreliable, making it impossible to learn from her, and thus knowledge fails to transmit.

background belief that prevents them from reliably transmitting information that can be used by its recipient as grounds for the formation a justifiable true belief (i.e., knowledge). This begs a question: where do these false background beliefs come from? The answer: a lot of them arise from the disinformation being deliberately circulated by bad actors (Rosling, 2018; Ghanem et al., 2020; Kapantai et al., 2020).[8]

Next, characteristics of the epistemological ecosystem can also cause knowledge formation failures (Graham and Bachman, 2019). A classic example is Goldman's box of thermometers, wherein Bob reaches into a box of thermometers in which all but one are broken (Goldman, 1986, p. 45). Bob uses the good thermometer to take his temperature and the reading is correct. Yet, because Bob only picked the working thermometer by chance, he cannot reliably come to know his temperature – the reading could just as easily have been incorrect. Removing the other broken thermometers would allow the knowledge to transmit reliably. Our current disordered information ecosystem is like Bob's broken box of thermometers: it has become unreliable. There is so much disinformation and misinformation floating around – the broken thermometers – that no matter if we read news that is true, we cannot really know whether we can rely upon it.

Why has our information ecosystem become so unreliable? There are several interconnected factors to consider. Scholars from a variety of disciplines have noted important institutional shifts in our knowledge transmission ecosystem that have created the conditions for disinformation to flourish. It used to be that the mainstream media filtered our news. They were the authoritative gatekeepers of what we could rely upon as trustworthy information, providing, as Lazer et al. (2018, p. 1094) state, "institutional bulwarks" against disinformation. Now, however, trust in mainstream media is at an all-time low in many countries, according to the annual Edelman Trust surveys (see Chapter 2). Mistrust in traditional mainstream media has often been encouraged by politicians and government officials who have benefitted from manipulating the news. Some politicians have been "weaponizing" (Liberman, 2017) claims of fake news, disparaging news stories they dislike as false.[9] Attempts to delegitimize the reports of journalists as fake news have also been accompanied by threats to publish embarrassing or harmful personal information about them online. This

---

[8] A number of researchers have explored how disinformation triggers strong emotions that mislead people into believing false information (Rosling, 2018; Ghanem et al., 2020; Kapantai et al., 2020). As Wardle (2019, p. 88) writes, "Stress testing technology in the context of the worst moments in history might have illuminated what social scientists and propagandists have long known: that humans are wired to respond to emotional triggers and share misinformation if it reinforces existing beliefs and prejudices."

[9] Chief among these has been the former United States President Donald Trump who, following the 2016 election, used the term "fake news" frequently (Derakhshan and Wardle, 2017).

tactic of discrediting and intimidating perceived opponents – called "doxxing" – has frequently been used against female journalists, who are perceived to be more vulnerable to this type of attack (Occeñola, 2018; Posetti, 2018).

What was once viewed as "responsible journalism," delivered by the mainstream media, is under pressure, both politically and financially, from the rise of new entrants – the social media platforms (Lazer et al., 2018). A 2017 report from the Brookings Institute (West, 2017) noted the following:

- Since 2017, 93 percent of Americans say they receive news online.
- Of the now vast array of online content creation and dissemination channels, many people are now using social media as their primary news source. In 2012–13 in the United States, for example, 27 percent relied upon social media sites, compared to 51 percent who did so in 2017.
- In contrast, the percentage of Americans relying upon print news had dropped from 38 to 22 percent.
- Social media sites are very popular in the developing world. Eighty-six percent of Middle Eastern Internet users rely upon social networks, compared to 82 percent in Latin America, 76 percent in Africa, 71 percent in the United States, 66 percent in Asia and the Pacific, and 65 percent in Europe.

Social media has both fragmented the media landscape and given bad actors powerful new tools to create and disseminate their message (Blumler, 2016). While sensationalism, or "yellow journalism," has been used widely in the past to sell newspapers, it is now being used to generate social media clickbait (Ireton and Posetti, 2018). These types of communications ultimately generate more money in advertising for social media and legitimate news sites, so their algorithms keep feeding people the content even if there is an awareness that this ultimately undermines the trustworthiness of information (Wardle and Derakhshan, 2017; Wardle, 2019). As it turns out, disinformation is very engaging, and engaging information makes money (Weeks, 2015). This business model is working so well for social media platforms that Canadian mainstream media news outlets were prompted in early 2021 to print blank front pages to draw attention to concerns that the platforms "use their monopoly power to pocket 80% of online advertising revenues" (Boynton, 2021). Backed by the power of their revenues and global reach, the platforms have become emboldened: Google's reaction to a proposed new Australian law designed to require it and other tech companies to pay media outlets for their news content was to threaten legislators in that country with removal of its search engine (BBC, 2021).[10]

---

[10] In addition, the platforms are also funding journalism schools and projects, further extending their influence over the news media landscape (see Rashidian, 2020).

A recipient of testimony is more likely to believe it if it is consistent with the recipient's other beliefs and if the recipient has no obvious grounds for disbelieving the giver of the testimony. This is more often the case when testimony originates from friends. Why? Because we trust our friends and see them – and the evidence they provide us – as being trustworthy. Trust is an inimitable aspect of coming to know something and of what we count as trustworthy evidence (Hardwig, 1991; Hinchman, 2005; Faulkner, 2007b; Nickel, 2012).[11] As Renee Hobbs, professor of Communication Studies at the Harrington School of Communication and Media, has observed, with the rise of social media, "we have a pool of content that is no longer controlled by the mass media. It's controlled by a network of friends, using the criteria of their social network" (quoted in Liberman, 2017). Information coming through our social networks, particularly from people with whom we are directly familiar, is a powerful "trust elixir." In a world in which we are bombarded with so much information and need to make assessments quickly about which sources of information to believe – with little information about the processes of production or the provenance of that information – we need a quick heuristic for deciding. This is often done by means of trusting the source of the information, if the source is known to us, or the reputation of the source if not directly known to us (Origgi, 2019). This kind of heuristic – a form of "fast thinking" – can trigger cognitive biases, however (Kahneman, 2011).

Further, when news is consumed as "unbundled snippets" – as it is on so many social media platforms – we are less likely to think critically about news content and ask media literacy questions, such as, "Who is the author and what is the purpose?" (Liberman, 2017). Instead, rather like "guilt by association," we assign greater trustworthiness to the information coming from sources we already trust, like friends (Kahneman, 2011; Origgi, 2019).[12] As Nguyen (in press) puts it, we adopt an "unquestioning attitude." Unsurprisingly, news received via our own social group reflects and reinforces prior beliefs – what Nickerson (1998) refers to as "confirmation bias" (Flynn et al., 1996; Dutton et al., 2017).

---

[11] Koenig and McMyler (2019, p. 104) write that "Many in psychology and philosophy treat testimony as a species of evidence, testimonial acceptance and rejection as evidence-based decisions, and the speakers who provide it as mere instruments of transmission ... While we don't deny that we can indeed take an evidential stance toward what we are told and an instrumental stance toward sources of information, we argue that evidential views fail to capture the fact that when speakers offer their testimony to others and implicitly commit or vouch for it, they offer learners a distinct kind of reason, and something other than mere inductive evidence." That reason, arguably, is based on trust.

[12] See also the bandwagon effect discussed in Leibenstein (1950), normative influence theory discussed by Deutsch and Gerard (1955), as social identity theory (Ashforth and Mael, 1989), and availability cascade discussed by Kuran and Sunstein (1999).

These cognitive processes are amplified by a self-reinforcing process in which collective memory forms around what is repeated in discourse within our social group (the "validity effect") and a "manufacturing of consensus" around the production of "echo chambers" (Jamieson and Cappella, 2008; Dutton et al., 2017; Woolley and Guilbeault, 2017). The danger here is that "A lie told once remains a lie, but a lie told a thousand times becomes the truth" (Hasher et al., 1977).[13] Research from the field of psychology on the formation of collective memory supports Wardle's observation (Spinney, 2017). Once the information is trusted and takes root as part of how an individual perceives the world, conservatism bias and the fact that individuals have a greater tendency to reject what does not conform to their established norms and beliefs may mean that it is difficult to dislodge the perception, even when individuals are presented with new evidence (Baker, 1987; Basu, 1997).

As disinformation makes the rounds on social media, eventually it might mistakenly be picked up and amplified as fact in the mainstream media. Wardle (quoted in Matthews and Posetti, 2020) describes this as an "Easter Egg" because the disinformation has been transmitted beyond a specific social network or group of social actors to the mainstream media where institutional-ized, society-wide manufacturing and legitimization of social facts occur. According to the Stanford Internet Observatory (DiResta, 2019), this has been a favorite tactic of the GRU, Russia's intelligence arm:

> The GRU was running narrative laundering operations globally, creating media front, fake think tanks, fake journalists who got articles placed in authentic popular independent media outlets – this all served to legitimize or conceal the origin of state-sponsored propaganda.

This sort of narrative laundering has also been used to manufacture a wide variety of fake sources, from fake academic profiles to entirely fake publications.

In all the above cases, the process of knowledge formation must be reliable or else the knowledge does not transmit. This is known as *reliabilism* (Goldman and Beddor, 2016). Though a widely accepted principle in epistemology, it is not without detractors, including those who argue that there must be some way to identify which processes are reliable and, by implication, a standard by which they might be judged to be so. This is not straightforward, since it requires that there exists some legitimate authority that sets the standard and the rules by which the truth is determined and whose judgement on matters of truth will be accepted by all. In our current fragmented epistemological

---

[13] The original saying is attributed to Joseph Goebbels.

ecosystem, in which trust in the authoritative "voice" of the mainstream media has declined, the source of authority is no longer easily identified.

In times of institutional mistrust, knowledge that is contingent upon a legitimate authority raises the spectre of *relativism*, since there might exist many competing authorities. When social actors share norms of truth – that is, when they operate according to the same system of knowledge production and share the same social values – the relationship between what is perceived to be true and what is considered a legitimate epistemic authority might be well-aligned and go relatively unobserved. But where norms of truth and values differ, epistemic conflicts become evident and what is true can become epistemically and socially contested.

Competing norms of truth often arise when an authority that was seen as trusted and, by extension, legitimate is no longer trusted as the arbiter of the truth. Our present era is not the first occurrence of this phenomenon. The story of Galileo's dispute with Pope Urban the VIII's chief inquisitor, Father Vincenzo Maculani da Firenzuola, in 1633 presents an earlier example. Galileo was ordered to turn himself in to stand trial for holding the belief that the Earth revolves around the sun, which was deemed to be a heretical belief by the Catholic Church. At that time, the Church was the ultimate authority and arbiter of the truth. Here, we see the clash of two knowledge systems, or two different norms of establishing the truth. On the one hand, the Church based its justifiable belief upon scripture, while Galileo saw this standard as being unreliable and based his justifiable belief upon scientific observation using his telescope. Their frames of reference were so far apart that neither could justifiably come to believe, or acquire the knowledge of, the other. So how was the matter resolved? Students of history will know that the Church asserted its power: Galileo was condemned to live out the rest of his days in prison. So, although there might be a way such epistemological disputes can be solved without resort to the exercise of power (e.g., epistemological pluralism), what so often happens in these cases – at least in the short term – is that the more powerful authority exercises its power and suppresses the truth claims of the other, as in the case of Galileo or, nowadays, the doxxing of journalists.

To acknowledge that truth may be relative to some authority, that there is a plurality of meaning-formation systems, and that truth may be determined in some cases by force or the relative power of one party over another might suggest that there is no such thing as universal truth. I do not wish to assert this.[14] I do wish to highlight, however, that philosophical solutions to resolve

---

[14] My claim, which draws upon two complementary ontological theories – Bunge's ontology of substantive "things" with intrinsic properties and Seale's social ontology of subjective entities with socially constructed properties – is that the truth of claims relating to social

contradictory truth claims remain open to debate in social epistemology and that, even before matters of competing truth claims can be resolved, we very often see in human history that power and force are invoked to resolve the dispute. Standpoint theory has dealt with the impact of positionality and power in epistemological matters. As Skarpelis notes, referencing the work of Hill Collins, "distinct epistemologies [are] localized, partial and situated forms of knowledge, and ... some epistemologies have historically trumped others: Far from being the apolitical study of truth, epistemology points to the ways in which power relations shape who is believed and why" (Skarpelis, 2019, p. 1, citing Hill Collins, 2015, p. 252).[15] For this reason, I prefer to think of truth claims as being authoritative, rather than necessarily objectively true, since it is very difficult from within the frame of one knowledge system to ascertain the scope, or eternal universality, of a given truth claim – even those that relate to the natural world, as we learn from the Galileo example.

4.5 Combatting Disinformation

In response to the significant effects of disinformation and associated information disorders on a global scale, widespread efforts are being made to understand and combat the phenomenon. Initiatives combatting disinformation are taking various forms (see Table 4.2). The diversity of approaches reflects that the pernicious problem of disinformation is, as noted in a report of the European Commission's High Level Expert Group on Fake News and Online Disinformation, a "multi-faceted and evolving problem that does not have one single root cause" (European Commission, 2018, p. 3). In this section, we review some of the key strategies being used to tackle disinformation. Each approach has its pros and cons and none has yet proven to be wholly effective in meeting the disinformation challenge.

Several initiatives target recipients of transmitted communications as contributing to, if not a root cause of, societal disinformation disorders. These initiatives, led by nonprofits and governments alike, seek to improve the digital media literacy of news consumers. As an example of this strategy, a report of the European Commission's High Level Group on Fake News and Online Disinformation

---

institutions (as subjective entities) will reflect a social reality. For a more detailed discussion of these ideas see Lemieux and Limonad (2011).

[15] Skarpelis (2019, p. 1) also observes that "Both perspectives overlap with anthropological and postcolonial engagements with the archive that ask us to see state actors as 'cultural agents of "fact" production' and that caution scholars to engage in ethnographic, rather than purely extractive, ways with the archive" (on this point, see also Stoler, 2002, 2010).

Table 4.2 *Major counter-disinformation strategies*

Type of intervention	Focus of intervention	Advantages	Limitations
Public education and information literacy	Recipients of communications	Teaches critical thinking skills; raises awareness and sensitizes recipients to disinformation techniques	False beliefs formed on the basis of disinformation are difficult to dislodge; difficult to scale; may increase individuals' perception that all information is untrustworthy
Inoculation	Recipients of communications	Uses cognitive behavioral science techniques aimed at dislodging beliefs formed on the basis of disinformation	Difficult to scale; may increase individuals' perception that all information is untrustworthy
Disrupting economic incentives	Knowledge transmission ecosystem	Reduces the incentives for some types of creators of disinformation	Does not address all types of disinformation creators; does not address the economic incentives of the online content providers nor necessarily provide financial support for traditional mainstream media
Government regulation	Knowledge transmission ecosystem	Can contribute to cleaning up the information environment	Concerns about freedom of speech
Platform self-regulation	Knowledge transmission ecosystem	Can contribute to cleaning up the information environment	Concerns about freedom of speech
Fact-checking	Sender of communications	Can detect disinformation	Difficult to scale unless automated; may not fundamentally alter recipients' beliefs over time
Automated detection and blocking	Sender of communications	Scalable approach to disinformation detection	Models used to identify and classify disinformation may be flawed or difficult to apply; can produce erroneous and biased results; possible for bad actors to "hack"
Human-in-the-loop detection and blocking	Sender of communications	Addresses some limitations of purely automated techniques while still being scalable	May still produce erroneous and biased results; possible for bad actors to "hack"

(European Commission, 2018, p. 5) recommended using media and information literacy as one of a number of approaches in a multidimensional strategy to counter disinformation.

Such initiatives are premised upon the belief that news consumers' susceptibility contributes to the problem of disinformation and misinformation online and that disinformation, therefore, may be solved by increasing news consumers' ability to

> access and identify information needed to inform decisions and behaviours; evaluate the reliability and credibility of authors, sources, and information presented in varied forms and mediums; assess the processes used to create information products (e.g., were rigorous journalistic standards applied? Were rigorous research processes employed?); [and] synthesize information from multiple sources.
>
> *(Huguet et al., 2021, p. 8)*

Digital media literacy initiatives, proponents argue, can protect news consumers against disinformation by helping them to gauge what sources they can trust in the midst of increasing disagreement about facts; reduce the spread of disinformation by teaching consumers to be more reflective about what they post; restore respect for and the authoritativeness of traditional news media or scientific sources by educating people about the rigorous processes they use in the production of their information products; highlight potential sources of bias by educating people about the sources and transmission of information; and debunk inaccurate beliefs once formed (Huguet et al., 2021). However, Huguet et al. (2021) point to a dearth of causal, evaluative research in the digital media literacy field that isolates the effects of interventions. Results are mixed: some studies indicate that digital literacy interventions may increase individuals' mistrust in all news, not only false news, highlighting concerns that interventions focused on critical media literacy could create cynicism damaging to trust in even credible sources of information (Lazer et al., 2018; Guess et al., 2020). The study also did not eliminate the possibility that false information appearing in mainstream media would be believed, suggesting that perceptions of source trustworthiness may play a dominant role in how individuals assess information. Even today, as Harsin (2018a) observes, readers have difficulties distinguishing the satirical news presented in *The Onion* from legitimate mainstream news media stories because of *The Onion*'s official-looking format. It is also questionable whether these initiatives are scalable from a human cognitive perspective. Faced with processing high volumes of heterogeneous information, as discussed above, human cognition increasingly relies on heuristics to increase the speed of information processing. This is not conducive to the more deliberative and critical cognition required by proponents of media literacy

(Kahneman, 2011; Huguet et al., 2021). For this reason, governments and other stakeholders are exploring other avenues for identifying and responding to the spread of disinformation.

Lewandowsky and van der Linden (2021) highlight initiatives aimed at inoculation, or "prebunking" as it is sometimes called. Research indicates that misinformation often can be corrected only when accompanied by an alternate causal explanation of the facts or if suspicion about the original source of the information is raised. Thus, according to Cook et al. (2017, p. 4), inoculation against misinformation or disinformation must consist of "(1) an explicit warning of an impending threat, and (2) a refutation of an anticipated argument that exposes [an] imminent fallacy." In one example of the approach, researchers created a game that exposed players to typical disinformation techniques by asking them to use emotional language, polarization, conspiratorial reasoning, trolling, discrediting others, and impersonation of experts online to generate fake news content.[16] Basol et al. (2020) report that playing the game significantly improved players' resistance to misinformation and increased their ability to spot it, thereby providing effective inoculation against misinformation and disinformation.

Initiatives that target the recipients of disinformation can only go so far. Problems in the transmission ecosystem can also lead to disinformation; thus, approaches to "fixing the broken thermometers," or targeting the transmission ecosystem are also needed. One of the key shifts in the transmission ecosystem has been in the economic incentives that drive disinformation creation. Disrupting these incentives has been identified as one way of discouraging producers of online disordered information. Facebook, for example, announced in 2018 that it was targeting "spammers [who] make money by masquerading as legitimate news publishers ... posting hoaxes that get people to visit their sites, which are often mostly ads" by "making it as difficult as possible for people posting false news to buy ads" through strict policy enforcement (Mosseri, 2017). At the same time, as discussed above, online platforms such as Facebook have undercut the business models of traditional news media, reducing traditional media's ability to maintain the investment it has made historically in verifying claims in news stories and providing editorial oversight of news content. While online platforms and mainstream media appear willing to block spammers from profiting by generating clickbait, neither seem willing, or able, to give up such lucrative practices themselves.

Given the difficulties of platform self-regulation, governments have begun to step in to fix our broken knowledge transmission ecosystems. In 2017,

---

[16] You can play the game yourself at www.getbadnews.com/#next.

Germany passed the Network Enforcement Act, which came into force on October 1, 2017, and explicitly aims to combat hate speech and fake news in social networks (Federal Republic of Germany, 2017). The German law requires social media companies with more than two million users to delete illegal, racist, or slanderous comments and posts within 24 hours. Companies can be fined up to $57 million for content – such as Nazi symbols, Holocaust denials, or language classified as hate speech – that is not deleted (Tworek and Leerssen, 2019).

Other governments have also taken similar action: in 2017, Indonesia established a government agency to "monitor news circulating online" and "tackle fake news" (Straits Times, 2017, as cited in West, 2017); in 2018, the government of Malaysia enacted anti-fake news legislation; and in 2019, the government of the Philippines sought to introduce anti-fake news legislation to "protect the public from the deleterious effects of false and deceiving content online" (Johnson, 2019).

Though these government regulatory initiatives aim to address the problem of fake news and disinformation, critics have pointed out that the cure may be worse than the illness due to the potential to curtail freedom of expression. Definitions in legislation and regulations of terms such as "social media platforms," "fake news," and "hate speech" are often so broad as to encompass what is normally considered to be positive forms of communication – such as investigative journalistic content – or, conversely, so narrow as to create loopholes for social media platforms that need regulating. Such concerns motivated a 2017 declaration by the United Nations Special Rapporteur on Freedom of Opinion and Expression, the Organization for Security and Co-operation in Europe (OSCE), the Organization of American States, and the African Commission on Human and People's Rights, which emphasized that "the human right to impart information and ideas is not limited to 'correct' statements, that the right also protects information and ideas that may shock, offend and disturb" (OSCE, 2017). Many fear that laws aimed at controlling disinformation and fake news could set dangerous precedents that might give licence to authoritarian regimes to justify the continuation or expansion of censorship (West, 2017). Still, given ongoing concerns over disinformation, some argue that it is a case of "when, not if" we will see more government regulation (Rochefort, 2020).

Sensing that more government regulation might be on its way, social media platforms have taken preemptive steps to regulate themselves by providing "minimalist public governance" on such issues as privacy protection, freedom of expression, and the maintenance of democratic institutions such as the electoral system (Gorwa, 2019; Rochefort, 2020). For example, Nunziato (2020, p. 2) observes that

Twitter has evolved from being the non-interventionist "free speech wing of the free speech party" to designing and operating an immense operation for regulating speech on its platform – epitomized by its recent removal and labeling of President Donald Trump's (and Donald Trump, Jr.'s) misleading tweets. Facebook for its part has evolved from being a notorious haven for fake news in the 2016 election cycle to standing up an extensive global network of independent fact-checkers to remove and label millions of posts on its platform – including by removing a post from President Trump's campaign account, as well as by labeling 90 million such posts in March and April 2020, involving false or misleading medical information in the context of the pandemic. Google for its part has abandoned its hands-off approach to its search algorithm results and has committed to removing false political content in the context of the 2020 election and to serving up prominent information by trusted health authorities in response to COVID-19 related searches on its platforms.

Platform self-regulation most often takes the form of content moderation, which can be, according to Riedl et al. (2021, p. 2) conducted "ex-ante, or ex-post (Klonick, 2017), the latter of which can be done by moderation teams wading through forums, or by responding to audience members flagging content (Naab et al., 2018). Moderation is further enabled by computational means, for example through machine learning and filtering (Myers West, 2018)." Just as with government regulation of online content, platform self-regulation gives rise to concerns about suppression of freedom of expression. A Pew Research Center report from 2020, for example, found that about 70 percent of Americans believe that social media platforms censor political viewpoints (Vogels et al., 2020). Moreover, efforts to block spammers have frequently resulted in blocking those documenting human rights violations as well (Deutch, 2020). At the same time, the platforms are often perceived not to be removing content such as terrorist propaganda, child pornography, or hate speech (Elghawaby, 2018).[17] Others question whether decisions about such complex public policy issues should be left to private sector platforms (Elghawaby, 2018).

Fact-checking is another popular approach aimed at rooting out the spread of disinformation online. Initially developed for use in traditional mainstream journalism, the process of fact-checking "aims to assess news authenticity by comparing the knowledge extracted from to-be-verified news content (e.g., its claims or statement) with well-known facts" (Zhou and Zafarani, 2020). It can be performed manually by experts or crowds, or by machines operating in the

---

[17] Elghawaby (2018) notes, "A website called onlinecensorship.org – which is run by the Electronic Frontier Foundation and Visualizing Impact – chronicles these examples. The site invites users to report on the takedown of their content, in order to 'shine a light' on the decisions made by social media companies and their impacts on freedom of expression. For instance, it highlights how, in 2017, 77 social and racial justice organizations wrote to Facebook about 'censorship of Facebook users of colour and takedowns of images discussing racism.'"

context of traditional news media, online platforms, and independent fact-checking sites. Well-known examples of fact-checking sites include Classify. news, FactCheck.org, Factnata.com, Fiskkit, GossipCop, Hoaxy.iuni.iu.edu, Hoax-Slayer.com, PolitiFact.com, Snopes.com, TruthorFiction.com and the Washington Post's Fact Checker (Zhang and Ghorbani, 2020; Zhou and Zafarani, 2020). Fact-checking sites can be categorized into those that debunk hoaxes and online rumors (e.g., Snopes.com); those focused on verifying political and public claims (e.g., Politifact.com); and those concentrating on specific controversies and topics (e.g., Climate Feedback.org). The practice also entails evaluations of news reports by traditional news media, such as the *Washington Post* (United States) and *JTBC* (South Korea) (Lazer et al., 2018; Choi and Haigh, 2019).

Expert fact-checking, performed by domain experts, is highly accurate but does not scale well (Zhou and Zafarani, 2020). Crowdsourcing, an approach that relies on a large population – usually online platform users – to verify truth claims, can help to scale the fact-checking process but can be difficult to manage, less accurate, and subject to bias (Zhou and Zafarani, 2020). These difficulties often require that crowdsourced fact-checking be filtered and reviewed by experts, taking away from the scalability of the solution. Nevertheless, the major online platforms – Google, Facebook, Twitter, and Sina Weibo – are all experimenting with this approach (Gingras, 2016; Mosseri, 2016; Xiao and Chen, 2020; Lyons, 2021).

Though crowdsourcing helps with the problem of how to scale fact-checking, it is still unable to cope with the scale and speed of information flow in our highly digitized knowledge transmission ecosystems. As the saying goes, "A lie gets halfway around the world before the truth has a chance to get its boots on."[18] Many thus call for automation to ensure that platforms can respond rapidly to disinformation. Zhou and Zafarani (2020) outline several different approaches to automated fact-checking. These solutions all rely upon the preexistence of a trustworthy repository of facts – a knowledge-base – against which the facts can be verified; Zhou and Zafarani (2020), for example, suggest using the "Open Web"; however, given the possibility of bias in such sources, relying upon the Web to identify disinformation could produce erroneous results (Caplan et al., 2018). This approach relies upon making inferences about the veracity or "facticity" (defined as the degree to which news and content rely on facts [Tandoc et al., 2018; Newman et al., 2018]) of a communication's content. As Zhang and Ghorbani (2020) point out in their

---

[18] This quote has been attributed to various famous personalities from Jonathan Swift to Mark Twain and Winston Churchill. On this point, see https://quoteinvestigator.com/2014/07/13/truth.

survey of online fake news detection techniques, online communications are diverse and the truth of any factual claim is not easily ascertained.

Inferences about the veracity of factual claims are subject to cultural, institutional, and political bias, which is why reliance upon knowledge bases to proffer the truth can be problematic. Moreover, such approaches tend to view information extracted from sources as "raw fact," which Uscinski and Butler (2013) see as being highly problematic; facts cannot be understood devoid of their context, they argue.

Uscinski and Butler (2013)[19] also argue that fact-checking might rely upon a "naïve epistemology" incapable of addressing the complexities of various types of assertions and the complexity of our current knowledge transmission ecosystems. The partisan nature of some fact-checking sites and the inherent bias in even the most well-meaning fact-checking also undermine the perceived trustworthiness of fact-checking as a strategy to counter disinformation (see, e.g., Brandtzaeg and Følstad, 2017; Ceci and Williams, 2020). Lack of transparency is another issue, prompting Brandtzaeg and Følstad (2017) to call for fact-checkers to increase transparency around the processes they use to check facts and to work collaboratively and in a networked manner across partisan lines, following an approach recommended by Hermida (2013). The Content Authenticity Initiative's standard-setting efforts around content attribution and verification is a recent attempt to address this gap (Rosenthol, 2020). Even if standardized and more transparent, fact-checking still might not effectively prevent individuals' belief in disinformation owing to the tendencies of individual and collective cognition that make it extremely difficult to dislodge false beliefs once they take root (Lazer et al., 2018; Lewandowsky, 2020). As Walter et al. (2020, p. 367) found in a study they conducted on the effectiveness of fact-checking, "the effects ... on beliefs are quite weak and gradually become negligible the more the study design resembles a real-world scenario of exposure to fact-checking." Thus, while fact-checking – whether manual or automated – can be helpful in identifying falsified news and disinformation, it is, like so many other strategies, imperfect. Despite these concerns, fact-checking is likely to remain important in efforts to combat disinformation in our epistemically challenged age.

Beyond fact-checking, automated techniques are also being used in an attempt to identify and weed out the purveyors of disinformation. Typically, these techniques use data mining, natural language processing, and machine or deep learning to analyze large datasets of communications,[20] such as social

---

[19] See Amazeen (2015) for a critique of the arguments in Uscinski and Butler (2013), and see also Uscinski's (2015) rejoinder.

[20] Commonly used machine-learning algorithms include Decision Tree, Random Forest, Support Vector Machine, Logistic Regression, and K-nearest Neighbour, while commonly

media posts, in order to look for features in the data – for example, the identity of the sender or grammatical mistakes – that can be used to identify it as a form of disinformation (Zhang and Ghorbani, 2020; Zhou and Zafarani, 2020). They may also sometimes use graph-based network analysis to reveal the patterns of communication between sender and receivers that are indicative of disinformation (see, e.g., Ferrara et al., 2016; Ma et al., 2016; Karataş and Şahin, 2017; Vosoughi et al., 2018).

Such techniques rely upon imputation of the intention of a communication's sender (Kapantai et al., 2020) based, for example, upon inferences about such characteristics as the source of the communication, the communication's propagation pattern, or the style of communication (Zhou and Zafarani, 2020). This might be a fool's errand given the context of disinformation. In the first place, it is extremely difficult to discern the intentions of a particular communicator of information through our current highly mediated information landscape; indeed, it might be impossible if that communicator is intent upon hiding their identity and aiming to deceive. This conundrum points to an inherent weakness in many typologies of disinformation and related "problematic" forms of communication: they might be satisfactory for labeling these different forms of communication once we have determined the identity and intent of communications creators, but they are impossibly flawed if we hope to use them to discern or make predictions about whether the sender of a particular communication is up to no good.

In addition, such techniques typically rely upon mapping a set of features (latent [derived] or non-latent; see, e.g., Pérez-Rosas et al., 2018; Zhou et al., 2019) associated with the intentions of the message sender (e.g., mapping characteristics associated with deceptive communications senders). We might come to know these features by means of detailed qualitative studies of the patterns of communication of purveyors of disinformation or by means of unsupervised machine or deep learning that infers features from analyses of large corpora of bad communications (LeCun et al., 2015; Ma et al., 2016; Ruchansky et al., 2017; Zhang and Ghorbani, 2020). Zhang and Ghorbani (2020), in their survey of fake news detection approaches, suggest that there are four main strategies: user profiling analysis; temporal and posting behavior analysis; credibility-related analysis; and sentiment-based analysis. Each mapping likely relies on different underlying conceptualizations of disinformation and theories about its causation; for example, a high intensity of reply and mention behaviors might indicate a high suspicion level of a social

---

used deep-learning algorithms include CNN, LTSM, bi-directional LTSM, Gated Recurrent Unit, and Recurrent Neural Network (Zhang and Ghorbani, 2020).

account (Zhang and Ghorbani, 2020, p. 3). User profiling might target communications originating from specific geographic locations on the assumption that these locations are more likely to be associated with fake news. The use of sentiment analysis relies upon an assumption that propagators of fake news use polarizing language and that polarizing language is associated with strongly negative or positive sentiment. Zhang and Ghorbani's (2020) analysis, for example, yields a model of fake news features comprised of three categories – creator/user-based features, news-content-based features, and social-context-based features – each of which includes a further set of sub-features. Aside from the fact that some of the underlying causal assumptions might be false, the problem then arises that such solutions can be reverse engineered by propagators of disinformation, resulting in a disinformation detection arms race: as soon as bad actors become aware that a particular communication feature is being used to detect and block their communications, they can alter their strategy to evade detection. For all these reasons, these techniques are not entirely effective.

To address these shortcomings, Zhang and Ghorbani (2020, p. 1) call for collaboration between humans and technology, sometimes called "human-in-the-loop" or "mixed initiative" approaches, in the detection of disinformation and other disordered forms of information. Human-in-the-loop or mixed initiative approaches refer to strategies that rely upon the involvement of humans (users or experts) to support artificial intelligence (AI) algorithms in doing their job, for example, by creating training data or manually validating the decisions made by these algorithms. Even with the aid of humans – which again reduces the value of AI-based solutions as a scalable alternative to manual forms of disinformation detection that are conducted either by experts or human recipients of communications – automated efforts to detect disinformation require further development to improve their effectiveness.

4.6 Getting to the Root of Disinformation

Zhou and Zafarani (2020, 109, p. 7) identify three broad phases of the fake news life cycle: fake news creation, fake news publication online, and fake news propagation through social media. They further elaborate on the complex information ecosystem surrounding the production of fake news in their description of the automatic fact-checking process. Zhou and Zafarani's model captures well the idea that most of the information we rely upon – whether that information is trustworthy or not – comes to us by means of a long, attenuated chain of knowledge formation. What their model captures less well, however, is the idea of primary sources as the evidential foundation of truth claims.

To elaborate, in large, complex societies where direct knowledge of people and events is often impossible, we must rely mostly upon information that comes from indirect – or secondary – sources of knowledge, in the form of news reports and analyses provided by other people.[21] Indirect sources contain testimony, or at least attestations, about truth claims concerning events and actions of which their authors do not necessarily have direct knowledge. At the beginning of this long chain of knowledge production, however, we should ideally expect to find either a primary source with direct knowledge of the events and actions who can testify to the truth of claims about them (e.g., an eyewitness) or a *record* which serves, as discussed in Chapter 3, as a socially institutionalized participant in and eyewitness to facts about events and actions. The length of this chain of knowledge formation, however, makes it quite difficult for us to trace back and substantiate each claim in relation to a direct source of knowledge, even if we have the interest or the time in our busy lives to do so. Yet, primary sources of knowledge, such as records, constitute the evidential foundation that undergirds the knowledge formation ecosystems upon which we rely for trust.

Records, as primary documentary sources of evidence that frequently under-pin attenuated knowledge formation chains, have received relatively little attention in the discourse on disinformation until relatively recently (see, e.g., Deutch, 2020) – dominated as it is by journalism, media studies, computer science, and engineering. The world of records, or archival documents, and recordkeeping is not something individuals within these fields typically con-template. It *is* a world that archival scientists think about, however.

One recent example is the work by the archival scholar Laura Millar. In her 2019 book *A Matter of Facts: The Value of Evidence in an Information Age*, which seeks to engage audiences beyond archivists and archival scholars, Millar (2019, p. xix) argues that the only remedy to descent into the "toxicity of a post-truth, post-fact world" is to fight for truth and combat lies by protect-ing and respecting recorded evidence. In a vein similar to some of the themes raised in Yeo's (2013) discussion of trust in records in the era of "cyberspace," Millar (2019) discusses the nature of digital information and describes how our ability to easily produce massive amounts of it, coupled with our inability to properly authenticate it, has compromised our ability to differentiate between

---

[21] An exception to this norm might be material produced by citizen journalists, but even in such cases content attribution is not easy (Rosenthol, 2020).

truths and lies. She also attributes the "post-truth" age to postmodernist ideas, which, she argues, have resulted in a world where everything, including the existence of objective truths, can be questioned (Millar, 2019, p. 4).

Archival theorist Luciana Duranti (2018), in a book chapter directed mainly to an archival audience, has also pointed to the connection between post-truth toxicity and processes of records creation, management, and preservation that have been complicated by political and economic interests and complex technical infrastructures. We must ask, Duranti (2018, p. 24) argues, how much trust we might be able to place in knowledge formation processes when

> records and actions of decisions are not generated; if those that are created are quickly destroyed as transitory records before entering such systems so that freedom of information can be evaded; if the content of the records that are made or received and properly maintained is selectively taken and used out of context; if claims, news and collected clips are neither traced nor traceable to authoritative documentary sources; and if users of data and information disseminated by broadcasts and social media do not know how to verify their sources and thus lose interest in doing so?

It is often only when there is deep disagreement between opposing epistemic viewpoints that we seek to verify the trustworthiness of records. Archivists have traditionally supported this by means of documenting the context of records creation and keeping, to present information pertinent to establishing the reliability of the records in relation to the facts they are about and to preserve records' authenticity.

Beyond the work of Millar and Duranti – which directly connects to perceived threats to the trustworthiness of records – there are literally scores of archival scholars who have been writing about these issues for decades, mostly exploring them from the perspective of technological change as well as cultural and political change. Solving the problem of uncertainty about the trustworthiness of records was, to a great extent, what the early Blockchain 2.0 proponents sought to do and what many – as we will discuss in the next chapter – blockchain projects continue to be concerned with: a way to create and keep evidence that can be trusted in an age of disinformation.

4.7 Concluding Thoughts

Trust – upon which complex societies depend to enable a wide variety of collective and coordinated activities that generate economic and social value – in turn depends upon knowledge about the likely trustworthiness of the person or thing to be trusted. Problems associated with the trustworthiness of the information upon which we base our assessments about the trustworthiness of other actors – the sorts of information disorders associated with the age of disinformation – can therefore have profoundly negative repercussions for societal trust. We have seen this time and time again in the past few years, whether those repercussions are in connection with disputed election results that foment social discord; suppression of, or efforts to delegitimize, social protest; whipping up public sentiment against public health measures; or denial of scientific facts relating to climate change. All have dangerous consequences for humanity. It is no wonder then that there is an enormous concern with finding solutions to the problem of fake news and other forms of disinformation. The search for solutions, however, often stops short of getting to an important epistemological root of the problem; that is to say, acknowledging the need to consider the evidential foundations of propositions. In the next chapter, I take a closer look at the trustworthiness of these primary sources of evidence, since unless they are trustworthy, they cannot contribute to a reliable epistemic foundation for societal trust.

5

Faking It

In this chapter, we turn to a topic that, as discussed in the previous chapter, has received relatively little attention in the discourse on causes of disinformation but which is becoming of growing concern – forgery or manipulation of the evidential basis of societal knowledge formation. This problem goes much beyond disputes about which "facts" to rely upon in determinations of the truth or about how to frame the agreed facts. Rather, it concerns the erosion of what I prefer to refer to as "evidentials," meaning the evidential foundations of propositions – the very basis of what we rely upon to anchor our beliefs. In daily life, we tend to think uncritically of evidentials as atomic, naturally occurring phenomena. Just as with the production of the news we consume, much of how evidential foundations of truth claims are created and preserved is obscured and we seldom give the process much attention beyond sometimes using evidentials to support claims in propositions. However, evidentials are as socio-technically produced as the news. Our blindness to the day-to-day "techne" of the production of the evidential grounds for the formation of our beliefs has rendered invisible the ways in which our "fact infrastructure" – including the means by which socially agreed sources of evidence supporting truth claims are produced, "fixed," and made persistent over space and time – can be manipulated at scale in the age of disinformation, with dire consequences for the epistemic foundations needed for the proper functioning of societal trust.

5.1 Seeing Is (No Longer) Believing

The age of disinformation has been marked by a rise in forged or manipulated content, and there is no better example of this than "deepfakes." This term derives from a combination of "deep learning" – the computational technique used to create deepfake videos – and "fakes," the result of this technique. More precisely, deepfakes involve the use of deep learning artificial intelligence (AI) processes to train visual manipulation algorithms (Kietzmann et al., 2020). Quite often, deepfakes replace the face of a real person in a video with that of another person, creating deceptive video content that seems to be real but is not. The term went viral in 2017 when AI-manipulated porn was uploaded to the discussion website Reddit (Maddocks, 2020). Although the capability to generate such fake videos has been available for some time in the entertainment industry, 2017 marked the moment when such advanced technological capabilities became available to the masses. Within a month of that Reddit post, tens of thousands of people were sharing their online "deepfake" porn (Maddocks, 2020; Mirsky and Lee, 2021).

The entanglement of deepfake porn and disinformation is illustrated well by the case of investigative journalist Rana Ayyub, who became the victim of this type of faked evidential after she took a stand against supporters of those accused of the gang rape of an eight-year-old in Kathua, India (Ayyub, 2018). Ayyub recounts that she was sitting in a café when she was sent a message letting her know that a pornographic video in which she featured was circulating on WhatsApp and, ultimately, phones throughout India (Ayyub, 2018). The effect of the video on Ayyub was devastating. In her own words,

> From the day the video was published, I have not been the same person. I used to be very opinionated, now I'm much more cautious about what I post online. I've self-censored quite a bit out of necessity.
>
> Now I don't post anything on Facebook. I'm constantly thinking what if someone does something to me again. I'm someone who is very outspoken so to go from that to this person has been a big change.
>
> ... [Deepfake] is a very, very dangerous tool and I don't know where we're headed with it.
>
> *(Ayyub, 2018)*

Images – especially video images – provide powerful evidence for the formation of beliefs. "I've seen it with my own eyes" is an expression often invoked by those arguing for the irrefutable truth of a matter that would otherwise be unbelievable. When we watch a video of something taking place, it is as if we are there directly witnessing the event (Witten and Knudsen, 2005; Sundar, 2008; Frenda et al., 2013; Liv and Greenbaum, 2020). We forget that the video is only a form of *testimony* (in the sense of being a means by which an alleged state of affairs is established or disproved). We adopt an unquestioning attitude toward such images (Nguyen, in press). Even if we might be inclined to question images, the veil of invisibility thrown over most of the ways that such evidentials are shaped and operate in an increasingly complex epistemic environment makes it extremely difficult for us to "cross-examine" a documentary witness. But what happens when evidentials are forged or manipulated? In an age of disinformation, we need to think carefully about the possibility.

5.2 The Invisibility of Evidentials

Most of us tend to assume the reliability and authenticity of the basis of our propositions rather than examining their features closely; in other words, we start from a position of trust (Hinchman, 2005; Nguyen, in press).[1] Our linguistic treatment of evidentials is revealing on this point, since the deep structure of language expresses social reality and practices (Mead, 1934; Dasgupta, 2014; van Elswyk, 2019, p. 136). Whatever we have no words or grammar to express in our language usually does not form part of our socio-cognitive reality and practices, as we have no easy way of communicating with one another about such concepts or phenomenon. It is telling, then, that only about 25 percent of the world's languages have obligatory linguistic evidentials, that is, a particular grammar that has evidentiality as a category (van Elswyk, 2019).

Evidentials are often expressed as verb conjugations indicating whether the proposition is at issue, the evidentiary strength of the source, whether the giver of the testimony bases their proposition upon direct knowledge or knowledge they might have received indirectly (i.e., hearsay, or knowledge passed on from another person), and how believable the giver of testimony finds the evidence. For example, in Cheyenne, "É-némene-sétse Sandy" expresses "Sandy sang, I hear(d)," with the use of the verb form sétse – the grammatical evidential – indicating that the speaker only has hearsay evidence of the proposition that Sandy sang (van Elswyk, 2019, p. 136).

Typically, the evidential operates in the background; that is, we might take issue with the proposition that it was Sandy who was heard to be singing but not with the proposition that the speaker heard about this indirectly (van Elswyk, 2019, p. 136). Thus, in language morphology, as Korotkova (2016) finds, the contribution of an evidential is usually a non-challengeable proposition. For

---

[1] Hinchman (2005) argues that testimony is "an invitation to trust" in the sense that grounds for trust need not be based on the weighing up of evidence in support of a proposition or the character of the giver of the testimony. Rather, when someone testifies to a claim, they invite the person to whom that testimony is directed to an entitlement to believe the claim. If the source of the testimony is generally a reliable source of the truth, then its hearer has no justifiable grounds not to believe.

example, in English the statement "It's raining, but I don't believe that it is raining" is considered paradoxical.[2]

In some languages there are linguistic devices to express relative strength or weakness of support for a proposition; that is, a speaker may use a grammatical form that expresses that evidence concerning the proposition was obtained indirectly rather than directly, with direct evidence being the more reliable source. Other languages allow for the expression of disbelief in a proposition based on indirect evidence, as in the case of Cuzco Quechua (van Elswyk, 2019, p. 138, citing Faller, 2002, p. 192) in which the phrase "Para sha ni si, ichaqua manic rei-ni-chu" expresses "It is raining (I heard), but I don't believe it." Outside those cultures where evidentials are a structural feature of the language, where the evidence for a proposition may be at issue the speaker's testimony must be interrogated to elicit evidence related to a proposition (e.g., whether direct or indirect [hearsay]) and information about its evidential weight, as we see during legal cases.[3]

In Western culture, in addition to physical evidence or oral testimony, we rely heavily upon documentary evidence. As with treatment of oral testimonials, the document as evidential will typically not be at issue, whether in a legal case or other contexts. Generally speaking, we take these sources "as read." In Western common law systems, for example, a legal principle known as the "business records exception to the hearsay rule" establishes that business records are exempt from the rule that oral or written testimony that is not presented by persons called as witnesses (i.e., persons who can be cross-examined) cannot be relied upon to ascertain the truth of a matter (The Law Dictionary, n.d.). Business records are treated differently because they are usually created in the course of fulfilling a regular business duty and are thus presumed to be reliable and authentic (Force, 2010; Baycara, 2014).[4] This

---

[2] This is a "Moorean" paradox, which captures the apparent absurdity involved in asserting a first-person present-tense sentence such as "It is raining, but I do not believe that it is raining" or "It is raining, but I believe that it is not raining." The first author to note this apparent absurdity was G. E. Moore. These Moorean sentences, as they have become known, are paradoxical in that, while they appear absurd, they nevertheless can be true, are (logically) consistent, and are not (obviously) contradictions.

[3] Van Elswyk (2019, p. 136) writes about the social consequences of this linguistic difference: "The significance of evidentials to grammatical practice is therefore immediate. In languages with obligatory evidentials, speakers are not capable of providing testimony by using a declarative without disclosing the source of their information. Merely stating how things are is grammatically impossible. . . . A speaker's reliability can be measured by whether she accurately uses evidentials or not. As a consequence, speakers whose language has obligatory evidentials often mistrust what other speakers say in another language that does not have obligatory evidentials. Aikhenvald (2004, p. 343) reports, for example, that 'Indians of the Vaupés area complain that when non-Indians speak Portuguese they are not explicit enough and often "lie".'"

[4] The court is not required to authenticate the documents. Legislation allows for business documents to be admitted to a proceeding with a presumption of authenticity if they have been created

presumption rests upon the circumstances surrounding the creation of certain documents, which, if they meet specific criteria, permit business records to serve as *prima facie* proof of the facts to which they attest. The most significant characteristic of admissible business records is that they spring from an originating action – a business activity or process – of which they are also the by-product and were created to represent. This is the reason that Thomassen (2015, p. 84) refers to the study of records as the study of "process bound information." The character of records creation in essence makes them direct participants in and witnesses to events and actions, even though it is not possible to cross-examine them like human witnesses. Records provide windows to the past, through which we can come closer than by any other available means to the historical moment to which they attest; nevertheless, we always need to recall that gazing at the past through a window is not equivalent to experiencing "history as it really happened" (*wie es eigentlich gewesen*) (von Ranke, 1824, pp. 13–14).

Legislation is often used to affirm that records generated in the usual and ordinary course of business, and which are relied upon routinely for accuracy, should be admitted without having to call the author or originator of the document to testify as to their reliability or to authenticate them; case law has further upheld and articulated the principle. Indeed, with blockchain and distributed ledger technology now being used in a growing number of business transactions, some jurisdictions have sought to establish smart contracts generated using these technologies as *prima facie* evidence on a par with other types of documents covered under the principle of the business records exemption of the hearsay rule.[5] These laws institutionalize the norms and standards by which we can adjudge such records as being reliable sources of evidence of propositions in the formation of justifiable true beliefs.

Baycara (2014) notes that the specific criteria that must be satisfied for business records to be non-challengeable – that is, to qualify under the business records exception to hearsay rule – generally include that the records must

- be made on some regular basis, routinely, and systematically
- pertain to an act, transaction, occurrence, or event

---

in the usual and ordinary course of business and according to the principles noted in, for example, Baycara (2014).

[5] For example, a law passed in 2016 in the State of Vermont (2016) – an act relating to miscellaneous economic development provisions – provides that a digital record electronically registered in a blockchain is to be considered authentic. Similarly, a law passed by the State of Arizona (2017) gives recognition to smart contracts, conferring upon them the status of an electronic record and specifying that a contract relating to a transaction may not be denied legal effect, validity, or enforceability solely because that contract contains a smart contract term.

- be made at the time of the act, transaction, occurrence, or event, or within a reasonable time thereof
- not express an opinion, diagnosis, impression, history, summary, or recommendation
- be made in the usual and ordinary course of business
- be created when it is within the usual and ordinary course of such business to make such record
- be made pursuant to a business duty
- be created under circumstances wherein both the record's creator and the informant are acting in the usual and ordinary course of business (where the records contain hearsay (indirect testimony)).

In common law legal systems, it is up to an opposing party to bring a motion questioning the accuracy, reliability, or authenticity of records introduced as evidence and to offer proof that the records do not meet the criteria (i.e., that they were not made in the usual and ordinary course of business, that they were not created by the person who claims to have created them, or that they were altered after their creation). In a manner similar to the handling of oral evidentials in testimony, when there is some issue to be resolved about a particular record – such as the circumstances surrounding its creation – this affects the evidential weight of the record as evidence rather than its admissibility as evidence of a claim (Baycara, 2014).

5.3 Examining the Evidence

Although we generally assume that evidence offered in support of truth claims is trustworthy, there can be many consequences when a trusting party bases their belief upon faulty evidence, some profoundly negative. As we discussed in Chapter 3, records and other evidentials anchor our assessment of the grounds for the trust that underpins complex human economic and social relations. These records and other evidentials are often how we determine whether a party to be trusted is (un)trustworthy. When the evidentials used to form this assessment are untrustworthy, a trusting party may form an incorrect or faulty belief about the other party's trustworthiness, resulting in "misplaced trust" (i.e., either trust is given when it is undeserved or it is not given when it is deserved, as in the Ayyub deepfake case). To avoid such negative consequences, it would seem to be wise for us to examine evidentials much more closely and critically than we might habitually be inclined to do. Indeed, Origgi counsels that

What a mature citizen of the digital age should be competent at is not spotting and confirming the veracity of the news. Rather, she should be competent at reconstructing the reputational path of the piece of information in question, evaluating the intentions of those who circulated it, and figuring out the agendas of those authorities that lent it credibility.

(Warburton, 2018)

Historians, for example, have developed finely honed techniques – the historical method – for critical examination of historical evidence. Though there are many debates about various points in relation to the historical method and changes in practice over time – as might be expected in any lively area of scholarship – in general, professional historians acquire knowledge of the past through the reading and interpretation, that is, criticism, of historical sources as part of a broader historical method involving the location of relevant sources, criticism of the spatial and temporal origins (aka provenance) of sources and their authenticity, and interpretation in relation to a historical question (Lorenz, 2001; MacNeil, 2013).

Writing about the use of archival documents in qualitative sociology, Skarpelis (2020) argues that it often relies upon an uncritical reading of the documentary evidence, or the making of "inferences from relics" (Goldthorpe, 1991, p. 213, as cited in Skarpelis, 2020, p. 388), prompting her to call for a greater interrogation of what she calls "life on file" and offering a methodology for doing so. Skarpelis (2020, p. 388) recommends, for example, that qualitative sociologists pursue a phenomenology[6] of the archives entailing

1. The *recovery* of life – whether persons, processes, or events – from files, where life is dislodged from paper, and persons and processes reanimated . . . ;
2. The creation of documentary evidence from social life, that is, *the turning of life into a record*;
3. The *archivization* of this documentary evidence, which follows the life of the file as it moves through institutional, physical, and intellectual spaces.

What Skarpelis describes is what archivists understand as the "archival method." Like the historical method, the archival method involves textual criticism and historical and even forensic research, but it is a method that is

---

[6] This phenomenology, asserts Skarpelis (2020, p. 388), draws upon approaches from disparate disciplines, which she cites as including history, anthropology, the history of science, documentation studies, archaeology, and library and information science. Given that Skarpelis is discussing archives and archival research, it is rather surprising that she does not cite archival science.

not directed at examining the evidence in relation to a particular historical question or truth claim. Rather, the method seeks to understand "life on file," as Skarpelis describes it, for the purpose of understanding records in relation to the past actions they have been created to give effect to and memorialize (Duranti and Michetti, 2016; MacNeil, 2016; Lustig, 2020). The archival method, then, uses a special form of criticism that seeks to "reconstruct relationships among internal and external elements of . . . records, their structure and their context," employing tools drawn from the philological disciplines such as philology, paleography, chronology, sigillography, heraldry, codicology, toponymy, epigraphy and textual criticism, and diplomatics (Duranti and Michetti, 2016, p. 90). Like the method proposed by Skarpelis, the aim of the archival method is to better understand the context of records creation and subsequent preservation in relation to a record's purpose, effects, and character as trustworthy grounds for belief in the actions to which it attests.

While these methods achieve the goal of critically examining the trustworthiness of evidentials, is the detailed analysis of "life on file" suitable as an everyday practice for the average person? Though we should be more critical of grounds for the evidence on which we base our beliefs, to question every record and closely examine "life on file" in the usual course of our daily activities would be extraordinarily taxing both cognitively and socially. Cognitively, we only have so much "bandwidth," given the speed of communication and transactional processing (Simon, 2013). If we were to stop to examine the trustworthiness of every record, even if we had the knowledge and skill to do so, the costs of transacting would also skyrocket and the speed with which transactions are processed would slow and potentially grind to a halt. We rely on being able to place our trust in the evidentiary character of records every single day to carry out various transactions in a reasonable amount of time with a reasonable amount of effort.

Moreover, even if we could examine every single source of evidence to determine its trustworthiness as support for propositions purporting to convey the truth of a matter, would we be able to accurately determine whether we could place our trust in these sources? The effectiveness of relying on individuals to conduct a form of textual criticism as a means of preventing phishing attacks suggests that the answer is no. Phishing is a social engineering technique where an attacker masquerades as a legitimate entity with which the victim might do business in order to prompt the victim to reveal some confidential information – very frequently authentication credentials – that can later be used by the attacker to gain unauthorized access to confidential information (Mitre Corporation, 2020).[7]

---

[7] Phillips and Wilder (2020) discuss how a number of these attacks are targeting individuals' cryptocurrency accounts, noting that many of the attacks operate on interconnected inauthentic websites advertised by malicious social media accounts that manufacture public blockchain

Quite literally, the attacker is fishing for information. To launch this type of attack, an email, an instant message, or a text message is made to look authentic to trick the victim into taking some action that reveals the desired confidential information. Often the victim is enticed into clicking on a link that redirects them to a fake but authentic-looking website (posing as the legitimate website of a financial institution or commercial service provider), where they are prompted to provide their login credentials. If the victim is fooled and enters their information, the attacker succeeds in gaining access to their account, at which point further financial damage can be done. According to the United States Federal Bureau of Investigation (FBI) Crime Complaint Center, individuals in the United States lost USD 57 million to phishing attacks in 2019 (FBI, 2019).

Prevention strategies to combat phishing attacks typically ask individuals to practice a form of textual criticism akin to the call to examine "life on file" – detailed analysis of textual variants of phishing emails and critical evaluation of their use of language and special signs and their provenance – to prevent attackers from fooling recipients and gaining unauthorized access to confidential information (see Figure 5.1). The fact that phishing attacks continue to be so successful points to the ineffectiveness of this strategy. Most people are not very good at the kind of textual criticism needed to assess the trustworthiness of digital records they receive. To determine the reliability and authenticity of digital records, people need to understand the complex processes that are involved in creating and transmitting them; they might lack the knowledge and skills needed to do this. Equally, they might simply lack the time and attention to do so effectively, or they might simply adopt an unquestioning attitude toward emails, text, and so on, owing to a natural predisposition to do so. Moreover, as the sophistication of the attackers increases, it becomes more and more difficult for individuals to spot red flags that might help them differentiate authentic messages from those that are fake even if they do adopt a more questioning attitude to such texts.

As if phishing emails were not bad enough, an increasing number of images and videos are being deliberately faked or altered. Strategies of forgery or manipulation might target any or a combination of different video components. Interrogation of visual images to determine their reliability and authenticity is even more challenging for us because visual images transmit direct to our visual cortex, triggering "fast thinking" and bypassing parts of our brain that

---

activity to create the appearance that their scams are genuine. The authentic-looking nature of the phishing communications tricks the victim into clicking on a link or opening an attachment that launches malware and steals data such as login credentials or credit card numbers. The target supplies their login credentials and is then notified that their account has been unlocked and that everything is fine.

Figure 5.1 Phishing attack protection as textual and literary criticism. To prevent phishing attacks, people are advised on the "red flags" that indicate a message may be inauthentic
(Federal Trade Commission, 2019)

might engage in more critical evaluation (Treisman, 1985; Witten and Knudsen, 2005; Stenberg, 2006). In other words, humans are "hard wired" to believe images.

The visual forgery and manipulation commonly seen in the age of disinformation can be grouped into two broad categories: shallowfakes and deepfakes (discussed previously). Table 5.1 outlines different "types" of each based on their manner of generation, along with a real-life example to illustrate them.

The generation of shallowfakes (Schick, 2020) can involve a range of techniques to manipulate the visual, audio, or textual components of videos, as shown in Table 5.1. These include altering the visual frames of videos by attaching short clips from one video to an unrelated second video, removing short clips from a video, or slowing down or fast-forwarding the playback speed of the visual frames. The audio of a video can be manipulated by cutting sound bites from one video and reattaching them to another, muting parts of the audio, or slowing down or fast-forwarding audio playback. Data used to

Table 5.1 *Types and examples of video forgery and manipulation*

Type	Examples
Shallowfakes	
Slowing down playback speed of video visual frames	Video of United States Democratic House Speaker Nancy Pelosi that was slowed down to give the impression that she was intoxicated.
Cutting visual frames	Video instance tweeted by former United States Press Secretary Sarah Sanders from the Infowars site in November 2018. It shows Jim Acosta, CNN's chief White House correspondent holding a microphone that an intern is trying to take away from him during a press conference with former United States President Donald Trump. Frames of the Infowars instance of the Acosta video were cut to make it appear that Acosta had aggressively placed his hands on the intern.
Altering audio	In the original Acosta video, Acosta says "Pardon ma'am" to the intern, but the instance of the video edited by Infowars mutes Acosta's voice.
Misrepresentation through alteration of descriptive text	Video posted by Facebook user Hendry Moya Duran purporting to show the devastation being caused by "Hurricane Irma," which took place in September 2017. The original video was actually captured in Uruguay after a tornado hit Dolores in April 2016.
Deepfakes	
Reenactment	Video of former United States President Barack Obama produced by Jordan Peel in which Obama appears to call his political successor, Donald Trump, a "dipshit."
Replacement	Video of former President Donald Trump's State of the Union address that replaces his face with that of actor Nicolas Cage.
Editing and synthesis	Altered video tweeted by former United States President Donald Trump showing a Nickelback video in which the photo in the video has been doctored to feature a photoshopped image designed to promote the claim that former United States Vice-President and now President Joe Biden was involved in corruption in the Ukraine.

Note: Readers can play back the original and manipulated example videos here: https://youtu.be/3u3SDzi8rFA. This compilation of sample manipulated videos was prepared by Hoda Hamouda, who at the time of writing is one of my doctoral students, for work described in Hamouda et al. (2019). See if you can spot the real from the fake. The *Washington Post* has also produced a guide to manipulated video (Ajaka et al., 2019).

describe a video (metadata) – such as the title (or caption) of a video, its location or date, or the introduction of an anchor – can be falsified or altered so that it misleads as to the visual or audio components of the video.

Deepfakes, the second major category of visual forgery or manipulation, are becoming increasingly problematic, as previously discussed. Mirsky and Lee (2021) identify four main categories of deepfakes: reenactment, replacement, editing, and synthesis (see Table 5.1). Disinformation involving reenactments is produced when a bad actor drives the expression, mouth, gaze, pose, or body of another person in the video. Facial reenactment focuses on changing the features of facial movements, rather than the identity of the source (Nirkin et al., 2019). As Mirsky and Lee (2021, p. 4) explain,

> Reenactment deep fakes give attackers the ability to impersonate an identity, controlling what he or she says or does. This enables an attacker to perform acts of defamation, cause discredibility, spread misinformation, and tamper with evidence.

Replacement occurs when new content is used to replace content in the original video in a manner that preserves the identity of an identifiable individual in the replacement video. This can be achieved either via transfer (such as facial transfer) or swap (such as face swaps commonly used to generate memes or satirical content) (Mirsky and Lee, 2021). When used with mal-intent, the aim is to make it seem as though the target is doing something they did not actually do, such as in the Ayyub deepfake porn video (Dale et al., 2011). Editing and synthesis involve the addition of attributes to an altered video, such as changing a person's clothes, facial hair, age, weight, ethnicity, tone of voice, and so on (e.g., Zhou et al., 2019). As Mirsky and Lee (2021) explain, using this type of deepfake a sick leader can be made to look healthy or fake online personas can be created.

Early fake videos, that is, those produced around 2017 and 2018, exhibited little "tells" of their inauthenticity – for example, glitches, flickers, poor image blending, unrealistic eye and mouth movements, bad lip syncing, lack of blinking, and jerkiness – that made it at least possible for humans to detect that they were fake. As deepfake technology has continued to improve through the application of new techniques – such as using generative adversarial networks, or GANs[8] (Mirsky and Lee, 2021) – and more professional

---

[8] As explained by Knight (2018), "A GAN consists of two components. The first, known as the 'actor,' tries to learn the statistical patterns in a data set, such as a set of images or videos, and then generate convincing synthetic pieces of data. The second, called the 'critic,' tries to distinguish between real and fake examples. Feedback from the critic enables the actor to produce ever-more-realistic examples. And because GANs are designed to outwit an AI system already, it is unclear if any automated system could catch them."

production (e.g., by intelligence organizations, states, big companies, and even terrorist groups), they have become increasingly difficult to detect with the human eye.

While the risks associated with deepfakes receive much of the attention in the current climate, other less visible but no less harmful forms of manipulation that target stored records also exist and are tightly interconnected with other forms of spreading disinformation. This is not a new phenomenon by any means, as we will come to in the following chapter, but we have become vulnerable to it in an era when so much of our information is stored digitally in centralized servers or the cloud (see, e.g., Kandukuri et al., 2009; Singh and Chatterjee, 2017). The vulnerabilities of these complex records' storage infrastructures present opportunities for unauthorized access to vast stores of even the most sensitive and confidential information. Though detailed, systematic studies of these types of attacks are not widely available, anecdotal evidence from a range of sources suggests that forgery and manipulation of stored evidentials could be on the rise. What happens when the underlying data used in machine-based analysis is forged or corrupted?

Given the rise of tools and techniques specifically designed for the manipulation of data at scale, trustworthy records are not guaranteed. As an example of this type of "content spoofing" (Mitre Corporation, 2020),[9] in December 2020, the European Medicines Agency (EMA) suffered a breach of COVID-19 vaccine data relating to records obtained from Moderna, Pfizer, and other third parties (EMA, 2021). The compromised records included confidential internal email correspondence relating to evaluation processes for COVID-19 vaccines. Though gaining unauthorized access to this data was serious enough, this was not the endgame of the hackers who conducted the exploit. Instead, their goal was to release a manipulated version of the records to sow public distrust of the results of the companies' vaccine clinical trials (EMA, 2021). Ultimately, in a climate of uncertainty, the attackers' goal was to foment

---

[9] Content spoofing involves scenarios in which "an adversary modifies content to make it contain something other than what the original content producer intended while keeping the apparent source of the content unchanged. The term content spoofing is most often used to describe modification of web pages hosted by a target to display the adversary's content instead of the owner's content. However, any content can be spoofed, including the content of email messages, file transfers, or the content of other network communication protocols. Content can be modified at the source (e.g., modifying the source file for a web page) or in transit (e.g., intercepting and modifying a message between the sender and recipient). Usually, the adversary will attempt to hide the fact that the content has been modified, but in some cases, such as with web site defacement, this is not necessary. Content Spoofing can lead to malware exposure, financial fraud (if the content governs financial transactions), privacy violations, and other unwanted outcomes" (Mitre Corporation, 2020).

mistrust of the evidentials – mistrust that could lead to social discontent and be politically costly but which also could have cost lives.

Another similar high-profile example involved the 2016 breach and manipulation of records of the World Anti-Doping Agency (WADA)'s Therapeutic Use Exemptions (TUE) process (WADA, 2016). The goal of the manipulation was to undermine the TUE process to cast suspicion upon WADA prior to the 2016 Olympic Games, from which Russian athletes found to be doping had been excluded. Not surprisingly the hack was ultimately attributed to the Russian hacking group "Fancy Bear" (Carmen, 2016; Thielman, 2016). This group was also linked to a hack of the United States Democratic National Committee (DNC) during the 2016 United States presidential campaign in which approximately 20,000 emails were stolen from DNC computers with the aim of uncovering information that would generate mistrust and undermine presidential candidate Hillary Clinton's campaign (Carmen, 2016; Thielman, 2016).

Aside from directly sowing uncertainty and mistrust, the manipulation of records has the potential to indirectly cause harm through machine learning dependencies on the underlying trustworthiness of evidentials. AI techniques are dependent upon data for the formation of training models. Data "poisoning attacks" can occur when machine learning systems are trained on user-provided records into which false training data has been injected with the aim of corrupting the learned model (Charikar et al., 2017). In essence, in this type of exploit, the uncritical reading of input data by AI algorithms mirrors our human blind spots, but at scale.

With an increasing amount of AI decision-making in everything from e-commerce recommender systems and stock market prediction to autonomous vehicles and healthcare, any malicious change in the underlying records upon which these AI algorithms train, or in the algorithms themselves, affects the end results of the analysis with the potential for serious consequences (Duddu, 2018; Pitropakis et al., 2019; X. Wang et al., 2019). Public availability of tools such as OpenAI's GP3, which uses AI techniques to produce "the next frontier of generative writing" (DiResta, 2020) – in other words, fake (non-human authored) text – creates even greater potential for widescale poisoning attacks.

Vast stores of scholarly and cultural records held in centralized memory institutions could also be at risk. As Clifford Lynch (2018, p.1) of the Coalition for Networked Information writes,

> This new centralized world offers few checks, tripwires, or other mechanisms to prevent an attacker from rewriting pieces of the scholarly or cultural record (including legal or government records) once the central server is compromised. I want to explicitly note here the difference between the act of quietly rewriting the record and enjoying the results of the rewrites that are accepted as truth and that of

deliberately destroying the confidence of the public (including the scholarly community) by creating compromise, confusion, and ambiguity to suggest that the record cannot be trusted. Both acts are very dangerous and damaging, but they serve different objectives.

An exploratory survey of how 15 archivists, librarians, directors, and technicians detected malicious actors, protected their collections from physical damage and viruses, or otherwise protected their digital collections' integrity, confidentiality, and availability suggests that curatorial professionals do not necessarily know if their collections have been subjected to the type of attack Lynch describes (Donaldson and Bell, 2019).

Lynch raises an important point about the lack of trust that can be generated by even a hint of manipulation of the scholarly and cultural record. Memory institutions involved in the preservation of archival documents have traditionally enjoyed a special public trust (Duranti, 1996; Lemieux, 2019). When public archives fail to behave according to the higher expectations of trustworthiness to which they are held, the resulting sense of public betrayal can lead to widespread outrage, as occurred in 2020 when the United States National Archives altered an image of a 2017 women's rights march by blurring signs appearing in it that were critical of former United States President Donald Trump (Cramer, 2020; Helm, 2020). Archivists are keenly aware of their special status as trusted custodians. But they are also aware that they might enjoy less trust today than they used to (Yeo, 2013; Plutchak, 2018) and that they operate in a world where digital content can be forged or manipulated with increasing ease. A paper by Green et al. (2018, p. 1) acknowledges this in asking,

> Is the archive trusted because of its people and practices or because of the sheer practical impossibility of altering or manipulating kilometres of physical records? What is the digital equivalent? The emerging challenge around trust is particularly relevant in relation to public archives preserving records of contentious histories; terms such as "fake news" and "post-truth" are frequently heard in the context of national and international politics. How do we ensure that researchers continue to trust that the records have not been tampered with, or that a document can be verified as being the same as the archived original?

The epistemic landscape in the age of disinformation leaves memory institutions vulnerable to attacks on their custodial credibility and the integrity of the historical record.

New, privately run types of cultural memory custodians, such as the Internet Archive,[10] might not have the same imprimatur of authenticity as public archives, yet historical researchers, legal disputants, and members of the public

---

[10] See https://archive.org.

alike rely upon such custodians to preserve "the authentic record" as if they were the equivalent of more traditional cultural memory institutions. Cohen (2015), for example, describes a legal case that hinged upon evidence from the Internet Archive's Wayback Machine, which can be used to "search the history of over 550 billion web pages on the Internet" (Internet Archive, n.d.). Cohen (2015, p. 13) recounts in detail some of the problematic aspects of relying upon such records as evidence, including how easily these types of digital records are altered:

> In the digital world, alteration can happen unintentionally or intentionally, the protection mechanisms of the Wayback Machine are not transparent and the adequacy of the machine and its mechanisms has not been established by a rigorous scientific process.

Many similar private and informal custodians in which we now place our trust for preservation of evidentials, assuming that the evidentials they keep are trustworthy, are also susceptible to alteration.

How to address the challenge of the forgery or manipulation of evidentials at scale is an open and active challenge. This type of activity renders fact-checking meaningless, since fact-checking is based on the premise that there is a ground-truth against which the facts can be checked. This might no longer be the case when the reliability and authenticity of evidentials is in question.

A range of solutions has emerged to address the problem of data manipulation, whether of images or textual documents, including (but not limited to) those that aim to "fight fire with fire," that is, to employ novel AI-aided techniques to augment what humans can do to identify faked or manipulated evidentials. For example, Konstantinov and Lampert (2019) discuss the development of adversarial machine learning techniques that allow algorithms to suppress irrelevant or corrupted data and thus to defend against content spoofing or data poisoning. In research on the detection and prevention of deepfakes, some AI-based detection algorithms use unique head and facial movements of a subject, such as a politician, as a sort of fingerprint of authenticity. Deepfakes are not always able to perfectly replicate these unique movements, even when the faked rendering looks nearly perfect to the human eye, so focusing AI tools on these details can help identify fake media. Another detection mechanism employs a browser-based plugin that warns users about synthetic media (Vincent, 2018). Using automatic detectors, the browser scans content on the screen and warns the user if it finds altered data. Social media tech giants are also coming together to develop tools to automatically detect deepfakes. Facebook, Google, Microsoft, Amazon, and other organizations have sponsored deepfake detection challenges that offer rewards to external researchers that develop the best deepfake detection tools (Wiggers, 2019). However, as with the challenges of detecting disinformation, very often these methods come up against the difficult challenge of identifying the real intention of the creator of the deepfake, especially when the content is political satire, and raise questions concerning freedom of expression and censorship.

Even setting aside these complex issues, some argue that machines can no longer keep up with the challenge of detecting and preventing fake evidentials. Researchers may be "outgunned": as soon as a technique is identified to detect some tiny flaw in a deepfake that marks it as a forgery, deepfake creators invent new ways to create more realistic content (Harwell, 2019). In an example of the limitations of AI in combatting the manipulation of records at scale, Israeli researchers have demonstrated that algorithms used to generate deepfakes (3D conditional GAN) could be used to manipulate stored patient CT scans to make it appear as though patients have cancer (Mirsky et al., 2019). In tests of expert human and AI approaches to detecting such manipulation, the researchers found that even AI detection tools were fooled. The dystopian possibilities of this type of attack are deeply worrying (Mirsky et al., 2019).

Even if the evidential manipulation "arms race" can be won, the mere fact that individuals know records and images supporting factual claims could be manipulated raises doubt and leads to questioning of evidence (Lynch, 2018; Vaccari and Chadwick, 2020). As Pomerantsev (2015) observes, writing about Russian disinformation operations, the aim of altering records is "to trash the information space so the audience gives up looking for any truth amid the chaos." A perfect example of this dynamic is a 2019 attempted coup in Gabon, a relatively stable country compared to its African neighbors, which was caused not by an inauthentic image but by one that was suspected as being inauthentic and was actually genuine. The background to this story is a rumor that emerged in October 2018 about the poor health of the country's president, Ali Bongo Ondimba, when he was at a summit in Riyadh, Saudi Arabia. As reported by the *Washington Post* (Cahlan, 2020),

> Shortly after the start of the program, on Oct. 25, 2018, Saudi state media transmitted a report saying Bongo had been hospitalized. Over the next few months, questions about Bongo's health grew as the government provided little [information] and evolving health reports. In October, the president's spokesperson said Bongo had suffered "severe fatigue." By mid-November, it was "bleeding." A month later, the vice president said it was a stroke. The statements and lack thereof – the administration released only a few images and a silent video of Bongo – helped feed rumors mainly from the opposition that Bongo was dead or replaced with a body double.

After months of silence, Bongo finally released a video on December 31, 2018. Some found the video suspicious, however, because Bongo appeared to be wearing a great deal of makeup and neither side of his face was moving. The strangeness of the video caused Elvine Belinda Andjembe Etogho, spokesperson for the Gabonese Council of Resistance, to question its authenticity and to form the belief that the president was being propped up by those around him to ensure that they would be able to hold on to power. Even though the video was subsequently found to be genuine, the belief that it was a deepfake created by those manipulating a president who had lost his faculties led directly to an attempted coup in early January (Cahlan, 2020). In the age of disinformation, the biggest threat to the epistemic foundations of societal trusting relations may be opening to question the basis of our claims of truth. In the long term, these effects can ripple out to online civic culture, potentially making individuals less likely to cooperate in contexts where trust is low, particularly in the case of highly polarized political situations (Balliet and Van Lange, 2013; Vaccari and Chadwick, 2020). Rising levels of uncertainty created by faked evidentials of all types might deprive people of the ability to make up their own minds. As Arendt (1978) warned, "And with such a people you can then do what you please."

5.4 Concluding Thoughts

As we have discussed in this chapter, forgery and manipulation of the evidential basis of our truth claims – the means by which we may come to know something – is on the rise due to novel, largely AI-driven techniques, combined with factors discussed in the previous chapter such as the rising dominance of social media as the primary source of news for many people and the increasing "weaponization" of information for economic or political gain. We are not always aware of the way in which evidentials are being undermined, since we have become socially accustomed – and, in the case of visual images, are cognitively hard wired – to see evidentials as non-challengeable (i.e., to trust them) unless there are exceptional circumstances or this sort of critical examination of evidence is part of our professional purpose and methods, as is the case for archivists. This leaves us open to the formation of false beliefs or, if we become aware of the extent to which the evidentiary underpinnings of our propositions might be untrustworthy, to feel uncertain about the basis of the "facts" upon which we might rely. In the age of disinformation, the rise of uncertainty might be the biggest threat to the epistemic foundations of societal trusting relations. In the next chapter, we will explore how it is that we find ourselves in this predicament and how blockchain technology might provide new capabilities that enable us to do something about it.

PART IV

Blockchain and Distributed Ledger Technology

6

The "Moral Defense of the Archive"

The forgery and manipulation of evidentials taking place in our present age is not a new phenomenon, although one can argue it is taking place at an unprecedented scale owing to the capabilities and availability of new technologies. Humanity has faced such moments in history before. A similar epistemic climate existed in many parts of the world during World War II, for example. Decrying the disinformation that was rife during this period, Sir Hilary Jenkinson (1882–1961),[1] a British archival theorist and practitioner of the twentieth century, saw the archivist's duty as protecting the "physical and moral defence of the archive" in support of "the truth." For Jenkinson, this entailed preserving the intellectual properties of records and their relationships to one another as much as protecting the records physically (Jenkinson, 1937, p. 83). In an article written in England during World War II, Jenkinson reflected that

of all the persons who pay service to the cause of Truth, the good Archivist is the most absolute, the most complete, the most selfless devotee. It is his duty and privilege not merely to be as truthful as he can himself, but to be the guardian for the benefit of others of countless truths of all kinds – truths which interest him personally and truths which do not; yes, and truths of which he himself does not perceive the existence. The whole of his professional labours, rightly understood, are directed to that one end. In an age which has allowed important people to publish important books describing and differentiating with nice precision the possible uses of lies; which conceals lies of every variety, from *suppressio* to *imitatio veri*, from the subtler garbling to the lie direct, lies of all degrees of magnitude and turpitude, under fine names, such as "Propaganda" and "Publicity" and "News Value"; an age which witnesses with complacency the daily perversion by journalists and others of every word descriptive of importance, quantity or value; an age which permits not merely that bad and ill-informed teaching but the

---

[1] Sir Hilary Jenkinson was Deputy Keeper of the Public Record Office (which is now part of the United Kingdom National Archives) between 1947 and 1954.

deliberate misleading of children and childish persons; an age in which the *ersatz* is admitted . . .; one which has called to the assistance of misrepresentation all the resources of science – in such an age the thoughtful Archivist cannot but reflect that his professional point of view seems to be one which distinguishes him sharply from a very large proportion of the population. He may in an expansive moment, go so far as to suggest that had his doctrine of the sanctity of evidence (which in four words is the Archivist's creed [*respect pour les fonds*]) been generally accepted in the world, the world would not now be at war. He may even be tempted to wonder whether that lost ideal of which everyone is in search, that standard for the better conduct of life which seems so difficult to determine, may after all be nothing more out of the way than a general application of those which govern professionally his own imperfect endeavours – the ideal of mere truth, the standard of truthfulness pursued not occasionally, as a means, but invariably, as an end.

(Jenkinson, 1944, reprinted in Daniels and Walch, 1984, p. 21)

Of course, looking back from our present-day vantage point, we can see that archivists do not preserve "the truth" per se (nor can they single-handedly prevent wars – or so I am told).[2] What they do instead is preserve records – those documents that individuals, groups, organizations, and governments create and keep in the course of their everyday activities and that, as a result of this preservation, present the possibility of providing evidentials in support of claims about what is "true," even if those same evidentials are used to support claims by those with competing versions of the "truth."

6.1 Evidentials: What's in a Name?

Over the centuries and in different cultures, these fixed evidentials have gone by many different names. During the Enlightenment in Europe, such fixed materialized representations came to be known as "documents." The term document derives from the Latin *docere*, to teach, and *documentum*, a lesson, proof, instance, or specimen (Oxford University Press, 2021c). In its early form, usage of the term "document" was not necessarily limited to written texts and could also extend to objects, such as rings, knives, and collected artifacts (Clanchy, 2012; Lund and Skare, 2017). Over time, the term evolved to mean "something written, inscribed, etc. which furnishes evidence or information upon any subject, as a manuscript, title-deed, tomb-stone, coin, picture, etc.," or "a proof given of any fact asserted" (Oxford University

---

[2] Archivists, being human, are fallible recordkeepers of course, and the organizations charged with the preservation of the documentary heritage are fallible institutions. Neither archivists nor archival institutions can escape the social, cultural, and political milieux in which they operate.

Press, 2021c). Suzanne Briet (1894–1989), a French documentation theorist, drew on concepts from semiotics in defining a document as "any concrete or symbolic indexical sign [indice], preserved or recorded toward the ends of *representing, of reconstituting, or of proving* a physical or intellectual phenomenon [emphasis added]" (Briet, [1951] 2006, p. 10). The term "document" thus became associated with proving one's rights and entitlements, and in science with proving the truth of scientific claims (Lund and Skare, 2017, p. 1374).

A closely allied term is "record," which originated from the French word *record*, entering English common law after the Norman conquest and the subsequent introduction of French law into the English court. In English common law, a record came to denote "testimony, legal record, authority of a court of record (all 13th cent. or earlier in Anglo-Norman), witness (13th cent.), official record, document (14th cent. or earlier in Anglo-Norman), opinion (1349)" (Oxford University Press, 2021d). Modern legal usage of the term gradually evolved to encompass all written documents that were created and kept in the usual and ordinary course of business, as discussed in the previous chapter, thereby linking the concept of a record to the conduct of juridically relevant activity. The concept of a record as forming a part, and an evidentiary by-product, of organizational activities and events is reflected in the International Organization for Standardization (ISO) definition of a record (i.e., "information created or received and maintained as evidence and as an asset by an organization, in pursuit of legal obligations or in the course of conducting business" [ISO, 2020b, 3.2.10]) and also in archival theory of the record (see, e.g., Yeo, 2007, 2008).

Yet another term bearing a similar meaning is "archives." Yeo (2015, p. 315) notes that "In mid-twentieth-century Britain, the terms records and archives (the latter supposedly newly introduced from continental Europe) were considered largely synonymous." With mounting quantities of public records in the post–World War II period, however, the meanings of the two terms began to diverge, "records" coming to mean those documents that organizations of all types create and keep in the course of carrying out their daily activities and "archives" coming to signify, in Germany and Anglophone North America in particular, that subset of the totality of records deemed, through processes of archival appraisal, selection, and acquisition, to possess value as historical evidence beyond the instrumental purposes surrounding their creation (Brenneke, 1953; Schellenberg, 1956; Yeo, 2015). In English, this differentiation has opened a divide between usage of the two terms (Lemieux, 1993): the term "record" is customarily applied to documents that are still in current or semi-current use by their creators, whereas "archives" tends to be used when referring to the body of records of a single creator transferred to an archival repository. The same divide does not necessarily exist in other languages and cultures (e.g., French).

No matter what name is used, these terms all represent a common phenomenon. Beginning in the modern period with the expansion of literacy in Western Europe, they represent the fixing of human activity into a material and intellectual form capable of testifying to the events and actions[3] of which they form a part and conveying knowledge about them over space and time. As such, the terms were used to describe those specific written texts – documents, records, archives – that serve as grounds to prove truth claims, that is, as evidentials (which should not be confused with evidence or perfect representations of past action, as I will come to in Chapter 7).

6.2 Blockchain As a Defender of Evidentials?

We can see a clear through line from Jenkinson's archivist to the present day in proposals for the use of blockchains to solve the types of disinformation-age problems identified in the previous chapter and, in general, to guard against manipulation of evidentials. Even some of the hyperbole about blockchains being "permanent sources of truth" and an "'ultimate' record of truth" (Roon, 2016; Dwyer, 2017) – or what Woodall and Ringel (2020, p. 2208) label "archival imaginaries" – seems to echo Jenkinson's sentiments about archivists. Surveying the literature on blockchain and distributed ledger technology, Woodall and Ringel (2020, pp. 2205–2206) find that "integrity, authenticity, or reliability are used 360 times in combination" and that *"Trust in evidence* [is used to justify] blockchain . . . [and] capitalizes on the complexity of establishing fixity in digital records [emphasis in the original text]." Thus, it can be argued that blockchain and distributed ledger technology, or at a minimum rhetoric about it, is animated by the same idealistic spirit as Jenkinson's archetypical twentieth-century archivist – the moral and physical defense of the archive – the only difference being that, with blockchains and distributed ledgers, realization of this utopian state is to be achieved technologically, rather than by human hand. Each blockchain solution seeks, in its own way, to defend the record, morally (read: intellectually) and physically against forgery and manipulation. Table 6.1 presents an illustrative selection of solutions drawn from a systematic search of two major repositories (i.e., the Association for Computing Machinery's [ACM] Digital Library and the Institute of Electrical

---

[3] Yeo, following usage of the term in philosophy, refers to these collectively as occurrents (see Yeo, 2018, pp. 130–132).

Table 6.1 *Examples of blockchain solutions relying upon trust in the ledger to address disinformation-age problems*

Example	Problem addressed by blockchain solution
Educational certificate anti-counterfeiting and anti-tampering	Xie et al. (2020, p. 1) note that "Traditional paper certificates and electronic certificates have difficulties in preservation and management, not to mention other problems concerning inconvenient verification, poor reliability, anti-counterfeiting and anti-tampering." They propose a blockchain scheme providing certificate services for a college students' innovation and entrepreneurship competition. Certificate issuing, verification, and revocation are realized via smart contract.
Electronic voting integrity	Bosri et al. (2019), Gani and Aşkaroğlu (2019), and Vivek et al. (2020) discuss issues of voter fraud and design a blockchain system to prevent data manipulation, deletion, and other security issues in the voting environment.
Fake video defense	Chan et al. (2020) propose a permissioned blockchain using Hyperledger Fabric 2.0 coupled with long short-term memory deep learning for audio/video/descriptive captioning for combating deepfake media. The solution requires that the original artist attest to the authenticity of digital media at point of reception.
Family deed certificate integrity	Sunarya et al. (2020) propose a solution to guarantee the integrity of, and guard against loss of, government-issued family certificates.
Integrity of government tenders	Yutia and Rahardjo (2019) outline a blockchain-based e-procurement system to protect against threat of vulnerability to fraud, collusion, and manipulation practices. The authors argue that by adopting blockchain, e-tendering can reduce the source of fraud arising from database manipulation.
International trade certificate authenticity and status	Q. Lu et al. (2020) set out a blockchain solution to enable trade participants to know about the authenticity and status of international trade certificates such as phytosanitary certificates, which record that exported plant based materials meet the biosecurity requirements of destination countries. The solution is advanced in the context of an electronic "ePhyto" certificate system to be operated by the United Nations.
Internet of Things (IoT) sensor data integrity	Lockl et al. (2020) have designed a blockchain-based IoT prototype that improves data integrity and addresses availability challenges.
Medical records integrity	S. Wang et al. (2019) and Du et al. (2020) propose that blockchains can be used to protect the integrity of medical records.
Power grid data protection	Bhattacharjee et al. (2020) notes that real-time power grid situational awareness, observability and state estimation, and online stability assessment depend upon the accurate and reliable measurement of samples inside the substations

Table 6.1 *(cont.)*

Example	Problem addressed by blockchain solution
	or in phasor data concentrators. These can become a target for cyberattacks, such as false data injection and data tampering attacks. The authors argue that blockchain can simultaneously ensure reliability, security, and integrity with decentralization properties in a peer-to-peer system. They propose a blockchain-based synchrophasor network protection framework to enhance the self-defensive capability of a power grid monitoring system.
Tamper-proof delegated storage in the cloud	Yang et al. (2020) highlight concerns about data integrity, security, user privacy, and the correctness of execution in the cloud due to untrusted remote data manipulation. Using blockchain, they propose a solution for efficient and transparent public verifiable delegation for both storage and computing and a smart contract application programming interface (API) for request handling and secure data query.
Trusted website certificates	Szalachowski (2019) similarly addresses issues with certificate management in the Transport Layer Security (TLS) protocol, the de facto standard for secure client–server communication on the Internet, noting that an adversary compromising a single trusted entity can impersonate any website, which is common in phishing attacks. The Persistent and Accountable Domain Validation solution is presented as a next-generation blockchain-based TLS notary service.

Note: The examples in Table 6.1 represent a selection of cases from a knowledge base compiled by the author's search of the ACM Digital Library and IEEE Xplore database in March 2021 using the following search terms: blockchain+phishing; blockchain+deepfakes; blockchain+fake+videos; blockchain+records+manipulation. The terms were chosen to represent issues of concern discussed in the previous chapter. The search yielded a total of 306 unique items. Given the acknowledged limitations of the search strategy (e.g., the term "distributed ledger" is not used, many other search terms might have been included, such as the terms that Woodall and Ringel [2020] use to build their corpus [i.e., integrity, authenticity, and reliability], and other databases might have been searched) and the fact that the examples were not randomly chosen by the author, no generalizations should be made from the chosen examples nor inferences about the efficacy of the solutions; rather, they have been chosen on the basis of relevance to the topic of discussion in this chapter to generate an impressionistic overview and for illustrative purposes only.

and Electronics Engineers' repository, IEEE Xplore) of research on blockchain technology that yielded hundreds of papers illustrating the wide variety of use cases for application of the capabilities of blockchains to safeguard data and information against the manipulation that has become increasingly commonplace in the age of disinformation.

Each solution expresses a desire, and a need, to insert consideration of the evidentiary character of information back into thinking about its creation and handling, or, as it has been described in the context of "big data," to consider "veracity" as well as "volume," "velocity," and "variety" (Laney, 2001; Cai and Zhu, 2015).

The capabilities of blockchains and distributed ledgers can be used to protect the intellectual integrity, or "fixity," of records to address the risks that datafication of records pose. At the same time, in an age of advances in information processing technologies and surveillance capabilities, it is also important to reflect upon the dangers of immutably preserving certain kinds of information, such as information that links individuals with descriptive attributes about them (e.g., race, gender, political affiliation, etc.) or that represents individuals in a certain light. Although we might prefer a world in which records are always created to achieve, or are used for, moral and just ends, the cases discussed in the previous chapter indicate that the world is not so black and white. It is safe to say that those who have been featured in fake pornographic videos would prefer that all copies of these records be deleted forever, not preserved immutably in a distributed ledger that protects the integrity of the videos for all time. But what of videos featuring human rights abuses of individuals? These would benefit from solutions that protect their integrity, such as blockchains. Even when records have been created by social actors who are not acting with good intent or who are later judged to have been acting immorally, it is often only because such actors took pains to protect the integrity of their records (e.g., in the case of the Iraqi secret police files [Montgomery, 2001]) or because others sought to capture evidence of such abuses and establish and preserve the authenticity of that evidence (e.g., in the case of the capture of records relating to the United States 2020 election in an effort to combat misinformation [Dotan, 2021]) that abuses of power and human rights are later discoverable and prosecutable. This is all to say that the moral defense of the archive is not always irrefutably moral. Answers to questions of what should be preserved over the long term and the principles that should be applied in balancing privacy rights and the public's right to know for purposes of accountability or scientific and social research cannot be found easily without reference to the contexts in which they arise. Archivists, as professionals working in institutions that acquire materials that frequently contain personal information about individuals, have long grappled with such questions and have developed relatively thoughtful strategies in response to them (MacNeil, 1992; Jo and Gebru, 2020). These strategies are not perfect, however, and are still vulnerable to abuse, which suggests that caution and humility are required in considerations of the universal "goodness" of the moral defense of the archive (Poole, 2020).

6.3 The Rise of Computing and the Transition to the Digital Record

How is it that we now perceive a need for a new "algorithmic archivist" in the form of blockchains and distributed ledgers? The transition from paper-based evidentials to digital evidentials in the post–World War II period has most certainly played a role. In the post–World War II period, computing emerged as a major new field that grew out of a desire for speed, accuracy, and reliability of numerical calculations (and as a replacement for slow and often inaccurate human calculations) (Hevner and Berndt, 2000; Dasgupta, 2014, p. 71).[4] Key to the new "machines as computers" paradigm were two developments: the mathematical theory of computing devised by Claude Shannon (1916–2001), which identified the bit as the fundamental unit of information and computing (Computer History Museum, 2021), and the "stored program" theory formulated by John von Neumann (1903–57), which introduced a program as a set of instructions stored in computer memory to enable the computer to perform a variety of tasks without human intervention (Dasgupta, 2014, pp. 138, 241; Lynch, 2017).[5] By the late 1940s, engineers in the United Kingdom and in the United States had already built stored program computers – for example, the Manchester Mark I in the United Kingdom and the EDVAC computer in the United States. (Dasgupta, 2014, p. 126).

Early computers were used to generate mortality and astronomical tables and as tabulators in accounting and other business-related statements (Dasgupta, 2014, p. 68). Throughout the 1950s and 1960s, the use of computers expanded to include the automation of routine activities, such as the sorting, searching, and organizing of business data (Hevner and Berndt, 2000). The period from 1965 to 1974 saw a maturation of business computing, when "the simplistic automation of basic business processes gave way to the full computerization of critical business functions at the center of major organizations" (Hevner and Berndt, 2000, p. 10). As records of business activities of all types came to be created using software programs, such as Wordstar, Microsoft Word, and VisiCalc (Computer History Museum, 2003), paper business records were gradually replaced by digital ones. The 1990s saw a surge in the use of

---

[4] Readers might recall the popular depiction of a human computer from the 2016 film *Hidden Figures* about female mathematicians working for the United States National Aeronautics and Space Administration prior to the introduction of computing machines.

[5] Invention of the stored program architecture gave rise to a focus on computer programming and programming languages (Dasgupta, 2014). In the 1950s, distinct computing "cultures'" emerged around two different languages. On the one hand, there was the language of scientific computing and computer science represented by FORTRAN and, on the other hand, there was COBOL (Common Business-Oriented Language), the language of business computing and data processing (Dasgupta, 2014, pp. 202–204).

computing in public sector contexts, for example, with the introduction of new information systems aimed at improving government efficiency, service delivery, and accountability (see, e.g., Heintze and Bretschneider, 2000; Lee and Perry, 2002; Grönlund and Horan, 2005; Heeks, 2006).

With the advent of business computing, the previously fixed materiality of records – increasingly viewed as an encumbrance following a post–World War II paperwork explosion – was set free. Records became "liquid" (Smit et al., 2017). Capturing the spirit of the age but lamenting the passing of the previous era, Brown and Duguid (1996, p. 9) write,

> It is a gross oversimplification simply to denounce fixity and embrace transience as if we could have only one. Even if, then, we are not in the middle of an irreversible transition from fixity, what does seem to be inescapably different now is that the two, the transient and the immutable, are materially no longer mutually exclusive. Now it's possible to have mutability where once there was only fixity – in, for example, the digital document.

Despite Brown and Duguid's call to embrace both fixity and transience, the mundane fixed document – providing proof and evidence of everyday business activities – gave way to a new-found love of mutability and computability.

With digitization and the creation of records in native digital form, records became "datafied" (Mayer-Schönberger and Cukier, 2013); that is, their textual components could now be extracted, broken up, and reconfigured, rendering them "computable." The work of Mortimer Taube exemplifies this shift in focus and its attendant approach. As Saracevic (2017, p. 2222) explains,

> In the early 1950s Mortimer Taube (1910–1965), another IR pioneer and entrepreneur, founded a company named Documentation Inc. devoted to the development and operation of systems for the organization and retrieval of scientific and technical information. Taube broke away from the then-standard methods of subject headings and classification, by developing Uniterms and coordinate indexing. Uniterms were keywords extracted from documents; a card for a given Uniterm listed the documents that were indexed by that Uniterm. Coordinate indexing was actually a search and retrieval method for comparing (coordinating) document numbers appearing on different Uniterm cards by using a logical AND, OR, or, NOT operation. Although at the time the algorithm was not recognized as Boolean algebra by name, the operation was in effect the first application of a Boolean algorithm for information retrieval. Uniterms and coordinate indexing were controversial for a time but soon it was recognized that the technique was a natural for use as a base for computerized search and retrieval.

Datafication would ultimately enable the "information age" and, latterly, the "age of big data" (Castells, 2009; Mayer-Schönberger and Cukier, 2013). These historical moments were characterized, among other things, by processes enabling the extraction of data from once-fixed sources of information (such as records), rendering such data "transient" and thus independently subject to computational analysis. "Data is the new oil" became the mantra of the age, signifying both the extractive nature of datafication and the newly recognized value of the extracted substance – that is, data (Arthur, 2013; Hirsch, 2013).

6.4 The Datafication of Records

Datafication of records changes their evidentiary quality. In the pre-digital world, a written "testimonial" about an action taking place in the usual and ordinary course of business – a record – was recorded on a material substrate, which "fixed" in place the "facts" about the activities it participated in and represented – in essence, rendering the record "immutable." The fixing of states of affairs about activities on a stable material substrate helped to protect the integrity of the record as proof of facts about those activities (or at least to render any alterations more evident). Depending on the type of material substrate used, it was possible for the intellectual content of records to remain fixed in place for a very long time. Content recorded on linen-based paper, for example, might last for centuries, whereas poor quality newsprint might crumble after only a few decades (Library of Congress, n.d.). Regardless of the durability of the substrate, the materiality of these fixed representations of activities provided a large part of what was relied upon to protect and detect their evidential integrity – the quality of being complete and unaltered (ISO, 2020b, s. 3.2.8).

Despite the lack of fixity of digital records, they are not completely devoid of materiality. Following Dasgupta (2016), digital records can be described as comprising three classes of computational artifacts: material, abstract, and liminal. Material artifacts, such as computer hardware, are those that "obey the laws of physics" (Dasgupta, 2016, p. 23). A second class of computational artifact is the abstract: these are the algorithms, Turing machines, and software languages of computing. They are, argues Dasgupta, "symbol structures" devoid of any physicality (though they can be made physical by, e.g., printing them out on a piece of paper). Finally, there are the liminal artifacts, which Dasgupta describes as both abstract and material: they are themselves symbol structures, like abstract artifacts, but their operations cause changes in the physical world and their actions depend on an underlying material agent. Liminal artifacts can comprise user interfaces, microprocessors, and software programs. All of these classes of artifacts collaborate in the production of digital records. As liminal artifacts themselves, digital records come into being as the dynamic output of an interacting hierarchy of implemented computational artifacts that have a materiality but which also have symbolic meaning, as in the case of representing and embodying legal claims. In other words, digital records can be understood as dynamic virtual performances: "[in relation to a word processor], someone must have designed and implemented a computational artifact which when activated performs as TEXT, hiding the details of the mechanisms by which TEXT was realized" (Dasgupta, 2016, p. 15; see also Duranti and Thibodeau, 2006).

While it is possible to understand paper records in this manner as well – that is, to consider them as performances rendered by the assemblage of pen, ink, and paper – the abstract (i.e., nonphysical) nature of most of the artifacts that configure records as digital objects make such records different from the materiality of their paper counterparts. Pen, ink, and paper all have connections to the physical world, while software languages and programs that generate digital records exist as purely abstract or mixed artifacts. This makes it possible to arrange records in as many sequences as desired by those who might like to use them as evidence and knowledge sources, rather than setting them in fixed places in folders and boxes as it was necessary to do in the pre-digital world (Weinberger, 2007; Yeo, 2012). Unlike analog records, then, digital records are space–time continuous in nature as opposed to spatially discrete.[6]

Moreover, in its digital form, a record has many interconnected dependencies, most of which are hidden (or abstracted) away or oftentimes not even made evident or instantiated. What appears to our eyes as a visible unitary "thing," a text, is really a complex network of interdependencies that becomes increasingly less visible to humans the further down the computational hierarchy one goes (moving from the level of human-to-human or human-to-machine interaction, through programming, binary code, and ultimately to a circuit board that resolves to silicon and metal, particles and fields). As that network of interdependencies becomes less humanly visible, so too does the semantic meaning that it is the intent of the record's creator to convey (Hui, 2012). All of this complexity is tucked behind a veil of abstraction, providing the illusion of a stable and unitary digital text appearing before our eyes – the quintessential computational example of Latour's (1987) "black box," wherein the relations that construct the artifact become so embedded as to be made invisible.

Yet it is from the representation of the many interconnected dependencies that records derive their meaning. We recognize how remarks taken out of

---

[6] Like discrete data, a discrete object is one that can only have a certain representation and is only found at a fixed location, whereas a continuous object is one that can have many representations and locations (within a certain range). On this, see Weinberger (2007).

context can alter the meaning of what was said: in fact, this has been a common tactic of those spreading disinformation. The same principle also applies to records as evidentials. They derive their meaning from who created them and for what purpose, their relationship to the activity that originated them and of which they are a by-product, as well as from their relationships to the other records created in the course of the same and related activities. All of this provides important context for the knowledge that they were created to convey about the events and actions they document and of which they are a part.

System designers have often failed to provide the capability to instantiate the context of digital records creation (e.g., through the application of contextualizing metadata) or metadata about the context of records creation. Even if the context is represented in instantiated form, it is often stripped away through subsequent processes of datafication, thereby altering the meaning that the record conveys. In addition, the syntax of records – or configuration of their intellectual components – can now be easily altered, giving records a malleability that is convenient but can also subtly alter their semantic meaning. Moreover, unlike paper records, wherein a record's intellectual components are all to be found in one unitary object, the intellectual components of digital records can be scattered across several interdependent and dynamic computational components. Standard form consumer contracts, for example, now consist of hidden hyperlinks that can change at any time, often without notice, potentially significantly altering the contract's meaning (Cornelius, 2018, p. 8).

Peering within the black box, then, digital records are far from unitary, fixed, and immutable. Rather, they are fragile, contingent, and conditional. Lynch (2001, p. 13) observes,

> Digital documents in a distributed environment may not behave consistently; because they are presented both to people who want to view them and software systems that want to index them by computer programs, they can be changed, perhaps radically, for each presentation. Each presentation can be tailored for a specific recipient. Further, the information that a human takes away from a presentation of a document through mediating software such as a Web browser may be very different from what an indexing program extracts even from the identical source document, unless the indexing program is designed to consider the perceptual impact of the document on human beings.

It is as if, by analogy to the pre-digital world, each time we wish to view a digital record, the pen, the ink, and the paper must come together to write a copy of the record anew so that we are able see and derive meaning from the resulting artifact. If the pen (or a similar enough writing implement) is no longer available to do the writing, then the record can be neither written nor read; likewise, the required ink and paper must be made available each time the record is to be written, or viewed, anew. Finally, the elements of intellectual content must be arranged on the page in precisely the same order as in the first writing of the record in order to convey a consistent meaning to the reader.

With such complex dependencies, it is no wonder that digital records often do not persist. There are many issues to attend to: digital records are easy to destroy, lose, corrupt, and alter. They can become inaccessible if not protected and deliberately made to persist. Their content, structure, and form are not inextricably linked and stored as a unitary entity apart from their presentation to an application user (Duranti and Rogers, 2019, p. 1). The best we can do is to preserve the compositional artifacts that make it possible for us to reenact them and capture enough information about the records and the context of their creation and subsequent custody to achieve a descriptive, or intellectual, fixity in the absence of a material fixity, making it possible for those who might need to rely upon these evidentials to evaluate the trustworthiness of the evidence about the activities they represent (Duranti and Rogers, 2019, p. 1; Duranti and Thibodeau, 2006).

The highly malleable and mutable nature of digital records also begs the question, "How can we trust them?" Is it possible to determine the trustworthiness of an object so shape-shifting as a digital record? Early computer scientists did not worry about this. Theirs was a world of data and information in which factuality was considered self-evident (Yeo, 2018, p. 118).

6.5 From Records to Information and Data

As the digital overtook the paper world, theories linked to the former materiality of records and to notions of documents or records as proofs became less influential than notions of information and data, at least in the Anglophone world (Lund and Skare, 2017). Documentation theory, for example, gave way to information science, an interdisciplinary field primarily concerned with the *relevance* – often constructed as "aboutness," pertinence, or topical-relatedness – of the informational content of sources of knowledge (Saracevic, 2017, p. 2216). In universities around the world, programs of librarianship transformed into programs concerned with information science (Lund and Skare, 2017). The task of critically reflecting upon "life on file" fell to scholars outside of librarianship and information science, such as Michel Foucault (1926–84), Harold Garfinkel (1917–2011), and Dorothy E. Smith (1926–) (Foucault, 1980; Smith, 1990; Garfinkel, [1986] 2017; Lund and Skare, 2017). As information science evolved, it became less about the documentary paradigm than about the need for, use, and retrieval of information resources, motivated by the key problem of the postwar information explosion and how information and communication technology might be used as a solution (Saracevic, 2017, p. 2217).[7] Over time, two key branches of information science took shape: one branch heavily focused on information retrieval (IR) and the other broadly focused on the human dimension of IR, that is, on human-beings as seekers and users of knowledge sources (Saracevic, 2017).

IR evolved to focus on information systems and the development of novel algorithms for the retrieval of knowledge sources and, as such, had close ties with computing (Saracevic, 2017). The tight coupling that existed between the IR branch of information science and computer science is no better embodied than in the contributions to the field made by Gerard Salton (1927–95), a computer scientist and academic who ran IR experiments from the mid-1960s to the time of his death in 1995 and developed many novel IR algorithms and approaches that serve as the foundation of the IR field to this day (Saracevic, 2017).

Unlike information science, which had a documentary tradition, the discipline of computer science – which crystallized in the 1970s with the introduction of computer science programs at many Western universities – had no such tradition. From its origins, computer science has been a field concerned with information and data (Dasgupta, 2014). It is noteworthy that the etymology of the term "data" indicates no conceptual connection with notions of proof or evidence, unlike the terms "documents," "records," and "archives." "Data" is a borrowing from the Latin *data* (Oxford University Press, 2021b) and is used as both a count noun (as in "The verticall Angles, according to the diversity of the three Cases being by the foresaid Datas thus obtained," from 1645 [Oxford University Press, 2021b]) and a mass noun meaning "Related items of (chiefly numerical) information considered collectively, typically obtained by scientific work and used for reference, analysis, or calculation" (Oxford University Press, 2021b). In computing specifically, the term has come to mean "Quantities, characters, or symbols on which operations are performed by a computer, considered collectively" (Oxford University Press, 2021b), but diverse scholars working in the field of computing have conceptualized data and its relationship to information quite differently and often the terms data and

---

[7] Bates (1999) identifies three "Big Questions" for information science: 1. The physical question: What are the features and laws considerations in the design of new systems?; 2. The social question: How do people relate to, seek, retrieve, and use information?; and 3. The design question: How can access to recorded information be made most rapid and effective?

information are used interchangeably (Borgman, 2016, p. 28; Dasgupta, 2016, p. 5).

To some, data has a materiality that information does not (Hey, 2004; Wempen, 2014; Laudon and Laudon, 2015); data takes up space – the bits, bytes, and now zettabytes[8] of storage we commonly require. Donald Knuth sees data as a representation of information obtained by observation or measurement in some precise manner (Dasgupta, 2016, p. 5). Similarly, for artificial intelligence researchers Jeffrey Shrager and Pat Langley data is what is observed and selectively recorded; information does not figure into the mix (Dasgupta, 2016, p. 9). Russell Ackoff, on the other hand, conceptualizes data as a representation of objects and events preceding information (Dasgupta, 2016, p. 5). For some, data is without its own meaning (e.g., Ratzan, 2004; Wilson et al., 2013). Luciano Floridi, for example, argues that data only signifies the presence of difference and information is something that combines two or more elements of data to generate meaning (Dasgupta, 2016, p. 9).

In the context of computer science and data science, data is often treated as "raw fact," suggesting a belief that it represents a certain incontrovertible objectivity, or truth (Yeo, 2018, p. 118). No distinction is made between the truth-value of the states of affairs represented in the data – what might be called a historical truth – and the truth-value of the data as a *representation* of those facts – what might be called a documentary truth (Duranti, 1998, p. 82). It is as if, by analogy to the language of evidentials discussed in the previous chapter, there is no linguistic device to conceptually distinguish between evidentials and what they represent, nor in the language of computing or cognate disciplines to express the relative strength or weakness of evidentials as grounds for belief in a proposition; evidentials are taken at face value to be trustworthy "raw data" and challenges to that basic proposition might seem paradoxical (see Chapter 5).

No matter the vagueness of the meaning of the term "data" and what it represents, data has become the new currency of our age. As Cukier and Mayer-Schoenberger (2013, p. 35) put it, "Once we datafy things, we can transform their purpose and turn the information into new forms of value." This capability marks the arrival of the age of big data, in which data has become the building block in the creation of novel products (Arthur, 2013; O'Neil and Schutt, 2013). Against this background, a new discipline has taken shape – data science. Data science is often described as a data-driven process comprised of regularized steps of analysis that proceed in a linear manner. For example,

---

[8] A zettabyte is the equivalent of 1,024 exabytes; an exabyte is equal to 1,024 petabytes; a petabyte is 1,024 terabytes; a terabyte is 1,024 gigabytes; a gigabyte equates to 1,024 megabytes; a megabyte is 1024 kilobytes; and a kilobyte is 1024 bytes.

Ward et al. (2010) present visual analytics – which, at its most basic level, involves a combination of data science approaches and visualization techniques – as a "pipeline"[9] comprised of raw data acquisition, data/ flow transformations, visual mappings, and visual transformations with the end-goal of supporting some user task; Keim et al. (2010) discern three stages – data management, data modelling, and data visualization – while Kandel et al. (2012) identify five stages – discovery, wrangling, profiling, modelling, and reporting.

With the rise of data science, the manipulation of information and data – and, by extension, of human actors – has become a new and specialized field but one, like computer science and latter-day information science, with a very different intellectual architecture than those rooted in documentary traditions. As evidence of the conceptual separation of this field from those concerned with evidentials, such as archival science, van Bussel (2017, p. 19) notes that "an analysis of the contents and abstracts of five top journals each for computer and information science from 2010–2016 shows that both sciences do not really acknowledge the concepts records and archives. [The terms] are rarely used, even while there are many articles in these journals describing information. ... In the end, only 25 articles (from the 5,319 articles reviewed) mention the concept records or archive(s) (or both) in its title or abstract."

I have written elsewhere about the effects of the introduction of computing for transactional information processing in developing countries, accompanied as it has been by a replacement of traditions of recordkeeping with new computing paradigms (Lemieux, 2016a). It is worth reiterating the early concerns raised by scholars about this practical and conceptual shift. For example, Heeks (1998, p. 2) wrote,

> Where public managers lack a clear records management strategy, computerisation has often been associated with diminution or even loss of paper records-keeping. Yet computer records, because of their intangibility and malleability are a far poorer basis for accountability than paper records. "The medium is the message" when often-inaccurate public sector data is produced by computerised accountability systems it gains a mask of objectivity and an aura of credibility that it does not deserve. Recipients can be led to believe in the validity of invalid accountability information, thus undermining the process of accountability.

---

[9] While visual analytics was originally conceptualized as a neutral process in which the human barely intervenes, recent work drawing upon insights from science and technology studies problematizes this notion. As Muller et al. (2019, pp. 1–2) observe, "human expertise intervenes between the raw data and the analysis, crucially shaping the data, the choice of analysis, and in some cases the truth claims associated with the analysis."

There is now a significant body of evidence from a wide range of sources that indicates that in large parts of the world – in well-resourced countries as much as in less-well-resourced ones – the essential enhanced structures, controls, and skills necessary to manage digital records to ensure their long-term accessibility and integrity as evidentials have not been introduced (Lemieux, 2016a). It was just this concern – a concern about the manipulation of land records in Honduras – that motivated Factom's blockchain solution, previously mentioned in Chapter 3.

This is not to suggest that protecting the integrity of data – which is necessary to protect its evidentiality – was previously unheard of in computing; there were efforts and new technologies (e.g., digital signatures) aimed at doing so dating from at least the 1960s and 1970s (Diffie, 1988; Warner, 2012). However, with no tradition of creating, handling, preserving, or scrutinizing documentary evidence, these early efforts focused narrowly on protecting the integrity of the bit structure of data, which can be said to be only a small part of protecting the integrity of sources of evidence. Broader concern with protecting the evidentiary quality of data only came into sharper focus later in computing and its cognate disciplines.

Several factors contributed to the need to protect data as documentary evidence and to a growing concern with the design of systems capable of generating and preserving trustworthy data and information. As the use of computers expanded throughout the 1980s and 1990s with the rise of the PC and networked computing, an awareness began to take shape that computers could be used to commit crimes such as digital vandalism, theft of confidential data, attacks on core infrastructure, or distribution of child pornography. This awareness, and the need to investigate such crimes, motivated the emergence of the field of digital forensics (Pollitt, 2010; Warner, 2012). Many of the early pioneers in this field had both a computing and a law enforcement background and worked for government agencies, and thus understood evidence and issues associated with its preservation (Pollitt, 2010; Casey, 2019). The field grew such that, by 1993, the First International Conference on Computer Evidence at the FBI Academy in Quantico, Virginia, was attended by representatives from 26 countries (Pollitt, 2010, p. 7). Throughout the 1990s and into the 2000s, the field continued to formalize, with publication of digital forensic principles between 1999 and 2000, recognition of digital forensics as a laboratory discipline, and a growing number of academic programs and scholarly journals (Duranti, 2009; Pollitt, 2010, pp. 10–11). Nevertheless, digital forensics remains retrospective in outlook rather than focused on the design of information systems (Duranti, 2009).

New requirements for reproducible research also drove increased interest in the trustworthiness of data (Peng, 2011). Researchers needed to be able to demonstrate that their data had not been manipulated to suit a particular interest group or that they had not made a mistake in analysis leading to a spurious conclusion. These changes sparked greater concern with the veracity of data, which entered the discourse on big data analytics with the acknowledgement that data was increasingly obtained from unverified sources, was incomplete or inconsistent, and often of low or unknown levels of accuracy (Laney, 2001; Liu and Özsu, 2009; Shankaranarayanan et al., 2012).

Within the field of information systems, notions of the believability of data – that is, the extent to which data is accepted or regarded as true, real, and credible – were added to models of data quality, growing out of discussions on interorganizational data exchange and decision-support (Shankaranarayanan and Blake, 2017).

The concept of believability is also closely linked to a focus on data provenance and source credibility in literature on organizational data exchange, data mining, and analytics (see, e.g., Prat and Madnick, 2008). The first workshop on data provenance was organized in 2006, launching a community within computing and cognate fields of those interested in the study of provenance as a means to assuring and ascertaining the trustworthiness of data (Ludäscher, 2016).[10] While this rising interest in data provenance in its various forms connects to growing concerns and questions about source accuracy and credibility – or believability – the emerging theories of this community of scholars, at least in the early years of its formation, remained siloed from disciplines such as archival science, history, sociology of knowledge, or law,

---

[10] Since interest in data provenance first arose within the computing field, there have been different definitions and formulations of the term. Buneman and Tan (2007), working in the context of databases, defined data provenance – which they note is sometimes also called "pedigree" or "lineage" – as the description of the origins of a piece of data and the process by which it arrived in a database. Simmhan et al. (2005) define data provenance as information that helps determine the derivation history of a data product, starting from its original sources, while Prat and Madnick (2007) define it in terms of the origin and subsequent processing history of data and propose a computational model of believability based upon an analysis of provenance metadata. Moreau (2010) differentiates between (1) provenance as process, or the process that led to a piece of data, (2) provenance as annotations designed to provide structure and semantics to resources (e.g., through the addition of metadata concerning author, creation date, and version), and (3) event-oriented provenance, according to which provenance is a chain defined as a time-ordered sequence of provenance records capturing events affecting a document. Ram and Liu (2006) propose the W7 model, conceptualizing of provenance along seven dimensions: "what" (the events that happen to data), "when" (time), "where" (space), "how" (actions), "who" (actors), "which" (devices), and "why" (reason for events, including goals). In the context of linked open data on the web, the meaning of provenance has been codified by the W3C PROV-dictionary as "a record that describes the people, institutions, entities, and activities involved in producing, influencing, or delivering a piece of data or a thing" (Missier et al., 2013, p. 1).

which also traditionally were concerned with issues of documentary trust-worthiness and had evolved concepts, terminology, principles, and practices for the critical examination of these issues that predated, in some cases by centuries, the approaches being considered in computer science and cognate fields (Lemieux, 2016b).

6.6 Concluding Thoughts

Since the post–World War II period, the rise of computational information processing has gradually supplanted traditional records and recordkeeping that centered on the physical record. While this has brought many new and beneficial capabilities, the demise of traditional recordkeeping knowledge has undermined practices concerned with the physical and moral defense of the record and supplanted them with practices arising from a dominant ethos of datafication. This focus on data malleability over the defense of information from manipulation and corruption (the ancient task of the recordkeeper) has contributed to the current diminution of the trustworthi-ness of society's evidentials. Consequently, we have seen a great unravel-ling of the evidentiary foundations of society's "fact infrastructure." In computing and cognate fields, this issue has been only recently noted, with some attention paid to digital forensics and questions of data believ-ability and provenance, and research into the quality of data and credibility of knowledge sources.

Despite its roots in computing, however, blockchain and distributed ledger technology represents something different. By creating and relying upon an immutable ledger, blockchain and distributed ledger systems promise to halt the processes of datafication contributing to widespread manipulation of records. Instead, blockchain and distributed ledger technologies can crypto-graphically fix the record, chaining it in place so that any tampering is extremely difficult and immediately evident. Thus, the design and spirit of blockchain and distributed ledger technology (at least in theory) harkens back to a pre-digital past when the materiality of paper records more readily fixed in place transactional facts and protected their integrity from manipulation. The vocabulary used to describe blockchain technology (i.e., "distributed ledgers" and "ledger records" [ISO, 2020b, s. 3.22 and 3.44]) indicates the Janus-faced orientation of the technology: one face looking toward comput-ing and the other toward recordkeeping (or the keeping of evidentials). Applications of blockchains' recordkeeping capability can be seen clearly in solutions targeting the causes of faked evidentials and the prevention of data manipulation. As such, blockchains promise society an algorithmic archivist and a computational custodial space in which to defend archival documents physically and intellectually, and they also represent a possible means to stabilize the epistemic foundations of societal trusting relations. In the next chapter, we will discuss how well blockchain and distributed ledger systems actually deliver on this promise.

7

From "Archival Imaginaries" to Archival Realities

As discussed in the previous chapter, this is not our first disinformation age. We have been down this road several times in the past: in Europe during the Middle Ages (c. 500–1500 AD), for example. Throughout the middle and later medieval period, document forgery and manipulation were widespread (Tout, 1919; Clanchy, 1980; Hiatt, 2004). Even the "Donation of Constantine" giving the papacy dominion over all the Western Empire was forged in the ninth century. Monks of the eleventh and twelfth centuries were said to have forged charters entitling them to property and jurisdiction all the time. So much a matter of course was document forgery and manipulation that the Archdeacon of Canterbury wrote to Pope Gregory IX in 1238, "Holy Father, there is not a single sort of forgery that is not perpetrated in the church of Canterbury" (Clanchy, 1980, p. 123) and the Bollandist[1] monk and hagiographer Daniel von Papebroch[2] (1628–1714) was later prompted to write that *all* documents contained in ancient cartularies[3] were deliberately falsified by eleventh-century monks and should be held in suspicion (Tout, 1919, p. 219). Tout (1919) offers several explanations for the widespread medieval practice of document forgery, including excessive pride in house and family, and a desire to confuse an enemy with false news.

While we might conclude from this information that the medieval period was populated by rogues of the highest order, willing to forge documents at the drop of a hat for personal and political gain, there is an alternate explanation that is quite relevant to our times. In the transition from an oral culture – in which

---

[1] The Bollandists are an association of scholars, philologists, and historians (originally all Jesuits but now including non-Jesuits), who since the early seventeenth century have studied hagiography and the cult of the saints in Christianity (Hayes, 2011).
[2] Sometimes spelled von Papenbroeck.
[3] The Oxford English Dictionary defines a cartulary as "'A place where papers or records are kept' (Johnson); whence the whole collection of records (belonging to a monastery, etc.); or the book in which they are entered; a register." (Oxford University Press, 2021a).

many transactions were completed by custom with the exchange of a token such as a ring, knife, or sword – to a written culture, the lords of great estates desired to have their land titles confirmed in writing by a charter under the great seal or a deed of land (Tout, 1919, p. 215). Indeed, as written documents supplanted customary rights (i.e., land held by evidence of common knowledge), it was increasingly required of them to provide such written evidence of their title (Tout, 1919, p. 215; Clanchy, 1980).

One way for landholders to obtain written title was to present an original title deed to a chancery office, which could then be confirmed in writing under the great seal (Tout, 1919, pp. 215–216). In the absence of having such original titles, the lords simply solved their problem by forging the required documents. The forger naturally tried to make the forgery look authentic, but as Tout (1919, p. 216) explains,

> He [the forger] could not understand that each age has its particular forms and technicalities. He knew best those of his own age, and he imagined that what he found in the document he was most familiar with belonged to all time. He was a reformer too in his way and wanted his charter to be up to date. He was, therefore, ... prone to copy out the technical forms in vogue in his own age. And the methods which innocence might adopt from sheer lack of historical sense, art and fraud, could also appropriate from entire ignorance of how things were really done in remote ages.

In thinking about the transition from paper to digital over the past several decades, it is possible to see a similar lack of historical sense at play. Paper documents are frequently copied (i.e., digitized) or made anew, without a historical sense of their technicalities – indeed, they are seen as being nontechnical – with the result that elements necessary to establish their evidentiary status are not translated into digital form or are somehow oddly out of place. New forms of records often lack the qualities needed for them to serve as evidentials. This is no less true of blockchain and distributed ledger records than it is of other forms of digital records, as I will come to in this chapter.

Back to Daniel von Papebroch, who had disparaged every eleventh-century document as a forgery. In 1675, he proved that a charter guaranteeing certain privileges to the Benedictines, supposedly issued by the Merovingian King Dagobert in 646, was a forgery. As we can imagine, the Benedictines were not well pleased with von Papebroch's finding and they set about to prove him wrong. One of the best and the brightest of their order was Dom Jean Mabillon (1632–1707) (Knowles, 1959). Mabillon spent several years drawing up a systematic way to test the authenticity of medieval documents to prove von Papebroch had been incorrect (he wasn't). In the course of doing so, however, Mabillon wrote *De re diplomatica* – completed in 1681 (Reynolds and Wilson,

1991, p. 189) – and invented a new discipline called "diplomatic," now more commonly referred to as "diplomatics" in North America (Yeo, 2017, p. 95).

Diplomatics, which drew upon theories and principles that had begun to be systematized in the Middle Ages with the first university course in notarial arts – offered in 1158 at the University of Bologna, according to Duranti (1995) – refers to "the science or study of documents and records, including their forms, language, script, and meaning. It involves knowledge of such matters as the established wording and procedures of particular kinds of documents, the deciphering of writing, and document analysis and authentication" (Beal, 2011, p. 121). Its purpose was to establish the authenticity of documents.

By the nineteenth century, diplomatics had evolved from its use in determining the authenticity of documents conferring legal rights to its adoption by historians as a tool for analyzing the authenticity of historical sources (MacNeil et al., 2001, p. 3). According to Williams (2005, p. 2, citing Brooke, 1970, p. 1),

> Christopher Brooke, formerly a teacher of diplomatic on the postgraduate archives programme at the University of Liverpool, when Professor of History at the University of London, referred to diplomatic as "the barbarous name given to the science of documents" which had the "reputation of a formidable and dismal science ... a kind of game played by a few scholars, most of them medievalists, harmless so long as it does not dominate or obscure historical enquiry."

As Williams (2005, p. 2) goes on to note, diplomatics has had something of a renaissance in recent years, emerging as a sub-specialty under the broader disciplinary umbrella of archival science, with consideration being given to how it applies to current recordkeeping theory and novel digital forms of records, most notably in the work of the InterPARES project that now spans more than 20 years of investigation on the question of the long-term preservation of the authenticity of digital records (Duranti and Preston, 2008; Duranti and Rogers, 2019). With this work, the application of diplomatics – coupled with concepts drawn from archival science, law, and computing – expanded into consideration of the design of records systems, and particularly how archival diplomatics might be developed to support the qualities of records' trustworthiness,[4] that is, the *prospective* application of archival science in addition to its *retrospective* application to analysis of historical documentary sources (Duranti, 1999, p. 165; MacNeil et al., 2001; Williams, 2005, p. 3).[5] To

---

[4] The addition of archival to diplomatics reflects a merging of the archival and diplomatic perspectives in the InterPARES framework. Diplomatics focuses mainly upon the individual record, while archival science tends to emphasize the record aggregate (e.g., files, series, and fonds) (MacNeil et al., 2001, p. 24).

[5] With the advent of the digital era, archivists realized a need to pay greater attention to records creation due to the challenges posed by preserving digital records. This perspective is reflected in the InterPARES project's research into the long-term preservation of the authenticity of digital

date, InterPARES has explored the application of archival diplomatic theory in a variety of digital contexts, most recently cloud technology (Duranti and Rogers, 2019).

Traditional diplomatics distinguishes between elements of *fact* in the document, that is, those elements describing the action of which the document forms a part, and elements of *form*, which are those relating to its physical and intellectual construction (Williams, 2005, p. 16). The work of mapping these elements to digital records has proven to be quite challenging because, while medieval documents contained all the necessary information to identify these elements in one unitary object, digital records, as we have already discussed, are dynamic and have complex system interdependencies. Many elements needed to ascertain or assure records' authenticity thus might be missing at the time of retrieval or might never have been created at all (Duranti and Thibodeau, 2006). This challenge has necessitated innovations in diplomatic theory, not the least of which has been to consider the characteristics of systems in addition to individual documents (Williams, 2005, pp. 11–13). The task has been made all the more urgent by the fact that, as discussed in the previous chapter, digital records are so fragile, contingent, and conditional.

The "diplomatics renaissance" and ongoing research demonstrating the continuing utility of diplomatics, albeit in an expanded and modernized form (known as "archival diplomatics"), show that it provides a useful framework for assessing how well blockchains and distributed ledgers meet their oft-stated goal of being "permanent sources of truth" or the "'ultimate' record of truth" as well as for guiding the prospective design of blockchain and distributed ledger-based records and records systems to imbue them with characteristics aimed at increasing the likelihood that they will be viewed as providing trustworthy evidence (Roon, 2016; Dwyer, 2017).

Archival diplomatics is not the only framework that has been used to evaluate the trustworthiness of records. Devan Ray Donaldson, for example, has proposed the Trust in Archives–Trust in Digital Archival Content (TIA–TDAC) framework, which he developed based on a synthesis of literature on users' trust in "digital archival content and relevant web credibility literature" and empirically tested by means of user surveys (Donaldson, 2019, p. 60). The

---

records, but it is a perspective not reflected in traditional archival theory. For instance, the Dutch Manual on the Arrangement of Archival Documents notes that "The rules which govern the composition, the arrangement and the formation of a [fonds], therefore, cannot be fixed by the archivist in advance; he can only study the organism and ascertain the rules under which it was formed. Every archival collection has, therefore, as it were, its own personality, its individuality, which the archivist must become acquainted with before he can proceed to its arrangement." (Muller et al., [1920] 2007).

crucial difference between archival diplomatics and Donaldson's framework (and those like it – see Meijer, 2003; Pattenden-Fail, 2008; Conway, 2010), aside from the fact that archival diplomatics has a longer tradition of theorical formation and evaluation, is that Donaldson's approach rests on how users *perceive* the trustworthiness of digital content and digital repositories rather than on any properties possessed of such content or repositories that might be used to infer trustworthiness (i.e., the "deep structure" of the object of analysis [Wand and Weber, 1995]); in other words, the TIA–TDAC framework is an *observer relative* and *retrospective* view of trustworthiness similar to the user trust discussed in Chapter 3.

However, working with records managers, records creators in large organizations – especially those that are highly regulated – often can and do take prospective steps to design digital systems that instantiate properties in records that they believe provide tractable and accessible signals of the records' trustworthiness, regardless of whether or how such properties are later perceived by subsequent users or readers of the record. Generally, these properties are broadly socio-culturally determined, although there will also be organization-specific variations. Thus, I would argue, trustworthiness of records is not strictly reducible to whether or how a specific user or group of users perceives these properties in the records *ex post*. Moreover, as discussed in Chapters 2 and 3, trustors can be mistaken in their assessments of the trustworthiness of trustees; trustees might be trustworthy whether perceived as being so or not, including when the "trustee" is a record or a records system. In the case of records, assessments might be missing full and complete information about processes of creation that would inform a user's perception of whether the record is reliable, for example. User perceptions, however, offer an important perspective on trust in records, including blockchains and distributed ledgers, that complements creator-oriented, observer-independent frameworks focused on the deep structure of objects and systems, such as archival diplomatics.

Another framework closely aligned with archival diplomatics is offered by the relatively new discipline of digital forensics. Both diplomatics and forensics were developed as practices for the purpose of retrospectively investigating existing material evidence, and both have the possibility of being extended for application to the prospective design of information systems (Duranti, 2009). Also, like diplomatics, digital forensics references the legal system and the geopolitical context in which that system operates (Duranti, 2009, p. 64). Unlike diplomatics, however, digital forensics studies objects, substances, and traces in digital systems that offer evidence. In her 2009 article presenting a detailed comparison of digital diplomatics and digital forensics, archival theorist Luciana Duranti discusses several concepts (e.g., computer stored, computer generated, and hybrid types of computer records) that she considers useful to all those fulfilling the function of trusted recordkeeper or custodian. She ultimately sees value in a merging of archival and diplomatics theory, principles, and practices with those of digital forensics, which she proposes to call "Digital Records Forensics" (Duranti, 2009, pp. 52, 64). Lee (see, e.g., Lee and Woods, 2014) has also called for the application of digital forensics tools and techniques to archival materials and related preservation functions. Thus, digital forensics adds a perspective, methods, and tools that are likely to complement archival diplomatics.

7.1 Records' Trustworthiness: An Archival Diplomatics View

Archival diplomatics defines the concept of a record in a very particular and precise manner, as might be expected of a discipline that proposes to advance theory-based principles that generalize to more than one case. A record is, thus, "a document made or received in the course of a practical activity as an instrument or a by-product of such activity, set aside for action or reference" (Pearce-Moses, 2018). Some might be skeptical of the notion that all records are documents. Ledger records, for example, might not, at first glance, fit the mold of what we typically think of as documents (e.g., a letter). However, the definition of the term "document" in archival diplomatics encompasses more than what might immediately come to mind in thinking about documentary evidentials. A document, according to InterPARES terminology, is "an indivisible unit of information constituted by a message affixed to a medium (recorded) in a stable syntactic manner. A document has fixed form and stable content" (InterPARES 2 Project, 2021a). Importantly, by incorporating the term "document" into its definition of a record, the InterPARES definition of the term establishes a continuity with notions of proof and evidence traditionally associated with the term "document." Indeed, the term "archival document" is treated as a synonym for records in archival diplomatics.

While the purpose of this volume is not to enter into archival theoretical debates, it is worth noting that the archival theorist Geoffrey Yeo does not use the word "documents" when defining records. Rather, he suggests that they are "persistent representations of activities or other occurrents, created by participants or observers of those occurrents or by their proxies; or sets of such representations representing particular occurrents" (Yeo, 2008, p. 136). In Lemieux (2014, p. 79), I build upon Lemieux and Limonad (2011) to extend Yeo's representational notion of records in the context of efforts to connect archival and information systems theory, arguing that records are "a type of information system that serves as a persistent representation of a set of beliefs[6] ... and of the other classes, roles, properties, restrictions and relationships that relate to ... interaction, which is created by actors or observers of that interaction, or by their proxies; or sets of such representations." While this assertion might seem contrary to my argument in the previous chapter that "information" and "records" do not share a common conceptual root, when I refer to records as being types of information systems I am not suggesting that records are a kind of information; rather, I am referring specifically to the representational[7] and other characteristics of information systems as discussed in information systems theory (see, e.g., Gregor, 2006; Straub, 2012; Recker et al., 2019). To explain, in traditional approaches to theorizing about records,

> records are viewed as objects or artifacts that reside *within* [emphasis added] a context. That is, they form part of the context in which they are found. Taking this view, records may be seen, in the traditional view, as the result of, the by-product of, or the execution mechanism of some transaction (e.g., a financial transaction) that takes place in a context (e.g., the Canadian financial system). However ... we can draw upon representation theory to merge traditions of viewing records as representations from archival theory with similar theories on the representational qualities of information systems.
>
> To elaborate, in information systems theory, an information system is defined as an artifact that pertains to three specific models: representational, state tracking, and good-decomposition. All three models rely on the premise that an information system is an iconic representation of concrete or conceived (i.e., in someone's mind) real-world systems (namely, the domain-of-discourse), as perceived by someone's or some group's view.
>
> *(Lemieux, 2014, pp. 75–76)*

---

[6] Yeo (2017) mistakenly concludes that the reference to beliefs in my 2014 definition of a record refers to the messages or "utterances" that records contain; instead, what I am referring to are the beliefs that a social group holds about how best to create a good representation of a perceived reality and what therefore will be accepted as a reliable source for the formation of justifiable true beliefs within a particular "domain of discourse." Nevertheless, I do think that all records communicate beliefs in some way, even those records that are *expressive* (express feelings or attitudes); *directive* (ask a question or attempt to get someone to do something); *commissive* (commit the writer to doing something); or *declarative* ("make changes in the world"), according to Searle's taxonomy adopted by Yeo (Searle, 1999, p. 150). Even when the record is created as an expression of feeling, a command, or a promise, the reader comes to know something. Since, according to broadly accepted epistemological principles, the receiver of a message cannot come to know something (i.e., hold a justified true belief) from a sender of a message that does not know that thing, we can assume that a record transmits a belief. It would seem odd to assert otherwise, since we clearly come to know about the states of mind, declarations of war, or promises made in the past through records.

[7] As Recker et al. (2019, p. 766) explain, "According to [representational theory], the essence of an [information system (IS)] is that it provides a representation of other real-world phenomena (the focal real-world phenomena). To the extent ISs provided more faithful representations of the focal real-world phenomena, they will be deemed more useful ... Humans can then employ them to obtain knowledge about real-world phenomena without having to observe the phenomena directly," such as in the case of using them to obtain knowledge about the past that would be otherwise inaccessible since past phenomena can no longer be directly observed.

This theoretical perspective is consistent with the expanded view of distributed ledgers as socio-informational-technical systems that I advance in Lemieux and Feng (2021) and rely upon in this volume, in the sense that distributed ledgers, like all records, are designed to faithfully represent certain real-world phenomena that their creators intend them to represent.[8] At the same time as they embed these systems, they also operate as objects or artifacts that exist and function within those systems; that is to say, they both represent, embody, and enact those systems. This notion is also consistent with Yeo's representational premise, though it extends it by suggesting that what is represented is not merely an activity or an occurrent (or sets of these) but entire perceived (or conceived) "domains of discourse" or real-world systems.

It might seem that this view is inconsistent with the archival diplomatics notion of records as instruments or by-products of activity. However, because representation is necessary in order for a record to fulfil its purpose as an instrument or by-product made in connection with practical activity (i.e., enact reality), I argue that there is no inconsistency. Representation is still critical for enactment (Recker et al., 2019). As a simple example, the signature of a party to a contract is a representation of the intention of that party to enter into and agree to the terms of the contract. This example also illustrates that, *contra* Yeo, though records are made or received in the course of practical activity, they are created to represent much more than an action or occurrent (or sets of these). They are created to represent intentions, institutionalized roles (e.g., the formal title of the signatory in the signature block), time (e.g., the date of the signature), and much more besides. Indeed, they can capture, depending on how well they are made, much about the context surrounding the originating action that has motivated their creation. It is for this reason that we can obtain knowledge about aspects of the past from an examination of records that extends beyond the purpose for which they were originally created; the circumstances of their creation mean that they embed a "life-world" (Husserl, [1954] 1970), in however fragmentary a form, connected to the originating activity to which they relate. If records were only to represent their originating activity, it would be very difficult for them to fulfil enactment purposes (e.g., conferring rights or entitlements) as they would be missing elements required by the juridical systems in which they function necessary to do so (e.g., signatures). It also

---

[8] This is not to say that records always perfectly and faithfully represent reality, or that records creators do not ever create records to present reality in a particular light or to advance their own points of view. This will become evident in discussions of blockchain and distributed ledger–based records in this chapter. This fact, however, does not invalidate the claim that creators of records intend to represent something when they create those records.

would be difficult to interpret their meaning (or to determine their trustworthiness) without access to representations of contextualizing elements (e.g., time, juridical or institutional authority, intentions to act, etc.).

The above observations point to another significant observation about records, which is that they are *not evidence* (although they provide evidence), but rather they are *instruments or by-products of human interactions*, which are said to "capture" the circumstances of interactions in which they participate, extending representations of the circumstances of those interactions over space and time and enabling subsequent beliefs and action based upon reference to them. As such, records also provide sources of proof or evidence of activities of which they are a part and to which they refer.[9] Moreover, as they are created as a part of those activities or as by-products of them, they are witnesses to those activities and testify to them – thus, as I discussed in Chapter 5, they fall within that linguistic category called evidentials (Aikhenvald, 2004). Indeed, it is their proximity to past actions that is said to raise records above hearsay, as evidentials capable of providing evidential grounds to support the "truth" of a matter.

In classical diplomatics, trustworthy records (1) accurately capture the facts, (2) are reliable as a "statement" of those facts (i.e., capable of representing the facts about the actions to which they refer), and (3) are authentic (i.e., are what they purport to be, or are genuine) are capable of serving as reliable grounds for the formation of justified true beliefs on the matters to which they refer and possibly a range of other matters as well (Roeder et al., 2008). It is important to emphasize, however, that achieving trustworthiness of records cannot be reduced to implementing an essentialist list of finite properties. Critics of diplomatics have often pointed to its essentialism and a tendency toward reductionism as one of its main weaknesses (on this point, see van Bussel, 2017; Yeo, 2017). The properties of trustworthy records as articulated in diplomatics are best viewed as socially negotiated, and in some cases institutionalized, reifications of processes that are intended to simplify complex realities in order to render them more tractable, representable, and, ultimately, recoverable. The goal is to use the reified properties identified as accuracy, reliability, and authenticity to better guide the design of systems capable of supporting the creation and preservation of records that are trusted, first of all, to give effect to and/or document the

---

[9] Archival theorists tend to debate whether records must be deliberately "set aside" in order to qualify as records, which is often interpreted as being "captured" into a recordkeeping system (see, e.g., Yeo, 2018 on this point). I tend to take a more relaxed view based on the fact that socio-cultural practices differ and thus interpret the "setting aside" as including more informal practices such as saving a document into a folder on a computer drive as well as more formal processes of capture and registration in records systems. The point for me is whether the social actors within the referent social group subsequently relying upon the record for action or reference believe it is authoritative. I will have more to say about this in Chapter 8.

actions motivating their creation and, second of all, to provide sufficient contextual information to serve as evidentials in support of propositions concerning the complex life-world surrounding the actions the records document. There will likely always be some gap between the reality of what records are created to represent and the generalized properties of trustworthy records as defined in archival diplomatics. This is no less true of any model of reality, however, and yet we often rely upon – indeed, must rely upon – such models as tools to manage that which our own cognition, or the tools we use to extend our cognition, cannot easily manage in full.

In contrast to the archival diplomatics definition of a record, the International Organization for Standardization (ISO) replaces the "traditional" reference to documents with the modernizing term "information" in its definition of a record. While still linking the term to its traditional association with evidence of an activity, it also connects it with what the record has become through processes of datafication – a source of economic value, an "asset" (i.e., a record as "information created, received and maintained as evidence and as an asset by an organization or person, in pursuit of legal obligations or in the transaction of business" [ISO, 2020b, s. 3.2.10]). For the purposes of my analyses of blockchain and distributed ledger records, I hew closely to archival diplomatics' definitions of the record, since I lean heavily upon diplomatic principles of analysis as understood through the lens of successive InterPARES projects.[10]

In archival diplomatics, as mentioned previously, there are three primary properties that signify the trustworthiness of archival documents, that is, their accuracy, their reliability, and their authenticity. These decompose further into sub-properties of the higher-level properties. Figure 7.1 illustrates the decomposition of the properties associated with trustworthy records. In the main, this taxonomy follows the same decomposition of an earlier InterPARES 2 Project – Ontology C: Trustworthiness of Records (the "IP2 Ontology," see InterPARES 2 Project, Terminology Cross-domain Task Force, 2008) but adds additional elements to emphasize characteristics of records that are generally not well understood but that are quite important to imbuing records with properties that signify their trustworthiness. All quoted element definitions in the remainder of this section are taken from the InterPARES 2 Glossary (InterPARES 2 Project, 2021b).

---

[10] This is not to suggest that the archival diplomatics conceptualization of a record is without limitations: it tends to assume that the record is reducible to a set of well-defined elements that are difficult to map to novel digital objects (Rogers, 2015, pp. 40–41). The elements that might comprise a record in classical diplomatics terms are, in the new digital environment, complex, interrelated digital system components, all the more dependent upon each other as technology continues to develop (MacNeil, 2004, p. 219; Duranti, 2009, pp. 42–43; Rogers, 2015, pp. 182–183).

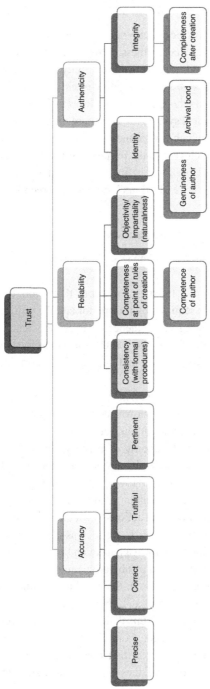

Figure 7.1 Taxonomy of trust
(Lemieux et al., 2019)

Accuracy

Accuracy pertains to the historical truth value of records and decomposes into the concepts of "precision," "correctness," "pertinence," and "truthfulness." Precision relates to "the quality of a record that strictly conforms in every detail of content and form to an established guideline or convention," while correctness is "the state of a record whose content and form fulfil the requirements set by the creator and the juridical system for the record to reach the consequences or produce the effects for which it was intended." Pertinence is "the quality of a record whose content is relevant to the purpose for which it is created and/or used." Lastly, truthfulness is "the quality of a record whose content is in accordance with the actual state of affairs" to which the record refers.

Reliability

Reliability decomposes into "completeness" and "creation procedure" in the IP2 Ontology.

Completeness is "the characteristic of a record that refers to the presence within it of all the elements required by the creator and the juridical system for it to be capable of generating consequences." These elements include such things as original signatures of competent authorities, required to give effect to a desired action, and dates to establish that the record is an original, not a draft or a copy.

Consistency (with formal procedures) of records creation procedure refers to "the procedure [body of written and unwritten rules] governing the formation of the record and/or its participation in the act."

To these two elements, the taxonomy of trust in Figure 7.1 adds a third: objectivity/impartiality (naturalness), which captures the idea that the trustworthiness of records rests fundamentally upon their being created as instruments and by-products of action contemporaneously (or nearly so, as in the case of minutes of a meeting) with the actions to which they refer. As such, they can bear witness to such action. Records are seen as being natural because of their contiguity to the actions they form a part of and reference, which is not to say that records present an impartial or objective view of historical actions or events; rather, when records are made in the usual and ordinary course of the conduct of affairs, they are impartial and objective with respect to providing grounds for believing future truth claims that the authors and preservers of the records could not have anticipated. Consider the example of minutes of a meeting. The minute taker might put their own slant on the proceedings of the meeting (e.g., by the level of detail they capture), but assuming they have no motive for failing to accurately record the proceedings – such as the names of all attendees – the minutes could be used as grounds to prove that a meeting attendee was not at some other location where a crime was being committed at the same time as the meeting was taking place. While this "naturalness" is generally considered to be a characteristic of all records, it is, at the same time, a property that proffers trustworthiness upon the records and thus is included as an additional element in the taxonomy of trust in Figure 7.1. Being one of the fundamental rules for creation of records, that is, that they tend to be made in the usual and ordinary course of business, naturalness might have been included as a sub-property of the creation procedure property; however, creation procedures generally focus on control over records creation processes, rather than temporal aspects of records creation. Thus, naturalness arguably deserves its own prominent placement in the schema.

Authenticity

Authenticity is the third major category. In the IP2 Ontology, this property consists of "integrity" and "identity." Integrity refers to "the quality of being complete and unaltered in all essential respects" after the moment of records creation. Identity is "the whole of the characteristics of a document or a record that uniquely identify it and distinguish it from any other document or record," which is a necessary precondition to being able to authenticate records.

The taxonomy of trust further decomposes identity into the identity of the author and the archival bond, highlighting two (though by no means all) of the most important characteristics of a record's identity that are needed to establish its authenticity. In terms of the author's identity, the author of an authentic record genuinely will be who they purport to be.

The archival bond is the "originary, necessary and determined relationship between and among records that participate in the same activity" (Cencetti, 1939). It speaks to a recognition in archival science that the identity and meaning of a record is not fully embodied in the "text" of a document but is, in fact, always "extra-textual," since the document indexes and represents an external action that is, in turn, embedded within and shaped by organizational, juridical, and wider socio-cultural contexts. In some cases, the term archival bond is described simply as a "link" (see, e.g., ISO [2016, s. 5.2.2.4], which states, "Linkages between records that document related business transactions should be maintained."). All the documents created as a part of completing a specific action are procedurally bound together; that is, they all share an archival bond to a specific action and to the other records involved in the same action. The network of relationships between the record and its originating action and other records concerning the same action, therefore, constitute the meaning that gives the record its unique identity. Because a record must have a unique identity before its authenticity can be determined, the archival bond also provides a foundation for establishing authenticity. Like the property of naturalness, the archival bond is described as a characteristic of records but is given prominence in the taxonomy of trust because it is an essential feature of trustworthy records that is so often absent from digital records systems.

Context Dependence of Signifiers of a Record's Trustworthiness

The specific embodiment of these signifiers of records' trustworthiness is context dependent, or, as I would argue, socio-technically constructed. Such properties are defined and determined (prior to a particular observer's gaze) by the socially agreed and institutionalized practices and technologies by which records are made and preserved to serve as both instruments and evidence of the actions to which they relate. To the extent that a record's "testimony" about such actions is physically and intellectually "fixed" and that fixity is maintained over space and time and sufficient contextual information about the circumstances of the record's creation and preservation is available, the trustworthiness-signifying properties of the record will persist and, in theory, be perceivable. Ideally, observers can then use those perceived properties to critically assess the trustworthiness of the record – in the manner of examining "life on file" – as evidential grounds for the formation of justifiable true belief about specific truth claims regarding the actions to which the record refers (or even to those that might have nothing to do with the original action that gave rise to the record, as in the example above relating to minutes of a meeting). Thus, archival diplomatics offers a perspective closer to the observer-independent notion of ledger trust discussed in Chapter 3. It also offers a body of theory that has been used over the centuries to determine the authenticity of archival documents in different documentary contexts and that can be extended both to critically evaluate claims of blockchains' and distributed ledgers' ability to establish "proof of facts" – the "archival imaginaries" of this technology – and to guide the prospective design of blockchain and distributed ledger systems so that the records they produce and preserve possess properties that enable assessment of the records' trustworthiness.[11]

---

[11] Consequently, I have drawn upon the work of the InterPARES project, within the context of advancing scholarship on computational archival science (Marciano, Lemieux et al., 2018), in

7.2 Assessing the Trustworthiness of Blockchain Records: An Archival Theoretic Perspective

In assessing the trustworthiness of different types of blockchain and distributed ledger records, the first challenge is, of course, to identify whether a given blockchain or distributed ledger system contains records and, if so, what kind of records they are and where the records can be found. This is challenging in blockchain and distributed ledger systems for several reasons. Firstly, much of the data that designers and users of such systems intend to serve as records (adjudged by their expressed intent to rely upon the ledger as a source of proof or evidence) does not adhere to archival diplomatics formalisms. Archival diplomatics holds that records must have several elements necessary to instantiate their evidentiary quality. These are a *medium*, that is, the physical carrier of the message; a *physical and intellectual form*, that is, the rules of representation that allow for communication of records' evidentiary content; the *content* itself, that is, the message that the record is intended to convey; an *action*, that is, the action or event that originates the record, as an exercise of the will of the record's author; *persons*, that is, the entities acting by means of the record (e.g., the author, the writer, and the addressee); an *archival bond*, that is, the relationship linking each record to its originating action and to other records associated with the same action; and a *context*, that is, traditionally, the juridical, administrative, procedural, documentary, and technological context in which the record is created (Duranti, 1999, p. 152; Duranti and Preston, 2008). Many of these elements are missing from the ledger records and associated documentation generated and retained in blockchain and distributed ledger systems. Table 7.1 provides an overview of the different types of records and documentation typically associated with such systems, recognizing that the entities described as "records" in the table might well fail the test of being records from the point of view of archival diplomatics and thus would not possess the characteristics they would need in order to serve as a trustworthy proof or evidence of a proposition.

As discussed in Chapter 1, the very first blockchain, Bitcoin, incorporated a ledger – the blockchain – to track transactions involving transfers of the bitcoin digital currency. A ledger is a very particular and circumscribed type of record, being a document containing entries of debits, credits, and other

much of my own work since 2016. This work primarily has been undertaken under the rubric of the "Records in the 'Chain' Project," which operated at the University of British Columbia between 2016 and 2018 and entailed conducting a series of case studies to analyze blockchain recordkeeping systems in terms of their trustworthiness as defined by archival diplomatics. For more information, I refer the interested reader to https://blogs.ubc.ca/recordsinthechain.

Table 7.1 *Types of blockchain records with examples and location*

Supporting documentation	Transaction records	Ledger records
Description: Documentation that provides background or supporting information relevant to a transaction with an archival bond to a transaction or ledger record, usually represented by a cryptographic hash link or metadata embedded into the associated ledger record.	Description: Records representing transactions, with an archival bond to a ledger record, usually represented by a cryptographic hashlink or metadata into an associated ledger record.	Description: Hashes that are recorded and stored in a distributed ledger that are instruments and by-products of a transaction or that are meant to establish proof of a truth claim.
Example: Images of a property offered for sale.	Example: Sale contract in digital form, where the sale was executed off-ledger.	Example: Transaction hash of a completed sale contract.
Location: May be in an organizational database, a cloud data store, or a decentralized data store, for example, the Interplanetary File System.	Location: May be stored on ledger as a ledger record output of a smart contract or be stored off-ledger in an organizational database, a cloud data store, or a decentralized data store.	Location: On-ledger.

Source: Updated from Lemieux et al., 2019, table 1.

financial transactions, typically organized into separate accounts (Poovey, 1998; Pearce-Moses, 2005; Maurer and DuPont, 2015). Each entry in the ledger is, itself, also a record. Like all ledgers, blockchain ledgers were designed to generate these simple records of financial debits and credits; they were *not* initially designed to capture records relating to actions other than the transfer of units of value from one person or entity to another. Most blockchains and distributed ledgers can store simple records relating to transfers of value from one account to another reasonably well. Records documenting cryptocurrency transactions are generated and stored in distributed ledgers as hashes, as already discussed. For purposes of clarity, these types of records are called "ledger records"[12] (ISO, 2020a, s. 3.44) to differentiate them from other types of records connected with the operation of blockchain and distributed ledger

---

[12] ISO (2020a) standard 22739 defines a ledger record as a "record containing transaction records, hash values of transaction records, or references to transaction records recorded on a distributed ledger." Note 1 to the terminological entry states that "[a] reference can be implemented as a cryptographic link."

systems, such as those wherein the associated activities occur off the ledger (i.e., off-ledger transactions).[13] Even so, such ledger records tell us nothing about the *reason* for the cryptocurrency transfer – was it to purchase a coffee, to pay a bill, to conduct a ransomware attack, or for some other purpose? Without context, we cannot know.

With the rise of Blockchain 2.0, discussed in Chapter 3, a variety of activities began to be recorded within blockchain systems (e.g., land transactions, supply chain transactions, and medical transactions to name but a few). Thus, ledger records began to represent a much more diverse and complex array of activities and to relate to a much greater number of associated transaction records and supporting documents, within a broader procedural and documentary context. These Blockchain 2.0 systems serve a variety of purposes and each leverage the capabilities of distributed ledgers in particular ways. Figure 7.2 provides a typology of Blockchain 2.0 type systems from a records perspective. The following sections present a discussion of the characteristics of these different types of blockchain and distributed ledger systems in relation to the goal of creating and keeping trustworthy records, and Table 7.2 presents an overview of the major (not all) barriers associated with these systems when it comes to establishing the authenticity of the records they generate and keep.

Table 7.2 *Major barriers to authenticity of records in blockchain and distributed ledger systems, by type of system*

Type | Property	Authenticity
Mirror	Bit-based integrity vs. records-based integrity can mean even alterations legitimately needed for digital preservation can invalidate a record.
Digital records	Operation of a poorly written smart contract might lead to inaccuracies or an unreliable record; missing contextual information (e.g., calendar dates, identities of contract signatories) and missing or broken links to related documentation can make it difficult to establish records' authenticity.
Tokenized	For non-fungible tokens (NFTs), broken or missing links to off-chain real-world or digital assets may occur; some decentralized identity systems that do not record transactions on-ledger might lack records needed for audit and accountability purposes.

---

[13] Off-ledger (or off-chain) transactions are those "related to a DLT [distributed ledger technology] system, but located, performed, or run outside that DLT system" (ISO, 2020a, s. 3.53).

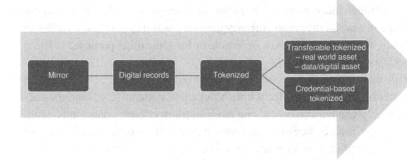

Figure 7.2 Typology of Blockchain 2.0 systems from a records perspective (updated from Lemieux, 2017b, figure 2)
Note: The typology is based upon research conducted between October 2015 and October 2017. The model posits a transition from types of systems that are closest to current recordkeeping practices, on the left, to the most innovative or novel (those least like current recordkeeping practices), on the right. Each innovation builds upon the range of available approaches to blockchain recordkeeping and within any given blockchain or distributed ledger system it is often possible to observe a combination of these practices being used.

Mirror Systems

The earliest type of Blockchain 2.0 system was used to embed hashes of records created off-ledger, whether in physical or digital form, into ledger records for the purpose of "fixing" those records in a stable (i.e., immutable) form. I call this a "mirror" blockchain recordkeeping system because the hashes simply mirrored, or fingerprinted, records in a preexisting (off-ledger) recordkeeping system and anchored them into the blockchain in the form of ledger records. This is the type of system that might very well be used to prevent the data manipulation discussed in Chapter 5. A mirror system uses distributed ledger technology as a means of validating the integrity of off-ledger transaction records, with the overarching aim of protecting those records from forgery and manipulation. This design pattern may be implemented using either a public blockchain or a permissioned blockchain or distributed ledger.[14] Early examples of this type include a prototype blockchain land-transfer system in Brazil, which hashed land transaction records kept by one of the country's municipal land registries and entered them into a blockchain ledger, and similar use of a distributed blockchain-like ledger to protect the integrity of

---

[14] A public distributed ledger (blockchain being a type of distributed ledger) is one which is accessible to the public for use (ISO, 2020a, s. 3.64); a permissioned distributed ledger is one requiring authorization to perform a particular activity or activities (ISO, 2020a, s. 3.57).

e-health records in Estonia (see Martinovic et al., 2017; Flores et al., 2018). This approach also underpinned Factom's proposed solution for managing the Honduras government's recording of land titles (Lemieux, 2016c).

A key limitation of the use of blockchains and distributed ledgers for protecting the integrity of transaction records is the difference between *data integrity* and *records integrity*. Data integrity is *bitwise* integrity; that is, a given transaction record will be considered to have integrity if each bit of data comprising that record remains unaltered. In contrast, records integrity allows for alteration of the bit structure of a transaction record and considers a record to have integrity if the record continues to provide trustworthy evidence of the facts about the actions to which it attests. Indeed, some alteration of the bit structure of digital records is an unavoidable aspect of digital preservation processes (Collomosse et al., 2018; Owens, 2018, p. 125). Figure 7.3 visually illustrates the point. If this record were digital, it would not be considered to have data integrity because parts of it are missing. Conversely, if sufficient information remains that the record can still provide evidence of the facts to which it attests, assuming that it can be determined that the missing information does not alter the author's intended meaning and its effect, it will possess records integrity.

Figure 7.3 Chinese oracle bones, circa 1200 BCE
("Shang dynasty inscribed scapula" by BabelStone, licenced under CC-BY-SA-3.0)

Project ARCHANGEL – a collaboration between the UK National Archives, the University of Surrey, and the Open Data Institute – has sought to address the need to protect records integrity rather than data integrity by an application of artificial intelligence (AI) combined with blockchain technology (Bui et al., 2019, 2020).[15] In this project, multiple archives maintain a "Proof of Authority" blockchain in which they store a hash that can verify the integrity of video records (e.g., videos of court proceedings). Unique identifiers link on- and off-ledger data, with two kinds of hash data stored on-ledger: (1) temporal content hashes (TCHs), protecting the audiovisual content from tampering, which are created by passing sub-sequences of the video through deep neural net (DNN) AI models to yield short binary "PQ" codes (codes which serve as start and stop markers for the videos), and (2) a binary hash of the DNNs and PQ encoders that guards against tampering with the TCH computation. The DNN models used in the TCH computation are trained to differentiate between natural format shifts affecting bitwise integrity and unnatural format shifts signalling tampering. This capability transforms data integrity into records integrity, since small transformations that result from digital preservation processes are allowed. Hashing the DNN models also protects the models used in the TCH computations from tampering. In this way, Project ARCHANGEL has developed one methodology for overcoming the challenge of using blockchains to address records integrity.

Digital Records Systems

A subsequent innovation in the development of blockchain and distributed ledger technology saw the emergence of "native" on-ledger transactions. In these systems, the activities in which the ledger records form a part take place entirely on-ledger, very often facilitated by smart contracts. I call such systems the "digital records" type in recognition of the fact that the transactional action results in the on-ledger creation of records. Among those I studied between 2015 and 2017, the Swedish land registry's prototype blockchain system represents this type (Lemieux, 2017a). Since that time, this type of system has become widespread in areas including trade finance, supply chain management, medical records management, art provenance tracking, and electric vehicle charging, to name only a few application areas.

---

[15] It should be noted that the core of this idea predates distributed ledgers and the ARCHANGEL Project; specifically, it can be found in the decades of work on digital preservation that precedes this project. The LOCKSS project, for example, developed by Stanford Libraries, used an "ex post" consensus mechanism and Merkle trees to make bitwise changes apparent to document custodians (Maniatis et al., 2005).

Smart contracts, typically used in digital records type blockchain and distributed systems, are "computer program[s] ... wherein the outcome of any execution of the program is recorded on the distributed ledger" (ISO, 2020a, s. 3.72). The concept of smart contracts is not new and is not unanimously understood. The idea was introduced in 1994 by Nick Szabo, who defined a smart contract as a "computerized transaction protocol that executes the terms of a contract" (Szabo, 1994). Later he defined them as "a set of promises," specified in digital form, including protocols within which the parties perform on these promises (Szabo, 1997). The initial purpose of smart contracts was to embed contractual clauses in hardware and software to make breach of contract expensive (Szabo, 1997) and also to "minimize the need for trusted intermediaries between transacting parties, and occurrence of malicious or accidental exceptions" (Christidis and Devetsikiotis, 2016, p. 2296). Smart contracts are implemented using programming languages, such as Solidity, which is the original language used for Ethereum smart contracts. On the Ethereum blockchain, when a contract is created it sets up the initial state of its database. After its creation, the contract "waits" to be initiated by a user of the blockchain system or by another contract. After the contract is initiated, each of the steps is executed "independently on every node of the network, with identical results" (Greenspan, 2015). Execution of the smart contract results in an output that is represented as a ledger record.

Quite often, smart contracts, and associated ledger records, connect to a larger procedural and documentary context; for instance, land transactions might involve the process of creating a cadastral mapping of a piece of land or securing a mortgage to finance purchase of the land. Thus, in digital records type systems, it has become increasingly common to see that ledger records that are recorded and stored on-ledger contain metadata about, or hash references to, other activities, and associated transaction records or supporting documentation (see Table 7.1), which the ledger record "fixes" on the blockchain as part of the documentary context of the transaction of which the ledger record forms a part. The transactional records to which the metadata or hash links refer are stored off-ledger, sometimes in traditional centralized storage (e.g., an organizational database or cloud data store) or, at other times, using decentralized storage (e.g., the Inter Planetary File System).[16] With concerns about recording and

---

[16] See https://ipfs.io. It should be noted that this system has important limitations as a store for records. In particular, there are privacy concerns: operators must act as peers in the system, thus requiring carrier relationships that allow them to run addressable servers, and they must carry certain traffic on behalf of others, thus making the system not incentive compatible. This issue might be addressed, for example, by using Tor onion services and addressing the storage concern with cheap encrypted Virtual Private Server shares (G. Goodell, personal communication, June 28, 2021). There are also issues of persistence: content must be propagated out to

storing records of transactions containing personally identifiable information – even if encrypted or stored as a hash – driven by the need to comply with privacy regulations such as the European Union's General Data Protection Regulation (Hofman et al., 2019), the use in ledger records of hash links that index off-ledger storage has become increasingly common.[17]

The accuracy of smart-contract-generated ledger records can be affected when the smart contract relies upon an external data source (e.g., an "oracle"),[18] which may contain errors or false information, or when it references an external asset incorrectly (such as when there is an erroneous or false claim that an artwork has been created by a certain person). The accuracy of smart-contract-generated ledger records might also be compromised if there is an error in the logic of the smart contract. This could result in an incorrect value of cryptocurrency being calculated or an amount of cryptocurrency being transferred on the wrong day.

A record's reliability might also be affected by smart contract programming. In particular, the computer code upon which smart contracts rely may not always perform as intended due to logic errors, "buggy" code, or unintended consequences of complex system dependencies. System performance problems can, and often do, result in data problems, which can affect the evidentiary quality of records (Delmolino et al., 2016; Rouhani and Deters, 2019). The reliability of smart contracts is an issue of concern in the emerging field of blockchain and distributed ledger technology because there have been a number of high-profile exploits involving smart contracts that have resulted in the loss of millions of dollars (Morisander, 2018; Nikolić et al., 2018).

The first significant event relating to the reliability of smart contracts involved a "DAO" – a decentralized autonomous organization – that used long-term smart contracts to raise funds for new ventures on the Ethereum blockchain (Buterin, 2013). The infamous "DAO hack" of 2016 resulted from a computer programming flaw – a "recursive call bug" – which an unknown attacker was able to use to drain millions from the DAO's account (Siegel, 2016).[19] Another significant smart contract breach was the Parity Wallet hack

---

peers, and those peers must remain accessible in order to retrieve the content (on this point, see Lemieux, 2017a).

[17] Personal data protection and privacy may remain a concern with this approach because transactions involving an individual's data are still recorded on the ledger, and therefore discoverable, even if to a limited set of system users. Those transactions may also contain personal information that an individual might not wish to reveal, such as that the individual has visited a particular doctor or participated in a study relating to a particular type of disease.

[18] ISO (2020a, s. 3.28) defines a distributed ledger technology oracle as a "service that updates a distributed ledger using data from outside of a DLT system."

[19] The goal of DAOs is to codify rules and decision-making tools, eliminating the need for people or physical documents in the governance of new blockchain-based ventures, i.e., governance

that happened in November 2017. Parity Technologies launched software for multisignature ("multisig") wallets (which allow for more than one private key signature) for smart contracts built to run on the Ethereum blockchain. The software consisted of two different contracts, one called "lightweight" that was used for every wallet creation and a "library" containing most of the wallet's logic (Lazarenko and Avdoshin, 2018). All Parity multisig users depended on the library contract, but since the contract's creators did not initialize it, the contract was left without ownership. A hacker used that gap to take control of the ownership of the library and then used another function to destroy it. All the wallets linked to that library were frozen as a result. The loss from this exploit was estimated at more than USD 150 million (Choy and Teng, 2017). Ultimately these kinds of errors, often the result of inexperienced smart contract developers or the practice of borrowing smart contract "recipes" that replicate logic errors, can render smart-contract-generated ledger records unreliable as evidence of business transactions, rights, and entitlements.

Record authenticity not only relies upon preserving the integrity of records after creation but also upon preserving the intention of the record's original author. To establish the author's intention requires interpretation of contract clauses, which, in turn, might be dependent upon access to external information such as master agreements or documentation communicating the intent of transacting parties at the time of signing. For this reason, it is particularly important to establish the archival bond of smart contracts to other related records and the procedural and documentary context of their creation.

Procedural and documentary context are often not evident in distributed ledgers, however. Figure 7.4 illustrates how difficult it is to interpret the meaning of a ledger record without some way to connect it to the context of its creation; certain snippets of information may give us clues as to a record's meaning and identity, such as the email address of the transacting parties or that there is an asset of some kind involved, but we cannot know for sure what it is without more explicit information.

In digital systems, the archival bond establishes the much-needed connection between a record and its procedural and documentary context. An archival bond is often made explicit by inserting metadata about the record's procedural context, which then connects it to all other records with the same piece of metadata to establish its documentary context. For example, a code linking the

with decentralized control, with stand-alone agreements requiring no interpretation of outside entities or jurisdictions (Siegel, 2016). The famous June 2016 attack on the DAO – an organization created by a German start-up in April 2016 – drained USD 60 million from its accounts, which had been buffered by an unexpectedly successful initial coin offering that raised in excess of USD 150 million.

(approvedUsers', ['commander.spock@mail.com'], 'assetHash',
'87bo1b5cd8a705c53038b1c9d3affeacdc447ac7o8c16721279b0d62a48a9el0ed044l8d40f1d8614a5580ccA3306999
71d594643bb9755b6ce0914ca780b89', 'assetId', '4614d610-8dd-11ea-ae64-17a1bfbae72', 'assetName' '38088399-
8423-42EC-9724-E825637FDE91.heic', 'assetOwner' 'peter.pan@mail.com', 'createTimestamp', '2020-03-
22T05.23.34.720Z', 'createBy', 'commanderspock@mail.com', 'lastModifiedBy', 'captain.kirk@mail.com',
'modFileHash',
'782421ad717la65086bl0bcc9c0a780675a33bc9e90cd7125cc85a85de9ac9012eff3072a3774bb7023058ee806ac30d
5560c2e9d809l84505d97bceb80', 'modFileName', 38088399-8423-42EC-9724-E825637FDE91_1584854797086.heic',
'modifiedTimestamp', 2020-03-22T05.26.38.266Z'),'lastModifiedBy', 'peter.pan@mail.com', 'modFileHash',
'ea093162d4g04721z3700227ce63d3b1570862234334ca4b4ea24797a76212810ca8aaa1el6785edcad6bd92e4563fd
a421ac3a37d9b3c9d5ba2oba117', 'modFileName', 38088399-8423-42EC-9724-
E825637FDE91_1584857461416.heic', modifiedTimestamp', '2020-03-22T06.11.02.172Z')], 'modifiedTimestamp'.
'2020-03-22T06.12.32.252Z', 'type', 'DigitalAsset')

Figure 7.4 Reproduction of a screenshot of ledger records on a blockchain. The meaning of the transactions is not obvious without instantiation of an archival bond, that is, until we understand the procedural and documentary context of their creation.

(Source: Author)

ledger record to its generative smart contract might be inserted into the object attributes for the ledger record as a means of instantiating the archival bond if the smart contract code contains business logic that reveals the purpose for which the ledger record has been created. Only when we are explicitly able to connect the record to its originating action – that is, the transfer of ownership of a specific tokenized digital image – and the context of that action does the record convey meaning and give effect to its author's intent.

To illustrate, Figure 7.4 shows a ledger record in a blockchain-based digital asset management system. The system includes a hash link to a digital asset stored in an off-ledger data store. A pre-programmed smart contract has generated the ledger record we see in the figure. The ledger record represents the transfer of an asset, in this case, a digital artwork. The image of the asset in the connected data store is not a record; rather it is a supporting document (and an asset in its own right) that forms an important part of the ledger record's documentary context. None of these important contextualizing elements are to be found in the ledger itself.

Dependencies between ledger records and supporting documents or transaction records stored off-ledger have given rise to the "broken link" problem, which occurs when a hash link that instantiates the archival bond between a ledger record and its originating action, and any other associated documents and records, is broken. While breaking links (i.e., archival bonds) to ledger records that index personally identifiable information might be a desirable feature of distributed ledgers aiming to be compliant with privacy regulations, it is decidedly not a desirable feature in other cases, as, for example, in those systems marketing artworks as "non-fungible tokens," or NFTs. In these systems, the broken link problem is a cause for great concern:

> Ultimately, you're buying a collection of metadata defining what you own.
> But there's one significant gap in the system ensuring that an NFT is held together: NFTs use *links* to direct you to somewhere else where the art and any details about it are being stored. And as anyone who has browsed the internet before should know, links can and do die. So what happens if your NFT breaks down and points to nothing?
>
> *(Kastrenakes, 2021)*

Though the broken link problem has been recently identified in connection with NFTs, this vulnerability was actually identified much earlier as a potential risk to the trustworthiness of blockchain and distributed ledger records and encompasses all forms of distributed ledger–based records that have external dependencies (Lemieux, 2017a). One early example of the problem can be found in broken links to external documentation observed in the case of a pilot blockchain solution for handling Brazilian land transfers (Lemieux, 2017a).

A separate but related issue is the status of smart contracts as legal contracts (Bartoletti and Pompianu, 2017; Werbach, 2018). Cornelius (2018, pp. 7–8; see also Cornelius, 2020) has observed that standard form consumer contracts often contain hyperlinks to contractual terms that can be changed at any time without the consumer's awareness, opening a similar possibility in distributed ledger smart contracts that embed links indexing dynamic and changeable external contractual clauses, even if the ledger record of the contract execution is "immutable."[20]

Another challenge lies in reconciling the unfamiliar form of ledger-based contracts with diplomatics formalisms based upon classical analog contract documents and very different types of digital records such as administrative databases (see, e.g., Duranti and Thibodeau, 2006; Roeder et al., 2008). Contracts created using blockchain and distributed ledger systems present a very foreign landscape.

To illustrate, dates have always been an important element of the execution of contracts, providing information that is often essential to determining a contract's authenticity and effectiveness. In contrast to analog records, as Duranti (1999, p. 153) explains, a digital record may have a number of dates, including

> the date given to the document by its author, which demonstrates the relationship between the author and the content; the date and time of transmission to either an

---

[20] Building flexibility into smart contracts remains an open challenge, which some say could be addressed through the application of AI (see, e.g., Dixit and Norta, 2018; Liu et al., 2019).

external or an internal addressee, which represent the moment in which a record begins to have consequences; the date and time of transmission to the dossier or class to which the record belongs, which reveals the development of the matter; and the date and time of each retrieval, which show every act of consultation.

Each and every one of these dates may be necessary to prove either the effectiveness of a contract or its authenticity over time. Dates present quite differently in ledger records than in both non-digital and other types of digital records. In blockchain and distributed ledger systems, the dating of a contract is often achieved by an embedded timestamp in a transaction record (see Figure 7.4). In some cases, transaction hashes might be published in external reference sources such as newspapers or social media to link a system-generated timestamp to an external source of proof about the time of the transaction (Anduck, 2018). Many blockchain systems (e.g., Bitcoin) also create a timestamp when transactions are grouped together into blocks, which forms part of the source input used to generate the block hash and cryptographically chain a block to its succeeding block. These different dates all have a bearing upon norms and laws applicable to consideration of the effectiveness of the ledger-based contract. Such dates include when a ledger record is validated, confirmed, and first entered into a ledger and when that entry is subsequently confirmed by participating nodes on a distributed ledger network. Finally, there might be a date upon which the ledger record is considered non-repudiable, but this depends on how many nodes must update their copies of the ledger before a transaction is considered confirmed, which, in turn, will vary according to the design of the blockchain, for example, the type of consensus mechanism used and who operates the nodes that participate in validation and confirmation (Bitcoin Wiki, 2018; Lemieux, 2019).

Similarly, signatures – which are used to determine whether a contract is complete and in effect and to authenticate it – are also very different in the context of ledger records. Whereas in analog contract documents of the twentieth century signatures typically appear at the bottom of a document (the "eschatocol" to use the diplomatics term [Storch, 1998]), for example, beneath the body of clauses constituting a contract's terms and conditions, in ledger records the "signature" is typically executed when the author of the record signs with their private cryptographic key. This act signals that the record is being created under the signer's will and authority. However, an important difference between traditional records and ledger records is that many blockchain and distributed ledger systems do not link the private key to the legal or natural identity of its holder. In such systems, transacting parties interact pseudonymously. Thus, many blockchain and distributed ledger systems lack the identity property required for authenticity according to archival diplomatics principles, which means that it might be difficult in these cases to determine the authenticity of a ledger record.

The private key is only one of two keys in a cryptographic key pair generated to execute a blockchain transaction, the other being the public key. The public key serves the same function as a seal in analog recordkeeping, as when documents were sealed with wax to prevent their alteration in an effort to guard against forgery and manipulation and as a means to declare that the document is what it purports to be (see Ferguson, 1960–1, pp. 755–756, cited in MacNeil, 1998, p. 9). In addition, though the digital signature seals the content of the ledger record – which then might also be subsequently sealed by inserting the transaction record (or the hash root of a set of such transactions) into a block data structure – it might not include the actual contractual terms and conditions. These may exist outside of the actual ledger record as logic encoded into a smart contract that has its own address in network storage (i.e., the Ethereum Virtual Machine) (Marino and Juels, 2016; Ethereum, 2021b), with the potential to create the previously mentioned problems identified by Cornelius (2018). Upon inclusion of a record in the ledger, we might consider it to be "delivered" (really it is an update to the ledger) to the public address of the other party to the transaction. In this way, the ledger record is "signed, sealed, and delivered" in a similar manner to the contract documents of the pre-digital age but in a novel fashion and subject to the provisos about effective date noted above.

Tokenized Systems

The final type of system that I identified in my 2015–17 research is the "tokenized" type. With this type of system, not only are ledger records captured on-ledger but assets are transformed into cryptographic representations, very often by linking them to an underlying cryptocurrency; that is, they are "tokenized." There has been tremendous innovation in the tokenized type of blockchain recordkeeping solution since the introduction of my original typology (Lemieux, 2017b).

In 2017, we saw the first type of tokenized solution, which we may describe as a "transferable" token. With this type of system, an asset (i.e., something of value) is represented on-chain as a cryptocurrency "token." Two subtypes of such systems can now be distinguished: those representing real-world assets and those that are digital assets. When these types of systems first appeared, the tokens represented physical assets of value – such as land, fine wine, food, diamonds, or artworks created off-ledger – and were usually represented by fungible tokens (i.e., tokens that could be divided into smaller units of exchange). Over time, the tokens began to represent digital assets of value, such as tradeable collectibles like "CryptoKitties,"[21] or even "bearer bonds," natively created on-ledger (see Batista et al., 2021). Many of these assets are represented by "non-fungible" tokens (NFTs), which uniquely identify an asset and cannot be divided up into smaller units of exchange. The first standard for these tokens was the ERC721 token standard (Ethereum, 2021b).[22] Ownership of NFTs is *transferable*, with the transfer of ownership rights given effect by a transaction recorded on-ledger in the form of a ledger record.

The use of tokens in these blockchain and distributed ledger systems harkens back to the early medieval period before members of European societies outside of the church came to rely upon written texts as evidentials (Lemieux, 2017b). As the historian M. T. Clanchy (1980) recounts, in the transition from a culture that relied on common knowledge to one based upon the written text, symbolic objects – such as knives, swords, rings, and cups – played a key role in proving a claim. During the early Middle Ages, many grants of land, for example, were conferred *nude verbo* (by bare word) accompanied by the gift of a symbolic object, a token, without a written charter or deed. As an example,

> the "ancient and rusty sword" which the Earl Warenne allegedly exhibited as evidence of title before Edward I's judges saying: "Look at this, my lords, this is my warrant!" A less familiar but better example, because it still exists, is the broken knife of Stephen de Bulmer kept in the archives of Durham cathedral. To its horn handle is attached a parchment label recording the details of the gift (made in the middle of the twelfth century) which the knife symbolizes. Likewise on the handle is inscribed "signum de capella de Iowic (the sign for the chapel of Lowick)". As the parchment label records details of the gift more clearly than the knife does, the interesting question arises of why the knife was kept. The best explanation is that to people at the time the knife was as important a record as the label, if not more so.
>
> *(Clanchy, 1980, p. 117)*

Like the NFTs of today's blockchain and distributed ledger systems, these medieval tokens were valuable symbolic objects in their own right, in addition to indexing human economic transactions. In its embodiment as a valuable asset and as evidence of a transaction, the record serves a dual role. In the era of datafication, records do have value, in the sense that they contain information that might be extracted or "mined" from them, to create new insights or revenue sources. With blockchain and distributed ledger systems, however, value is not derived from extraction of data but from the very fact that it *cannot* be extracted. The immutability of the ledger makes it possible to determine

[21] www.cryptokitties.co. [22] ERC stands for Ethereum Request for Comment.

when such alterations have occurred (i.e., tampering becomes evident). This solves a "data double-spending problem" as much as it solves a digital cash double-spending problem (see Chapter 1), restoring the ability to possess a record as a symbolic object or asset and as evidence, in the same way as one might possess a unit of digital currency, a ring, or another physical "token" (Sanitt, 2021). Where datafication has created the conditions to take away property rights in records and data, blockchain-based tokenization provides capabilities that once more enable assertion of property rights in records and data (Sanitt, 2021). Indeed, such rights have been upheld already in a number of legal decisions (Sanitt, 2021).[23] Not everyone agrees that this capability will be socially beneficial, but others see this development in a positive light, especially when it comes to reclaiming ownership and control of personal data or ongoing rights in creative works.[24]

In parallel to transferable tokens, a second subtype of the tokenized system has emerged, which we may refer to as "credential-based." Such systems are also known as decentralized identity systems, with self-sovereign identity (SSI) systems being a novel and growing variant of this class (see Mühle et al., 2018). With SSI credential-based tokenized systems, assets (e.g., university credentials, business licenses, health certificates) are transformed into cryptographic tokens that may be used to exchange identity claims or "proofs" based on the token. These tokens are not designed to be transferable (in the sense of being used to transfer legal rights of ownership) once issued, unlike in the case of NFTs; they currently are designed, therefore, to ensure that rights of ownership be *nontransferable*. The reason for their nontransferability is that they represent characteristics that identify and, in some way, embody a human being, especially in the case of health credentials. It makes sense, then, that such tokens should be designed not to be transferred, even if information based on the credentials can be shared with the consent of the individual who holds the token. Arguably, it is also the most ethical design choice since, if one accepts that verifiable credentials identify and embody individuals, the sale of such tokens is a little too close to trafficking in human beings. That said, the use of

---

[23] For case law, see *B2C2 v Quoine* [2020] SGCA(I) 02 in Singapore; *Moore v Cryptopia* [2020] NZHC 728 in New Zealand; and *AA v Persons Unknown* [2019] EWHC 3556 (Comm), *Robertson v Persons Unknown*, Case No. CL-2019–000444, July 15, 2019 and *Vorotyntseva v Money-4* in England. For reports, see, for instance, *Legal statement on cryptoassets and smart contracts*, LawTech Delivery Panel, November 2019, and *Issues of legal uncertainty arising in the context of virtual currencies,* July 2016, Financial Markets Law Committee (cited in Sanitt, 2021).

[24] A recent exchange on Twitter is critical of the "faux scarcity" created by NFTs (Ridge et al., 2021). The Twitter discussion focuses on the art and museum world, but even in that world, there are those who argue that NFTs empower artists to derive ongoing value from their creative works (Casey, 2021).

nontransferable identity tokens (i.e., tokens that are always inalienable from an individual) raises the specter of user profiling. Careful consideration of privacy protections is always necessary.

The exchange of proofs based on these verifiable credentials is not recorded on-ledger in the form of a ledger record. Rather, the distributed ledger is used only as a means to prove that assertions (i.e., claims, proofs) that a person makes using the credential as evidence are accurate, have integrity, and can be cryptographically verified as being based on an authentic credential, and thus assumed to be true. For example, in the Hyperledger Indy/Aries framework, the blockchain records and keeps only public decentralized identifiers, data schemas, credential definitions, and revocation registries in a blockchain (Tobin and Reed, 2016). In such systems, if the issuer of the credential is trusted, the facts provided by the issuer, such as whether a person has a university degree, can be trusted as being authentic. Subsequently, the person to whom the verifiable credential has been issued can make a provable claim (e.g., that they have a university degree). In short, the verifiable credential serves as the evidentiary foundation of the assertion. Cryptography, such as zero knowledge proofs (Goldwasser et al., 1989), is commonly used as the means of "proofing" the assertion without revealing detailed information contained in the verifiable credential, which thereby protects the privacy of the credential holder (Yang and Li, 2020). As an example, a person might be able to prove that they maintained an average above a certain grade-point during their time at university without revealing the actual grades they achieved.

Contrary to conventional blockchains, such as Bitcoin or Ethereum, some (though not all) SSI systems, to preserve privacy, do not capture the exchange of transactional data between interacting peers. Instead, such systems use the ledger only to register credential schemas, definitions, and credential revocations – all content laying the foundation for use of the ledger to verify claims, albeit claims for which no record is made and that are not captured on the ledger. While these types of SSI systems might have the advantage of complying with privacy regulations such as the EU's General Data Protection Regulation, they have the disadvantage of not capturing records of exchanges that have happened between interacting peers. Capture of records may be needed, however, for audit and accountability purposes, such as when the exchange of transaction data involves consent to participate in health-related research, such as clinical trials (Charles et al., 2019). Consequently, it might be necessary in some cases to develop a privacy-preserving, verifiable, and secure means of capturing transaction records. To give one example of how this capability can be achieved, it is possible to establish a "proof registry" that captures a record of a consent to participate in the clinical trial without revealing the individual's identity but also in a manner that allows for cryptographic verification that the consent comes from the authentic source of the claim (i.e., the individual agreeing to participate in the clinical trial) (Lemieux et al., 2021).

A final important issue is that, despite claims of building immutable records, and even a "new Library of Alexandria" (Haley, 2020), blockchains and distributed ledgers will no more last for an eternity than did the original Library of Alexandria. Blockchains and distributed ledgers comprise computational components the certain obsolescence of which requires ongoing human and technical intervention to achieve digital preservation of the records they inscribe and contain. As growing use of blockchain and distributed ledger technology for a wide variety of recordkeeping use cases leads to many alterations in records and recordkeeping – with the potential to introduce new risks to the evidentiary character of records – more difficult becomes the task of envisioning what long-term digital preservation challenges might need to be identified and solved in such a cryptography dependent, distributed ledger–based recordkeeping world. However, if the world is set upon increasing use of blockchain and distributed ledger technology for the creation and keeping of records, effective ways of preserving the authenticity of ledger records must be devised.

7.3 Designing for Ledger Trust

What the above examples reveal is that record creation and keeping in the digital environment is almost never guided by considerations of the preservation of trustworthy records over the long term (Eppard, 2008, p. 2), and this is also true of the creation of ledger records – or what might be viewed as "quasi-records" from an archival diplomatics standpoint, even if such systems purport to be creating objects that serve the same purpose as records.

The purpose of using the ledger might be to "set aside" transaction records to which the ledger record refers – as is the case for records created outside of a blockchain or distributed ledger system that are hashed and "fixed" on the ledger as a means of being able to validate the integrity of records held in mirrored recordkeeping systems – or to automatically execute a set of procedures resulting in an algorithmically secured and immutable record of a new transaction – as in the case of the transfer of a land title from one person to another using a smart contract on a blockchain system. Ledger records might also contain cryptographic hash links to real-world digital assets, such as artworks or music, or be used to create new tokenized digital assets, such as digital collectibles. What all these solutions have in common is that they rely upon trust in the ledger and the records the ledger contains.

Each type of blockchain system, however, still has limitations when judged against archival diplomatics standards of record trustworthiness, which demands the accuracy, reliability, and authenticity of records – concepts that are understood in very specific, technical ways in archival diplomatics. Blockchain systems might lack, for example, controls over how external data is incorporated into records on the ledger, thereby reducing the records' accuracy; they might lack the specific metadata needed to identify the procedural and documentary context of a ledger record, making it impossible to uniquely identify the record and interpret its meaning; they might preserve the bit structure of a ledger record while at the same time making it impossible to preserve the meaning of a ledger record over time in the face of technological obsolescence. These and a myriad of other problems can make it impossible to deem blockchain and distributed ledger–based records trustworthy in the sense of being accurate, reliable, and authentic, never mind the wider claim that they represent an irrefutable truth.

As the technology evolves, solutions to some of the issues identified in this chapter are being developed. However, designing blockchain and distributed ledger systems capable of creating and keeping what later observers might deem to be trustworthy records requires an awareness that records, as evidentials, differ in fundamental ways from information and data. It also requires knowledge, including a conceptual architecture, of how to design systems capable of producing records possessing properties that render evidence of past actions recoverable to subsequent readers of records. Very often, those engaged in the design and development of blockchain and distributed ledger systems have no such awareness or knowledge. Training in archival science among blockchain and distributed ledger systems designers and developers, and training for archival scientists in blockchain and distributed ledger technology, could help to predict and prevent a host of archival issues in these systems, such as the broken link problem or the absence of peer transaction records in SSI systems mentioned above. Raising awareness and filling the knowledge gap might be addressed by a new multidisciplinary, and even transdisciplinary, approach that draws together – into a holistic framework (Duranti, 2009; Marciano, Lemieux et al., 2018; Lemieux and Feng, 2021) – theories, principles, and practices from computing, the usual background for blockchain and distributed ledger system designers and developers, with those from archival science, in which archivists are trained, with, at the least, the goal of determining how digital systems should be designed "to create and maintain trustworthy digital records that can be regarded as [or rather, that can provide] material evidence of facts and acts" (Duranti, 2009, p. 65).

7.4 Concluding Thoughts

What lessons can we learn about blockchains and distributed ledgers in an age of disinformation from the limitations discussed in this chapter? Certainly, attention to designing for evidentials – for example, by prospectively applying archival science principles and practices – is likely to have a positive impact upon the epistemic desiderata of knowledge,[25] in the sense discussed in Goldman (1999) and McDowell (2002, p. 52). In *Knowledge in a Social World* (1999), Goldman points out that practices in society can be beneficial or detrimental to knowledge acquisition. He takes the goal of social epistemology to be that of identifying practices that have an impact on knowledge in society, assessing that impact as positive or negative, and recommending epistemically preferable practices. Practices have instrumental and, arguably, moral value insofar as they promote or impede the acquisition of fundamentally epistemically valuable states such as knowledge and the avoidance of error and ignorance (Goldman, 1999, p. 87). Given that the reliability of truth claims benefits from propositional support from evidentials, practices that improve the trustworthiness of records as evidentials can improve and protect knowledge formation in society and help to prevent the sort of manipulation discussed in Chapter 5. If designed according to principles that acknowledge their evidentiary character, blockchains and distributed ledgers can help to secure the intellectual and material fixity needed for trusting parties to place trust in distributed ledger records as epistemic grounds for belief. This is, however, a far cry from claiming that blockchains offer permanent sources of truth or are ultimate records of truth or that they can solve the complex epistemic problems that we face in the age of disinformation, as we will explore further in the next chapter.

---

[25] McDowell (2002, p. 53) makes a very important point about epistemic value, arguing that it does not trump all other values: "Assessing practices on one consequentialist framework does not mean that one cannot assess them on another. An epistemically desirable practice may be undesirable for moral, aesthetic, practical or other reasons. When this occurs, one needs to determine which of the values is the more important. If another value outweighs the epistemic value all things considered, overturning the epistemic evaluation's decision about which practice is preferable, the other value has 'trumped' the epistemic value."

PART V

The Theory of the Future

8

The "Life-World" on Ledger

8.1 From Archival Realities to Socio-Epistemic Realities

While there is much that can be done *ex ante* to strengthen blockchain and distributed ledger–based systems with respect to their prefigurative ability to generate and preserve trustworthy evidentials, this is insufficient on its own to enable trustors to trust in distributed ledger records as sources of "the truth." Evidentials only bear witness to past actions that they were involved in or specifically created to document. As Stoler (2002, p. 87, cited in van Bussel, 2017, p. 25) observes, "using poststructuralist arguments: the 'archival turn' means looking to archives more as epistemological experiments of the past than as historical sources, as cross-sections of contested knowledge, as transparencies inscribed with power relations, and technologies of rule." Thus, though records can be conceptualized as types of evidentials, this is not equivalent to understanding them as *being* evidence (Yeo, 2007, 2008) or truth.

The method used by archivists to uncover and describe life on file has always included studying the manner by which records come about (Duranti and Michetti, 2016).[1] Traditionally, archivists have applied the archival method to the arrangement and description of bodies of archival documents (i.e.,

---

[1] According to MacNeil (2009, p. 90), "Presuming the authenticity of an individual record is premised on establishing its identity and demonstrating its integrity; that is, was the record written by the person who purports to have written it? Has it been altered in any fundamental way since it was first written? The principles of archival arrangement allow for an extension of such presumption to an aggregation of records – typically, a *fonds*. Keeping the records of one creator separate from those of another is intended to preserve the unique identity of that aggregation, while keeping records in the order in which they were maintained by their creator aims to protect the integrity of the relationships between and among its parts. By explaining the records' arrangement and the circumstances in which they were created and preserved, an archival description communicates information relevant to a user's understanding of the records' identity and integrity."

archival *fonds*) by application of the principle of *respect des fonds*,[2] including respect for original order.[3] The archival method arises from practices that aim to enable both archivists and subsequent readers of the record to assess the meaning and trustworthiness of records from a deep understanding of the "lived experience" of record creators and the subsequent keepers of those records – in other words, from within its "life-world" (Husserl, [1954] 1970). Assessments of records' trustworthiness must take into consideration a subsequent reader's relationship with a record's life-world – for example, the reader's positionality with respect to a network of relations that includes the record's creators and keepers – as this also will bear upon how much trust a reader will place in a record as an evidential.[4]

The historiographical foundations upon which the archival method is premised originate in the Romantic period when many scholars held a

> belief in the possibility of entering into direct contact with a past reality. Such belief is embedded in a number of interlocking assumptions: that the surviving remains of the past can stand in for those that have disappeared; that those remains are, in some sense, a personification of the records creator; and that it is possible to enter into the consciousness of that creator and the past itself through its documentary remains.
> *(MacNeil, 2016, p. 184)*

This viewpoint found expression in the Dutch archival *Manual for the Arrangement and Description of Archives*, first published in 1898 and reissued

---

[2] *Respect des fonds* is defined as "The principle that the records of a person, family or corporate body must be kept together in their original order, if it exists or has been maintained, and not be mixed or combined with the records of another individual or corporate body" (Bureau of Canadian Archivists, 2008). This apparently simple definition belies the complexity and scholarly debate surrounding the concept.

[3] Archival theorist Heather MacNeil has written extensively about the principle of original order. She sums up the traditional view and application of this principle as follows: "The principle of original order is posited specifically on a presumed affinity between records and their creator in which the arrangement of the records acts as a kind of mirror, or personification, of the entity that produced them. The Italian archival theorist Giorgio Cencetti, for example, believed that an archival fonds, 'is the creator itself, in the sense that the original order of the archive, the order given to the archive by its creator, is the manifestation of the administrative structure, the history and, in some way, the very "essence" of the records creator.' That presumed affinity suggests an implicit connection with final authorial intentions. If we understand intention to be synonymous with a creator's purpose, aim, or design, then the records of that creator constitute the tangible remains of its intentions and the original order of the records, the final shape of those remains. Preserving that final shape is thus a means of preserving the creator's final intentions" (MacNeil, 2016, p. 175).

[4] A good example of this is Marciano and colleagues' work with Japanese Prisoner of War index cards created by the administrators of United States internment camps and preserved by the United States National Archives and Records Administration. The cards index reports that, in many cases, describe "misbehavior" on the part of Japanese prisoners. These reports cannot be viewed as objective "facts" about the behavior of Japanese prisoners but rather as how camp officials perceived and reported on the behavior of their captives (see Marciano, Underwood et al., 2018).

in a second edition in 1920, which views archival documents emanating from one creator as an "organic whole" that "comes into being as the result of the activities of an administrative body ... [and] is always the reflection of the functions of that body" (Muller et al., [1920] 2003, p. 19). In its original formulation, the archival method viewed records as providing direct access to the past. Today the widely held view is that records offer windows into knowing the past rather than in some way *being* the past (Lustig, 2020). Thus, we accept that records provide us with a means to gain knowledge of past actions and of the persons, organizations, and social institutional structures that have led to a record's formation.

The epistemology of the archives shares a common root with the work of several philosophical and social theorists of the late eighteenth, nineteenth, and early twentieth centuries, many of whom were trained in philology. MacNeil notes that

> Philology focused scholarly attention on the restoration of the past through the
> language, form and historical context of texts and, according to Donald Kelley,
> "established a new logos upon the assumption that language reproduced, if it did not
> actually create, the configurations of reality."
>
> *(Kelley, 2012 cited in MacNeil, 2016, p. 163)*

This idea found full flower in the "linguistic turn" in the humanities and the social sciences of the mid-twentieth century, referring to a fundamental discursive shift that posited language as generative of human behavior and social institutions (Lévi-Strauss, [1963] 1985; Austin, 1962, 1975; Berger and Luckmann, 1966; Rorty, 1992; Foucault, 1973; Habermas et al., 1984; Searle, 1985; Derrida, 1996). With the linguistic turn, what had been a theory of text (philology) was transformed into a theory of social behavior and formation.

The work of library scientist and document theorist Jesse Shera – who, writing in the 1960s with his colleague Margaret Egan, first advanced the idea of "social epistemology" – exemplifies this linguistic understanding of socio-epistemic reality. Shera saw the text as forming "the basic bonds through which individuals achieve unity in a culture," arguing that "[a] culture, almost by definition produces a 'transcript', a record in more or less permanent form that can be transmitted from generation to generation" (Shera, 1961, p. 169; 1968, pp. 8–9; 1972, p. 112 – all as cited in Martinez-Ávila and Zandonade, 2020). In this sense, society and culture is an ecosystem that forms around and, in turn, is formed by a shared record. Further, although Shera did not touch upon this, following Hardwig (1991), we can assume that trust among the social actors involved in the formation of the record is an essential part of this process of socio-epistemic formation.

While we might disagree with the notion that every action in society is transcribed or produces a text, or even that it should, if we contemplate the effects on personal privacy as described in Chapter 6 – and indeed, many archivists have called for reading the archive "against the grain" and interpreting archival "silences" (see, e.g., Carter, 2006; Cook, 2009) – the "speech act" theory of philosophers John Langshaw Austin (1911–60) and John Searle (1932–) argues for an understanding of speech, including speech that is captured in the form of text, as not only conveying information but as capable of performing declarative acts that summon a society into existence (Austin, 1975; Searle, 1985; see also Yeo, 2018). Through successive speech acts, a culture intersubjectively constructs and reproduces its life-world (Berger and Luckmann, 1966).

From this perspective, all societies are socio-informational-technical eco-systems constituted of, and by, social actors, communications, and technologies of cognition and communication that enable the constitution and continuation of the social group over time and space. To study and learn from life on file, then, is to study and learn from social life itself.

It is possible to understand blockchain and distributed ledgers systems as distinct microcosms, or simplified forms, of the socio-epistemic ecosystems that are, at one and the same time, configuring a record (i.e., the ledger) and configuring a life-world. By adopting the archival method of studying the origins of these records and the context of their creation and keeping, we can come to understand the unique epistemic and social communities associated with them. This strategy offers the potential for insights pertinent to the questions that face society in an age of disinformation, owing to the unique ways that blockchain and distributed ledger–based ecosystems operate (i.e., by the formation of a socio-epistemic consensus). This is especially true since all of these communities have a utopian vision of some sort – whether, like Bitcoin, they embody grand "social imaginaries" of the sort theorized by Taylor (2004) or (as in the case of Norway's seafood supply chain consortium) they aim at more modest improvements to socio-economic conditions well within existing neoliberal social-political, economic, and legal frameworks.

8.2 Ledger Records, Peer (Dis)agreement, and Socio-Epistemic World Formation

A distributed ledger, and the life-world that takes shape around it, emerges out of the formation of a socio-epistemic consensus, that is, by means of overcoming possible peer disagreements to arrive at what peers agree accurately, reliably, and authentically documents states of affairs. This state of affairs is embodied in what takes shape as a blockchain or, more broadly, a distributed ledger. In social epistemology, peer disagreements relate to the problem of and methods by which "an agent [should] adjust her initial belief about [a] specified proposition upon learning that her peer holds a contrary position" (Goldman and O'Connor, 2021). Social epistemologists have discussed several strategies by which peers, that is, epistemic equals, might settle their disagreements. They might, for example, practice "conciliationism" (Feldman, 2006, 2007; Christensen, 2007, 2009; Elga, 2007); that is, they might suspend judgement if both they and the other peer have good grounds for, simultaneously but respectively, believing and disbelieving a proposition to be true. In this view, the only way forward, when only one true belief can be held, is to hold back on a final judgement as to whose belief is justifiably true.[5] Another option is to discursively take into consideration the quality of the reasoning of each peer and adopt the beliefs of the peer who reasons best, which Kelly (2010) refers to as the "Total Evidence View." It is, of course, also possible to adopt pluralism, accepting that there can be many versions of "the truth," emblematic of postmodernism.

None of these approaches describes the strategies that peers use to resolve disagreements in the context of blockchains and other distributed ledgers.[6] The particular modus operandi of such systems requires an algorithmically arrived at single true belief, thus ruling out belief suspension, the weighing of evidence, or the holding of several different "true" beliefs by different actors. To explain this further, let us first be reminded of how peers reach agreement. Under normal conditions, agreement among peers on the ordering of transactions and what is to be included in the ledger is determined computationally by means of a consensus mechanism – the algorithmic rules and procedures for achieving a consensus.[7] The consensus mechanism addresses the problem of how widely distributed peers in a system come to form a single shared justifiable true belief about the state of transactions on the ledger when peers across a distributed ledger technology (DLT) network compete to add records. Consensus is defined as "agreement among DLT nodes [and, by extension, those who control

---

[5] Goldman and O'Connor (2021) succinctly observe that "One may worry that there is something wrong with a principle that tells you not to believe in its own truth. (For further discussion, see Christensen, 2013.)"

[6] A possible exception to this is the Starling Framework, which acknowledges that different groups of peers, or "trust circles," might hold different justified true beliefs about states of affairs and the authenticity of sources of evidence and which therefore seeks to address this via enabling interoperability among different ledgers representing different versions of "the truth" (see Dotan, 2021).

[7] Technically, ISO 22739 (2020a, s. 3.12) defines a consensus mechanism as "rules and procedures by which consensus is reached."

those peers] that 1) a transaction is validated and 2) that the distributed ledger contains a consistent set and ordering of validated transactions" (ISO, 2020a, s. 3.11). Once consensus has been reached, it reflects the accepted state of the ledger; that is, all participating peers come to share the same canonical, replicated belief in the state of the ledger and agree upon the records it contains. As discussed previously, consensus mechanisms produce the epistemological basis (i.e., the ledger) for transacting parties to form justified true beliefs in the trustworthiness of the other party to the transaction – the trustee – enabling them to act (if they wish) with a high degree of confidence (in theory) that they possess a certain amount of cryptocurrency, own a particular asset, or that a certain state of affairs persists. By providing an institutionalized foundation for engendering trust, the ledger provides a basis for social and economic coordination and cooperation and shared meaning necessary to socio-epistemic world formation, even among social actors who know almost nothing about one another.

There are several different consensus mechanisms by which validated trans-actions can be included in the ledger. Each of these takes a slightly different approach to determining the inclusion and ordering of transactions and settling disagreements among peers. These differing mechanisms afford the "settings, materials, and infrastructures for local episodes of individual, interactional, and organizational cognition, emotion, and action" (Steele et al., 2020, p. 3).

The most well-known of these, because of its use in the Bitcoin blockchain, is the Proof-of-Work (PoW) consensus mechanism. As discussed in Chapter 1, the PoW consensus mechanism requires that peers ("miners") compete to be the first to add to the ledger a block containing a set of new transactions by solving a computationally hard puzzle that involves finding a random number (i.e., a nonce) that, when combined with specified input data, will produce a hash value for the block smaller than some currently accepted difficulty target, usually expressed as a long string of zeros.

From time to time, two miners will solve the puzzle at the same time resulting in a peer disagreement. Bitcoin peers solve this disagreement by always trusting the longest chain – in other words, combined computing power over time represents the justified true belief. If two blocks are mined at the same time, the block that is accepted is the one that the majority, that is, 51 percent of the miners, decide to follow. The rejected block becomes what is often referred to as an "orphan" or "stale" block, since it is no longer part of the longest chain (Orphan block, 2019). In other words, that belief is discarded, and the holders of that belief lose out. In Bitcoin, there is no mechanism to bring these orphaned blocks back into the epistemic fold of the ledger. This can therefore sometimes result in a ledger split, as I will discuss further below.

In contrast, the Ethereum GHOST (Greediest Heaviest Object Subtree) protocol, which is a variant of the PoW protocol, incorporates a financial incentive (the "ommer" or "uncle" block reward) to encourage miners to mine orphaned blocks and bring them back into the fold of the canonical ledger (Ethereum, 2021a) – a sort of computational epistemic inclusiveness. This innovation was seen as necessary because of Ethereum's faster block formation time (circa 13 seconds versus every 10 minutes [Kenton, 2020]), which would naturally have resulted in a much higher number of orphan blocks without the addition of incentives to bring orphaned blocks onto the main chain. Without this innovation, peer disagreements about the state of the ledger might have become frequent, rendering the ledger untrustworthy as an epistemic source of evidence about transaction statuses.

Another popular type of consensus mechanism is known as Proof-of-Stake (PoS) (King and Nadal, 2012). PoS is based on the notion of coin age, which is computed from a combination of the amount of cryptocurrency held plus the period for which it has been held (King and Nadal, 2012). This approach has gained support because it reduces the amount of energy needed to confirm blocks compared with the PoW consensus mechanism and because it is seen as a way of aligning the interests of participants in the correct operation of the network, since to act against the rules would ultimately reduce the value of participants' economic stake. Moreover, assuming correct operation of the network, the longer the stake is held the more its value should increase over time, thereby incentivizing participants to continue their relationships on the network to provide greater network stability. This approach aligns well with Hardin's "encapsulated interest" notion of trust, which presupposes that trusted parties have an incentive to behave in a trustworthy manner because they have in interest in continuing relations from which they benefit (discussed in Chapter 2).

In a version of PoS proposed for use in a future release of the Ethereum blockchain, participants must stake their holdings of Ethereum's cryptocurrency, ETH, to become validators on the network – the equivalent of miners in the context of PoW. Validators, chosen pseudo-randomly, are responsible for ordering transactions and creating new blocks (Ethos.dev, 2020). The stake is used to incentivize good validator behavior: "For example, a user can lose a portion of their stake for things like going offline (failing to validate), or their entire stake for deliberate collusion" (Ethereum, 2020). The handling of peer consensus formation and potential disagreements in PoS differs significantly from that in PoW consensus. In the proposed Ethereum version of PoS, for instance, there are two types of ledgers (or chains): a "shard chain" with 64 instances and a "beacon chain" that acts as a sort of controller chain. For each shard chain, validators are algorithmically chosen and responsible for adding new transactions to a block. Validators who are not chosen to add a block are called upon instead to attest to another validator's block – to confirm that it conforms to protocol – which they must do within a specified time "slot." Only one valid block is created per slot. At least 128 validators, forming a "committee," are required to attest to each shard block. This attestation is recorded in the beacon chain, once the requisite number of attestations has been obtained, with a "crosslink" to the shard block confirming the inclusion of the block in the state of the shared ledger. After completing 32 rounds of attesting to blocks – called an "epoch" – a new committee of validators is formed with different, random participants so as to prevent collusion (Ethos.dev, 2020). Ethereum proposes to use the Casper protocol to work out transaction and block finality. This involves having validators check on the state of a block at a certain periodicity and, if two-thirds of the validators agree, the block is considered finalized (Ethereum, 2020).

As the above discussion illustrates, even when the same category of consensus mechanism is used in a distributed ledger system, the rules and procedures by which it operates to arrive at an agreed state of affairs can be quite different, with very different outcomes for how peer agreement is reached, how disagreements are ultimately settled, and how the ledger forms. Given this, it is important to consider where these rules and procedures come from and how they are enacted – in other words the juridical system from which they emerge. In archival diplomatics, a juridical system is "[a] social group that is organized on the basis of a system of rules and that includes three components: the social group, the organizational principle of the social group, and the system of binding rules recognized by the social group" (InterPARES 2 Project, 2021c). The concept of juridical system bears certain similarities to the notion of "macrofoundations" in the literature on sociology of institutions (Steele et al., 2020). As this body of literature points to, institutional macrofoundations co-constitute organizations with microfoundations, or localized and particular social interactions, "and are inscribed into the symbolic frameworks, bodies, emotional registers, and sensory apparatuses by which people experience world and self" (Steele et al., 2020, p. 3).

The juridical context of consensus is a broad topic considered in discussions on governance of blockchain and distributed ledger ecosystems, which tends to encompass both nontechnical and technical aspects of how agreement on the shared state of the ledger will be reached and maintained, and in more specific technical literature discussing specific consensus mechanisms. Interestingly, very little of this literature focuses on the settling of disagreements, even though there is much to be learned from the study of disagreements. Governance thus concerns the *formation* of the rules and procedures for knowledge generation – in other words, the conditions under which a justified true belief about a transaction is to be considered epistemically reliable – while specific consensus mechanisms *embody* those rules and procedures in operation *ex ante and under normal conditions*.

In Bitcoin, for example, the initial and ongoing acceptance of the validation mechanisms is set out in the rules forming the Bitcoin protocol (acting as informal laws) established by the set of social actors responsible for the design and ongoing governance of the system. These rules exist in the form of Bitcoin improvement proposals (BIPs), a design document providing technical specification of the attributes and rationale for a new feature of the platform's software code (BIPs, 2021). These BIPs are ultimately instantiated in code, either as experimental versions of the protocol to test new rules or, if agreed to collectively, in the form of the current version of the protocol. In theory, if we were to compare Bitcoin to a liberal democratic state, the social actors responsible for BIPs, usually the core developers, function as the delegated (though not elected) representatives of Bitcoin users as well as legislators and administrators (Walch, 2015). This, of course, differs from liberal democratic states wherein the legislative, administrative, and judicial aspects of governance are normally separated.

Core developers possess legitimacy as legislators and administrators on behalf of Bitcoin users primarily by virtue of community trust placed in their expertise, which makes Bitcoin a meritocracy – an organizing principle that tends to tightly meld epistemic authority with social power and authority. Bitcoin core developers demonstrate skill as software developers by the number of their "commits" to the Bitcoin codebase.[8] Maintenance of the codebase has only ever been the purview of a handful of "core (rather centralized) developers"[9] most of whom are perceived and trusted by other peers as having the competence and "virtue" – that is, the epistemic authority – to set the rules determining knowledge formation on the ledger. Initially, core developers' legitimacy also came from their degree of social proximity to the ledger's

---

[8] "Commits" refers to a revision or an individual change to a file (or set of files) on GitHub.

[9] Bitcoin maintains and publishes a list of individuals (ordered by the number of commits each has signed to Bitcoin Core's git repository) that it refers to as "Bitcoin Core contributors" (Bitcoin, 2021). At time of writing, this list is "led" by Wladimir van der Laan, the current lead maintainer of the Bitcoin repository on GitHub (succeeding Gavin Andresen), supported by the MIT Media Lab's Digital Currency Initiative (DCI). The DCI was founded in 2015 to fund Bitcoin developers, with a view to "allowing us to continue to improve the software that powers the currency without the worry of an intrusive corporate mandate or ideology" (Digital Currency Initiative, n. d.) Others on this list with more than 1,000 commits are Marko Falke, Pieter Wuille, fanquake, and Gavin Andresen (the lead maintainer from February 23, 2011 to April 7, 2014 [Lopp, 2018]).

original developer, the pseudonymous Satoshi Nakamoto. Thus, in the case of Bitcoin, developers like Gavin Andresen, who had corresponded directly with Nakamoto, had a proximal epistemic authority. Additionally, a core developer's legitimacy comes from their commitment to a set of core values; commonly, for example, a belief in the value of open-source software development and detachment from corporate incentives.

The tight-knit community of Bitcoin core developers thus was initially bound together by mutual trust based upon an understanding that each individual's interests encapsulated the others' interests, a common foundation of respect for software development competence associated with the project's founder, and shared norms and operating principles and practices that contributed to a perceived trustworthiness through independence of thought and action. In a manner very reminiscent of Shapin's (1994) account of the gentlemen-philosophers of the British Royal Academy, *early* Bitcoin core developers trusted one another and operated according to informal norms and values that determined the overarching rules and procedures by which Bitcoin operated, including how ledger consensus was achieved and disagreements settled.

The Bitcoin community has not always settled their disagreements by means of the sort of genteel scholarly debate that Shapin describes as characterizing the British Royal Academy gentlemen-philosophers, however. Rather, Andresen has been described as saying that "as 'lead maintainer' he always sought consensus, but on the few occasions when there was irresolvable disagreement, he made the final call, acting as a sort of 'benevolent dictator'" (Popper, 2016b), a rather corporatist approach. This statement aptly illustrates the deep interrelationship between the epistemic rules of the game – and the record that results from their operation – and social power and authority. The making of records, if not all evidentials, is deeply bound up with such matters through socio-epistemic processes that determine the rules and procedures by which evidentials are made and how states of affairs captured in them will be determined to be reliable – and therefore reliably and justifiably true.

In Bitcoin, peers are free to come and go as they please, but once participating in and maintaining the state of the platform, they must submit to the rules as instantiated in the platform's software code. Dispute resolution – or by analogy to the liberal democratic state, the judicial function – is handled computationally under normal operating conditions. Protesting rules by continuing to operate according to an older version of the Bitcoin software protocol or, conversely, adopting new code (if not backwards compatible with the currently accepted version of client software instantiating the new rules) will cause what is referred to as a "hard fork" or split in the state of the ledger, which essentially creates two competing ledgers (and thus potentially two versions of accepted truth). Once a ledger undergoes a hard fork, peers must choose which fork they want to continue transacting on, that is, the version of the truth that they wish to follow.

Hard forks typically reflect unresolved epistemic disagreements among those involved in the design and ongoing governance of a distributed ledger system (see, e.g., Hearn, 2020). Illustrative of this dynamic is the now infamous hard fork that occurred in Bitcoin Core and resulted in the creation of Bitcoin Cash in 2016–17. In this hard fork, the disagreement between different factions in the Bitcoin community was over how to scale the network, which requires changes to the rules configuring the ledger. The issue arose because, as the number of transactions on the Bitcoin network grew and the complexity of each transaction increased with use of the ledger extending beyond the exchange of cryptocurrency (i.e., the Blockchain 2.0 use cases discussed in Chapter 3), the transaction throughput of the network became slower since the size of each block remained fixed, as did the rate of new block formation. By 2016, the network had slowed to about three transactions per second from its 2011 rate of about seven transactions per second. This was already significantly slower than Visa (with a speed of about 1,700 transactions per second), which some Bitcoin community members viewed as an appropriate benchmark (Hearn, 2016).

By 2017, the situation had become untenable, with some transactions taking up to 14 hours to be mined and propagated to the network. There were also rapidly rising transaction fees and concerns about network (and ledger) reliability (Hearn, 2016). Many in the Bitcoin community argued for an increase in the block size to facilitate faster transactions; however, other community members resisted this idea.[10] Popper (2016a), writing in the *New York Times*, observed that the debate had "exposed fundamental differences about the basic aims of the Bitcoin project, and how online communities should be governed." Insiders characterized the disagreement as a "civil war" (Hearn, 2016) in which "Bitcoin has gone from being a transparent and open community to one that is dominated by rampant censorship and attacks on bitcoiners by other bitcoiners" (Hearn, 2016, as cited in Popper, 2016b). Popper's (2016b) article describes how vitriolic the dispute had become by that point: "The divide has led over the last six months to death threats against Bitcoin developers and hacking attacks that have taken down Internet providers. The sense of betrayal is strong on both

---

[10] Hearn attributed resistance to Chinese miners, just two of whom control more than 50 percent of the hash power. Hearn wrote in his 2016 post that "At a recent conference over 95% of hashing power was controlled by a handful of guys sitting on a single stage [the post links to a photo of group of Chinese miners]." Hearn went on to accuse miners of not allowing the block chain to grow because they knew that poor Chinese internet connections would not be able to keep pace if network speed increased (Hearn, 2016).

sides." Use of the word betrayal is telling: with this dispute, trusts were breached.

These epistemic problems stemmed, at least in part, from diverging economic interests among those within the community of Bitcoin core developers, which engendered a sense of mistrust among the social actors involved in rule formation. On the one hand were those, such as Hearn, who saw the future of Bitcoin, and thus their own economic stake in the system, as being enhanced by increasing the block size to Visa-level transaction speeds. On the other were those who were developing a "layer 2" approach to scaling the network, called Lightning Network, whose economic interests were served by retaining the existing 1MB block size.[11] The Lightning Network was intended to create an alternative blockchain – or a sidechain – that could handle many more transactions, but which was still anchored to the main Bitcoin chain (see, e.g., Poon and Dryja, 2016).

Further complicating the matter was the fact that the system had been evolving such that peers no longer had equal hash power. The rise of the miners and mining pools meant that some peers, or coalitions of peers, held much greater power than others to influence the outcome of proposals for rule changes. Additionally, these peers had an economic incentive to keep the network operating rules as they were, since a change could ultimately lead to a reduction in their power, earnings, and the value of investments in specialized Bitcoin mining equipment (e.g., application-specific integrated circuits [ASICs]). Not to be discounted, many of the powerful miners at the time of the disagreement were Chinese, while many of the core developers were North American or European, adding cultural difference to the divisions rending apart a previously cohesive, and trusting, socio-epistemic Bitcoin community (Hearn, 2016).

Approaches to resolving the increasingly acrimonious disagreement varied. While Andresen's "benevolent dictator" approach as lead maintainer of the Bitcoin code might have led him to step in and arbitrate the dispute, Wladimir J. van der Laan, a Dutch programmer who had by then taken over from Andresen as lead maintainer, did not wish to follow suit, stating, "I cannot be the decider for network-level issues," and further that "No one 'owns' Bitcoin. No one can decide over Bitcoin as if it's some kind of company" (Popper, 2016b). After Andresen's resignation from the position of Bitcoin Core maintainer, he and Mike Hearn put forward a new BIP – BIP 101 (Bitcoin, 2015a) – "to address several controversial ideas lacking the consensus required to be implemented in Bitcoin Core" (Hearn, 2016; Bitcoin XT, 2020). BIP 101 was

---

[11] For example, developers associated with the company Blockstream, founded by Adam Back.

implemented as Bitcoin XT and released on August 15, 2015 (Bitcoin, 2015b; Hearn, 2015a, 2015b, 2016). If a majority of peers had adopted Bitcoin XT, it would have been accepted as a new rule and block sizes would have increased; however, other community members viewed the introduction of what they considered to be a preemptive and divisive fork as a betrayal of the community's values and its commitment to reaching epistemic consensus (Popper, 2016b). BIP 101 was ultimately withdrawn in January 2016 but not before any talk of Bitcoin XT had been banned from the Bitcoin forum and cyberattacks were launched against peers running the new protocol (Hearn, 2016; Popper, 2016b; Bitcoin XT, 2020).

In the face of an impasse, some Bitcoin community members believed that setting up a workshop (Scaling Bitcoin) as a forum to "aid the technical consensus-building process … present proposals, and evaluate technical materials and data with academic discipline and analysis that fully considers the complex trade-offs between decentralization, utility, security, and operational realities" was the best approach to resolving the dispute – a sort of British Royal Academy of Bitcoin (Scaling Bitcoin, n.d.).[12] Others saw this as a waste of time (e.g., Hearn, 2016).

Another proposal, called Segregated Witness (SegWit), which had first been mooted as early as 2012 (van Wirdum, 2017), also gained support and was ultimately approved after machinations of operatic proportions and several high-level summits among Bitcoin core developers and miners (van Wirdum, 2017). The idea behind SegWit was to increase block capacity without increasing block size by stripping the digital signature required to check transaction validity (the "witness")[13] from the input to the transaction, moving it instead to the end of a transaction. This had the added advantage of enabling new developments, such as the Lightning Network and various "Altcoins" (alternative coins) building upon the basic framework of Bitcoin. While SegWit did

---

[12] To that end, this author was invited, in 2017, to submit a proposal for the University of British Columbia (UBC) to host Scaling Bitcoin, as academic institutions were trusted (at least by some) to provide an impartial forum for discussion. Research into the effects of different scaling proposals also began to be undertaken at the time, including work that researchers at UBC became involved with in collaboration with researchers associated with Bitcoin Unlimited (see www.bitcoinulimited.info) to explore the effects of a block size increase from 1MB to 1GB (see Suisani et al., 2017). This paper was presented at Scaling Bitcoin in 2017. UBC researchers also participated in the BSafe Network, which was set up to empirically test the effects of different rule change proposals for the Bitcoin network, serving as another forum to generate information that might inform decision-making on rule changes.

[13] Van Wirdum (2017) explains the idea of a "witness" as follows: "Bitcoin transactions consist of two main parts. One part is 'base transaction data.' That covers which bitcoins are being moved and where they are being moved to, as well as some other data. The second part is called the 'witness.' This contains a bit of code with cryptographic signature data, which proves that the owner of a bitcoin really did want to spend the bitcoin."

address the scalability issue to an extent, several community members continued to disagree with this approach. They preferred to directly increase the block size from 1MB to 8MB, arguing that an increase was necessary for the survival of the network. In addition, some of the large miners blocked the implementation of SegWit for "political reasons," but which Gregory Maxwell attributed at the time to the fact that the miners were using "patented AsicBoost technology" that was incompatible with the proposed SegWit changes (Maxwell, 2017; van Wirdum, 2017). By exploiting a flaw in the BIP 9 soft fork activation mechanism,[14] which set forth the rules on how new releases would be considered accepted by the community, the miners were able to prevent the upgrade (Segregated Witness, 2020).

With the economic majority controlling consensus, not the miners, the deadlock was solved in August 2017 by creating a user activated soft fork BIP 148, wherein the economic majority bypassed the blocking miners and activated SegWit on their own (Segregated Witness, 2020). Once SegWit was implemented, the portion of the Bitcoin community that supported a block size increase refused to update their clients to adopt the new protocol, causing a hard fork in the ledger that led to two versions of Bitcoin: the original and another with the larger block size that ultimately became Bitcoin Cash.[15]

The Bitcoin scaling dispute generated many alternate rules for the governance of the Bitcoin network. Among them were rules underpinning the formation of a new blockchain ecosystem, Decred. According to the history offered on Decred's website, "the [Bitcointalk] user, tacotime [also a founder of the cryptocurrency Monero], ... _ingsoc, another Bitcointalk user, and Jake Yocom-Piatt," launched Decred in 2016 as a cryptocurrency based upon the Bitcoin blockchain, but one that would combine the PoW and PoS consensus mechanisms based on a proposal for the Memcoin2 protocol (Decred, n.d.; Mackenzie, 2014). Decred was specifically designed to enable a community to update its protocol without resulting in the sort of acrimony and, ultimately, community and ledger split that occurred with Bitcoin over debates about scalability; in other words, it aimed to encourage and maintain community consensus (Yocom-Piatt, 2015). It also sought to implement a sustainable funding model for development, an issue with which many open-source projects struggle.

---

[14] According to the GitHub Bitcoin mediawiki repository, BIP 34, an existing rule change mechanism, only supported "one single change being rolled out at once, requiring coordination between proposals, and [would] not allow for permanent rejection: as long as one soft fork is not fully rolled out, no future one can be scheduled" (BIP-0009, 2020). BIP 9 changed this rule change protocol by allowing for multiple soft fork releases at once (BIP-0009, 2020).

[15] See https://bitcoincash.org for more information.

To achieve its goals, Decred implemented a governance model that combined the PoW and PoS consensus methods based on the principle of ticketholder voting both for validation of blocks and for voting on consensus rule changes. To purchase tickets to vote, users time-lock their coins. The process of confirming a block begins, as in Bitcoin, with the blocks being mined using the PoW mechanism; however, unlike in Bitcoin, miners only receive 60 percent of the block reward and the block is not confirmed for entry into the ledger until 20 ticket holders (called stakeholders), who are selected using a lottery process, vote to approve or reject it. These stakeholders receive 30 percent of the block reward for casting their vote. The remaining 10 percent is withheld by the treasury and used for development projects. If a majority of stakeholders vote to reject the previous block, the miner who produced that block loses their block reward and the transactions from that block are returned to the mempool. This procedure is intended to guard against malicious PoW miner behavior, such as the mining of empty blocks and acrimonious forks. Voting on "higher-level issues" – such as how to spend funds held back by treasury or significant policy decisions such as amendments to the Decred constitution – occur off-chain using a specially designed web platform, called Politia, following rules and procedures outlined in Decred's "constitution" (Decred, 2020; Decred, 2021).

Reflecting at the time upon the dispute that had erupted within the Bitcoin community surrounding the rules of representation to be used in the making of its community's transcript, Popper (2016b) noted that "The current dispute, though, is a reminder that the Bitcoin software – like all computer code – is an evolving product of the human mind, and its deployment is vulnerable to human frailties and divergent ideals," and, I would argue, it is also a product of social group trust, power, authority, rules, norms, and values. Bitcoin Core, as it is today, and each subsequent fork or blockchain variant of Nakamoto's original Bitcoin project – such as Bitcoin Cash or Decred – represents the outcome of the interaction of individual minds and social institutions in the, sometimes quite contentious, shaping of a record and, concomitantly, the shaping of a social group's shared epistemic and social reality.

This does not imply that all social actors within a social group necessarily hold the same justified true beliefs, even if they have adopted the shared institutional rules of the game of the social group. As discussed in reference to orphan blocks, different social actors might momentarily or permanently be out of step with a dominant socially accepted "truth." Most often this results in their having to adopt the dominant truths of the group (as in the case of the ommer blocks of Ethereum). Outside of blockchains, social actors might exist as an epistemic subgroup of the larger group; however, in the case of blockchain ecosystems that do not accept epistemic pluralism or other means of resolving peer disputes, epistemic exile (e.g., orphan blocks or a ledger split) is usually the only option. In time, such epistemic exile might lead also to social exit, as we observe in the case of Bitcoin Cash and Decred. Moreover, some social actors might have more epistemic authority than others, either by means of social power or computing power, and thus be able to impose their version of the truth. Over time, this might also translate into greater socio-economic power that, recursively, strengthens the source of these social actors' epistemic power. We see this in the epistemic strength of the Bitcoin miners, who receive many more block rewards owing to their superior computational power.

Thus far we have discussed public, permissionless blockchains, but what of private, permissioned blockchains and distributed ledgers, which instantiate their rules of operation primarily in human-made law rather than computational "law"? Typically, participants in such an ecosystem will be vetted to confirm their identity and ensure that they sign up to community operating principles, thereby maintaining trust and security (IBM, n.d.; Kshetri, 2018). That said, the security on private, permissioned blockchains is only as good as the honesty of the entities validating transactions. There are no mathematical guarantees behind the irreversibility of transactions in private, permissioned blockchains, in contrast to public, permissionless blockchains that rely upon mechanisms such as PoW or PoS. Nevertheless, private, permissioned blockchains and distributed ledgers still use cryptography to maintain the integrity of ledger records and consensus mechanisms, as in the case of the Practical Byzantine Fault Tolerance consensus mechanism used to manage agreement among interacting peer nodes. Once the rules are contractually set, ledger creation occurs according to the chosen consensus mechanism, with *ex post* recourse to the law should any one of those social actors try to manipulate the ledger or otherwise be in breach of contract.[16]

Hyperledger Fabric, an example of a permissioned ledger, was developed by Hyperledger, a community described as "a collaborative and global open source software community hosted by The Linux Foundation, and advancing blockchain technologies for business" (Hyperledger, 2019). The Linux Foundation is a 501(c)(6) nonprofit technology consortium founded in 2000 under the laws of the United States as a merger between Open Source Development Labs and the Free Standards Group (Hyperledger, 2019). Those

---

[16] For such systems, as Harvard computer scientist James Mickens (2018, 06:24), referenced in Chapter 1, observes, "a lot of these use cases participants have out-of-band relationships in real life . . . so what this means is that these real-life relationships for example between entities that have tax IDs . . . that's going to decrease the likelihood of malice because I can always sue you in the real legal system."

wishing to join the Hyperledger community must sign an agreement that sets out the various conditions of membership, including adherence to brand and intellectual property guidelines. Community members contribute to various open-source projects maintained on GitHub. Proposed and approved new rules are laid out as Requests for Comment (RFCs) that provide standardization across the ecosystem in such areas as architectural changes, substantial changes to component interfaces, new core features, backward incompatible changes, and changes that affect the security of communications or administration (Hyperledger / fabric-rfcs, 2021). The process of approving a new RFC, or amending or revoking an existing one, involves a review process during which "maintainers [a core group of technical experts responsible for maintaining the project and its documentation][17] may schedule meetings with the author and/or relevant stakeholders to discuss the issues in greater detail, and in some cases the topic may be discussed at a contributors meeting." The maintainers make the final decisions about RFCs "after the benefits and drawbacks are well understood" (Hyperledger / fabric-rfcs, 2021). One of the main differences between the Hyperledger Fabric community and the Bitcoin or Ethereum communities, however, is that Hyperledger Fabric community members typically implement different versions of their own private, permissioned distributed ledgers. This means that they can deviate from protocol standards if they wish in creating their own (not necessarily compatible) ledgers, unlike Bitcoin or Ethereum wherein peers participate in a single unifying ledger in which transactions will be rejected if not compatible with the canonical version of the shared ledger.

Groups of social actors, often taking the form of business consortia with a lead industry partner, can use the Hyperledger Fabric open-source software codebase to develop customized, use-case-specific applications, often running on use-case-specific private, permissioned distributed ledgers. The approach is exemplified by a blockchain-based supply chain project in Norway involving the Norwegian Seafood Association (Sjømatbedriftene) and led by a Norwegian IT infrastructure provider, Atea, and IBM (Bankole, 2019). This project is described as creating traceability along Norway's seafood supply chain platform, from "fjord" to "fork" (Askew, 2020).

The motivation for the project returns us to the theme of preventing forged documents and fraudulent claims (see Chapter 5) that has motivated so many of the Blockchain 2.0 projects, a capability said to give blockchain and distributed

---

[17] Maintainers are selected by other maintainers, from time to time, based on three criteria: "demonstrated track record of [pull request] reviews (both quality and quantity of reviews); demonstrated thought leadership in the project; [and] demonstrated shepherding of project work and contributors" (Hyperledger, 2020).

ledgers their place as a tool to combat disinformation (Hannam, 2017; van Ruth et al., 2018; Saberi et al., 2019; Bumblauskas et al., 2020). This capability, combined with the possibility of efficient and structured messaging, has attracted many businesses to the use of blockchains for supply chain management (Kshetri, 2018).

The Norwegian project uses IBM's Hyperledger Fabric-based Food Trust blockchain platform,[18] which proponents of the project see as capable of delivering a more "transparent and regulated supply chain" to "ensure that all parties involved in Norway's seafood industry are acting accordingly" (Wolfson, 2020). For the purposes of the Norwegian project, the Food Trust blockchain was customized to provide Norway's seafood industry consortium with their own governance model, including rules for membership management, sharing of documents, the creation of the history of physical and digital assets on the ledger, and ledger transparency (Wolfson, 2020). Norway's project sits within the larger Food Trust network, which is led by IBM and an advisory council of representatives of global businesses. The advisory council, according to IBM (2019, p. 12), "helps set the rules of engagement and leads accountability in adhering to the governance agreement for the blockchain community, ensuring that the solution benefits all. The council formally reviews and ensures the policies meet the needs and values of the global Food Trust community across various segments, sizes, geographies, and more," noting also that the governance model is continually updated "based on expansion of the solution, member needs, technology innovation, and regulatory changes" (IBM, 2019, p. 12). By this means, the rules, principles, practices, norms, and values constituting the unique socio-informational-technical ecosystem that is the IBM Food Trust, and the Norwegian seafood supply chain network operating as a sub-ecosystem within it, come into existence and constitute a new epistemic truth and social reality.

That truth is not a universal one, however. Epistemic authority only extends as far as the institutional power of the ecosystem responsible for the creation of the transcript, or ledger. Faced with two alternate justified true beliefs about a state of affairs in two different ledgers, both reliably arrived at according to their own juridical systems, we confront the problem of epistemic interoperability among ecosystems, which also might manifest technical, informational, and social interoperability issues. At a time when distributed ledgers are growing in number and variety, yet also remain siloed, obtaining agreement among these systems remains an open challenge and a growing area of research

---

[18] The Food Trust blockchain is led by IBM with Walmart, Nestlé SA, Unilever NV, and other global companies (IBM, n.d.).

interest in a manner very reminiscent of the lack of epistemic cohesiveness we see among different socio-economic and political groups more broadly in society in the current age of disinformation (Koens and Poll, 2019). To illustrate, ledger A might indicate that a person holds a token balance of X. If that person also wishes to transact on ledger B, that ledger must also recognize and be able to trust that the person holds a token balance of X.

Much of the research on blockchain and distributed ledger interoperability focuses on interoperability of the technical kind, that is, on how technical systems operating according to disparate consensus mechanisms or with different data structures can be made to recognize one another's accounts of a state of affairs without the use of a trusted intermediary (see, e.g., Wood, 2016; Herlihy, 2018; Borkowski et al., 2019; Yang, et al., 2019). Koens and Poll (2019) outline three common strategies, for example: (1) notary schemes, wherein "a group of parties together execute an action on ledger A when a specific event takes place on ledger B"; (2) relay schemes, wherein "a smart contract on a ledger can read, validate, and act upon state or events from another ledger"; and (3) hash-locking, wherein the cryptographic proof generated on ledger A triggers an event on ledger B (an atomic swap). Lafourcade and Lombard-Platet (2020), on the other hand, argue that blockchain interoperability is impossible according to the classical definition of a blockchain; it always requires a "2 in 1" blockchain containing both ledgers to work. That is, the ledgers (and their respective communities) must encompass one another's technical and epistemic reality.

Even given that technical interoperability can be achieved by various (still imperfect) means, social interoperability is another matter. A couple might register their marriage on a blockchain solution – such as Bitnation Pangea, which offers its adopters the ability to create their own "Decentralised Borderless Voluntary Nation ... [c]hoose [their] Code of Law and Decision Making Mechanism, write a Constitution and provide Governance Services to Citizens" (Bitnation, 2019) – and that couple's "lived experience" might be that they are married. Attendees at their wedding ceremony might even share that epistemic reality and justifiably believe that the couple is married. However, when that couple presents the ledger record as proof of their marriage to an employer or state for the purposes of obtaining benefits, they might find that their status as a married couple is questioned. This is because the ledger record bears no juridical authority in relation to the institutional structures of the juridical system with which the couple is interacting. In other words, their marriage record has no legitimate juridical authority (or "deontic power," if we prefer Searle's formulation [Searle, 2010]) for purposes of the epistemic claim (and its associated social world consequences) they are attempting to make and is therefore untrustworthy as grounds to support that claim. The couple is basing their understanding of what is true on their own socio-epistemic ecosystem, while those offering social benefits base their understanding of the truth on another, similar to the gulf between Galileo's understanding of reliably justifiable true beliefs versus that of the Church (as discussed in Chapter 4). For the couple to legitimately claim an entitlement, they must present a marriage certificate that is issued by a recognized juridical authority (i.e., government agency) within the juridical system with which they are interacting. Shaped by a specific social reality, ledger records therefore can only have socio-epistemic authority and consequences, no matter how well made and preserved they are, if the creator and preserver of those records (i.e., an originating ledger) is acknowledged by the verifier of a truth claim as being an authoritative and legitimate source with respect to that truth claim and any rights and entitlements that proof of the claim might confer. Recognizing that different social groups might hold different epistemic beliefs, in contrast to the operation of many blockchain and distributed ledger ecosystems, the Starling Framework, a joint initiative of the University of Southern California Shoah Foundation and Stanford Engineering, aims to configure a distributed ledger ecosystem that allows for epistemic pluralism in efforts to combat misinformation (Dotan, 2021), yet it remains to be seen what tensions and conflicts might emerge in this configuration and how they will be resolved.

8.3 Concluding Thoughts

What does a study of the rules and actualities of consensus formation and the handling of peer consensus and disagreements in blockchain and distributed ledger ecosystems tell us about the trustworthiness of ledger records and societal trusting relations? It suggests that the means by which ledger records come into existence are constituted by social actors who trust (or come to distrust) one another to hold institutional power and authority, and thus the resulting records reflect their worldview and socially constructed version of the "truth."

To the extent that the rules and practices by which the ledger takes shape are embodied in formal social, epistemic, and technical mechanisms, the resulting ledger expresses and constitutes a socially constructed socio-epistemic reality. Individual peers, however, may dissent and not share or wish to adopt the socio-epistemic reality that the ledger expresses, nor the rules by which that social reality takes shape, especially when they no longer trust the rule creators. This is often the case when the interests of the peers are not served well by those rules; for example, they might lose out economically or politically by adopting them. Given this, while ledgers are useful in protecting and providing certainty about the integrity of agreed peer consensus on a state of affairs, the extent to which they express and will be accepted as "proof," "truth," and evidence is socially constructed and bounded and, in some cases, can be quite socially divisive.

To elaborate, social actors that agree with the social rules of the game (the macrofoundations) by which these records come into existence are likely to accept them as evidentials and grounds for supporting truth claims – either about the actions from which the records arise or other types of truth claims for which they might serve as evidence – because they trust and view as legitimate the social actors who create those rules. In contrast, when trust breaks down, some social actors will disagree with the rules of the game, will be more likely to reject or suspect the ledger records as evidentials, and may even be forced, or wish, to exit the social group as a result. Given this, Nissenbaum's (2001, p. 663) admonishment to "take greater heed of the sanctioned harms of respectable insiders" because "evil hackers are not the only, nor are they the most important barriers to trust online" stands as an important reminder of the need to make visible and attend to questions of systemic power imbalances in the formation of rules concerning the operation of a ledger, since these imbalances will be reflected in the operation of the ledger's ecosystem and the "transcript" that ultimately results from the interactions of social actors within the ecosystem.

This is no less true of other types of records than it is of ledger records, and it is one of the reasons why records providing documentary evidence and grounds to support a particular truth claim might be rejected as grounds for the formation of justified true beliefs by particular individuals or groups, no matter how perfectly accurate, reliable, and authentic they might be considered to be. If there is social disagreement and lack of trust in the juridical and institutional mechanisms by which the records have come into existence or have been preserved, there will always be room for "facts," "alternative facts," and epistemic disagreement.

In a manner similar to the epistemic and social fragmentation that we have seen arise within some distributed ledger communities, the epistemic disagreements and the disinformation of our present times express deep social fragmentations and an absence of social cohesion with a recursive effect: social cohesion requires the formation of trusting social relations and the formation of trusting social relations requires trustworthy evidence about trustees as the basis for reliable formation of beliefs about whether trustees can be trusted, which, in turn, requires that social actors trust the juridical and institutional macrofoundations shaping sources of evidence. When that evidence is viewed as not being trustworthy because it embodies social power and authority mistrusted by a trustor, trustors might reject the evidence and fail to reliably form a belief supporting trust, like the "broken box of thermometers" example discussed in Chapter 5. Or, trustors might land on a false belief that a trustee cannot be trusted, when in fact the trustee is trustworthy. Even with a critical reading of "life on file" and careful examination of the evidence – which is cognitively and socially costly – trustors still might not form a reliable belief if the epistemic environment is corrupted or noisy. Is there a way out of this terrible recursive loop?

Paradoxically, we might turn to blockchains and distributed ledgers for answers, as they are expressions of, and can serve as sites for discourse on, the nature of trust in our society and its epistemic foundations. The various strategies that blockchain and distributed ledger system designers have devised for arriving at peer consensus, resolving disputes, and even engendering sustainable socio-informational-technical ecosystems point to insights into the effects – both epistemic and social – that we might expect if we were to deploy similar strategies more widely to solve the current problems of disinformation and social fragmentation. As such, blockchain and distributed ledger systems offer opportunities for experimentation from which we might learn, even when the experiments fail. For instance, there might be lessons in how Ethereum designs its PoW incentive mechanism to weave dissenters back into the epistemic fold through offering "ommer" rewards. We might learn from the effects of the greater weight being given to peers with a long-standing stake in an ecosystem, as in the case of PoS consensus mechanisms. Equally, we might gain insights from the social and other consequences of requiring that all social actors must agree on a canonical epistemic state or leave the social group (i.e., is this epistemic stance socially "good"?). What if we were to explore and seek to better understand the motivations of our own epistemic dissenters with a view to understanding what might encourage their inclusion back into the epistemic fold? What if we were to explore how much trust in the rules by which an ecosystem operates is necessary to achieve cohesion of the ecosystem? We might also explore what archival silences the rules around consensus formation prefigure; in other words, whose transactions are dropped or disallowed, and what is the effect on the communal life-world. We might consider the consequences as more of our life-world exists "on ledger." What are the effects if individual choice lessens concerning how much of ourselves and our lives to make visible through inscription on a ledger? We might consider what should be left invisible and what to remain silent about. We might also ask how to build epistemic bridges that connect ecosystems (i.e., interoperability). In other words, can experiments with the formation of the record in the context of blockchains and distributed ledger "micro-worlds" (Latour and Woolgar, 1979) provide us with opportunities to experiment with the formation of our own socio-epistemic world?

Some might argue that this is a rather utopian perspective of the contribution that blockchains and distributed ledgers can make to understanding and finding solutions to current socio-epistemic dilemmas. Utopianism, and especially techno-utopianism, has developed something of a bad name for itself in recent times. Techno-utopianism can just as easily engender techno-cynicism when utopian imaginaries turn out to be just wishful thinking or, worse, dystopian nightmares of unintended consequences. Blockchain and distributed ledgers have given rise to a good amount of worry and critical reflection upon the possible negative outcomes of techno-dreaming of this sort (Husain et al., 2020), from concerns about concentration of power in the hands of core developers to recentralization, lack of regulatory oversight, excessive individualism, and risk of worsening socio-economic inequalities (Atzori, 2015; Coeckelbergh and Reijers, 2016; Walch, 2018; Lemieux, 2019; Husain et al., 2020; Humphreys, 2021).

Yet, as much as there is a dark side to utopianism, it can provide a way, even if it fails to help us reach a desirable future state, to explore different standards to steer by (Taylor, 2004, pp. 23–24) through experimentation with different sorts of imagined communities (Anderson, 1991). As do all utopian imaginaries, the blockchain utopian imaginary takes the form of a "wish":

> This wish is the organizing principle which even moulds the way in which we experience time. The form in which events are ordered and the unconsciously emphatic rhythm, which the individual in his spontaneous observation of events imposes upon the flux of time, appears in the utopia as an immediately perceptible picture, or at least a directly intelligible set of meanings.
>
> *(Mannheim, [1929] 1954, p. 188, as cited in Turner, 2019, p. 37)*

Husain et al. (2020, p. 380) further speculate that "blockchain projects personify 'prefigurative politics' by design – the idea that their technical and organizational forms, to a large extent, embody the political imaginaries and power structures which they want to enable in society." Consequently, blockchains and distributed ledgers can be viewed as constitutive sorts of experiments in alternative social, epistemic, and technical forms.

As Turner (2019, p. 37) observes, however, even as we contemplate the idea of the cogenerative nature of the utopian wish, "we are still faced with the problem of where the wishes come from." This begs the question of whether it is possible to escape the epistemic troubles of our time with the same epistemo-logical systems that brought us to this point. Possibly not, but with imagination we might be able to transcend such thinking. Transcendence, I would argue, begins with a hermeneutic, phenomenological, and *archival* approach to the comparative study of diverse blockchain and distributed ledger imaginaries and possible future socio-epistemic realities.

To return to the title of the opening chapter of this volume, then, "What Good Is Blockchain?," my answer is that it is as good as we wish. Like all wishes, the original blockchain project, Bitcoin, and the public, permissionless and private, permissioned blockchains and distributed ledgers that have since come into existence embed and express feelings of collective hope and desire for a return to epistemic and social integrity and trust. This is not to suggest that these projects successfully realize such utopian visions; indeed, they, by and large, do not. But there is something to be learned from all of the projects. Is the utopianism of blockchain and distributed ledger technology all just wishful thinking then? Perhaps. But let's not forget Mannheim's words (Mannheim, [1929] 1954, p, 188, as cited in Turner, 2019, p. 37):

> It is the Utopian element – i.e., the nature of the dominant wish – which determines the sequence, order and evaluation of the dominant experiences.

References

Accenture. (2016). *Editing the uneditable blockchain: Why distributed ledger technology must adapt to an imperfect world.* www.accenture.com/t00010101T000000__w__/es-es/_acnmedia/PDF-33/Accenture-Editing-Uneditable-Blockchain.pdf

Aikhenvald, A. Y. (2004). *Evidentiality.* Oxford University Press.

Ajaka, N., Kessler, G., & Samuels, E. (2019). Seeing isn't believing: The fact checker's guide to manipulated video. *Washington Post.* www.washingtonpost.com/graphics/2019/politics/fact-checker/manipulated-video-guide

Alesina, A., & Wacziarg, R. (2000). The economics of civic trust. In S. J. Pharr & R. D. Putnam (Eds.), *Disaffected democracies: What's troubling the trilateral countries?* (pp. 149–170). Princeton University Press.

Amazeen, M. A. (2015). Revisiting the epistemology of fact-checking. *Critical Review, 27*(1), 1–22. https://doi.org/10.1080/08913811.2014.993890

Anderson, B. (1991). *Imagined communities: Reflections on the origin and spread of nationalism.* Verso.

Anduck. (2018). *Blockchain in words.* https://bitcoinstrings.com

Aneesh, A. (2002). *Technologically coded authority: The post-industrial decline in bureaucratic hierarchies* [Conference paper]. 4th International Summer Academy on Technology Studies: "Technology and the Public," Deutschlandsberg, Austria, July 7–13, 2002. www.researchgate.net/publication/254843955_Technologically_Coded_Authority_The_Post-Industrial_Decline_in_Bureaucratic_Hierarchies

Antonopoulos, A. (2014, February 20). Bitcoin security model: Trust by computation. A shift from trusting people to trusting math. *Radar.* http://radar.oreilly.com/2014/02/bitcoin-security-model-trust-by-computation.html

Arendt, H. (1978, October 26). Hannah Arendt: From an interview. *New York Review of Books.* www.nybooks.com/articles/1978/10/26/hannah-arendt-from-an-interview

Arizti, P., Brumby, J., Manning, N., Senderowitsch, R., & Thomas, T. (Eds.) (2010). *Results, performance budgeting and trust in government.* World Bank. http://hdl.handle.net/10986/27895

Arrow, K. J. (1972). Gifts and exchanges. *Philosophy & Public Affairs, 1*(4), 343–362. www.jstor.org/stable/2265097

Arrow, K. J. (1974). *The limits of organization.* W. W. Norton & Company.

Arthur, C. (2013, August 23). Tech giants may be huge, but nothing matches big data. *Guardian*. www.theguardian.com/technology/2013/aug/23/tech-giants-data

Ashforth, B. E., & Mael, F. (1989). Social identity theory and the organization. *Academy of Management Review*, *14*(1), 20–39. https://doi.org/10.2307/258189

Askew, K. (2020, July 1). From fjord to fork: Norwegian collaboration leverages blockchain for "safer, better seafood." *Food Navigator.com*. www.foodnavigator.com/Article/2020/07/01/Norwegian-collaboration-leverages-blockchain-for-safer-better-seafood

Atzori, M. (2015). Blockchain technology and decentralized governance: Is the state still necessary? http://dx.doi.org/10.2139/ssrn.2709713

Austin, J. L. (1962). *Sense and sensibilia* (G. J. Warnock, Ed.). Clarendon Press.

Austin, J. L. (1975). *How to do things with words* (2nd ed.). Oxford University Press.

Ayyub, R. (2018, November 21). I was the victim of a deepfake porn plot intended to silence me. *HuffPost UK*. www.huffingtonpost.co.uk/entry/deepfake-porn_uk_5bf2c126e4b0f32bd58ba316

Baier, A. (1986). Trust and antitrust. *Ethics*, *96*(2), 231–260. https://doi.org/10.1086/292745

Baker, J. (1987). Trust and rationality. *Pacific Philosophical Quarterly*, *68*(1), 1–13. https://doi.org/10.1111/j.1468-0114.1987.tb00280.x

Balliet, D., & Van Lange, P. A. M. (2013). Trust, conflict, and cooperation: A meta-analysis. *Psychological Bulletin*, *139*(5), 1090–1112. https://doi.org/10.1037/a0030939

Bandyopadhyay, P. (2018, December 3). The origin of blockchain – from cypherpunks to Satoshi to IBM. *Medium*. https://medium.com/datadriveninvestor/cypherpunks-to-satoshi-to-ibm-819ebcfdd674

Bankole, K. (2019, April 2). Code pattern: Deploy a blockchain network to regulate food shipments along a supply chain. IBM. https://developer.ibm.com/technologies/blockchain/patterns/monitor-food-shipments-using-blockchain/

Bannister, F., & Connolly, R. (2011). Trust and transformational government: A proposed framework for research. *Government Information Quarterly*, *28*(2), 137–147. https://doi.org/10.1016/j.giq.2010.06.010

Barber, B. (1983). *The logic and limits of trust*. Rutgers University Press.

Bartoletti, M., & Pompianu, L. (2017). An empirical analysis of smart contracts: Platforms, applications, and design patterns. In M. Brenner, K. Rohloff, J. Bonneau, A. Miller, P. Y. A. Ryan, V. Teague, A. Bracciali, M. Sala, F. Pintore, & M. Jakobsson (Eds.), *Financial Cryptography and Data Security, FC 2017*. Lecture notes in computer science, vol. 10323 (pp. 494–509). Springer. https://doi.org/10.1007/978-3-319-70278-0_31

Basol, M., Roozenbeek, J., & van der Linden, S. (2020). Good news about bad news: Gamified inoculation boosts confidence and cognitive immunity against fake news. *Journal of Cognition*, *3*(1), 2. http://doi.org/10.5334/joc.91

Basu, S. (1997). The conservatism principle and the asymmetric timeliness of earnings. *Journal of Accounting and Economics*, *24*(1), 3–37. https://doi.org/10.1016/S0165-4101(97)00014-1

Basu, S., & Waymire, G. B. (2006). Recordkeeping and human evolution. *Accounting Horizons*, *20*(3), 201–229. https://doi.org/10.2308/acch.2006.20.3.201

Basu, S., Kirk, M., & Waymire, G. (2009). Memory, transaction records, and "The Wealth of Nations." *Accounting, Organizations and Society, 34*(8), 895–917. https://doi.org/10.1016/j.aos.2009.07.002

Bates, M. J. (1999). The invisible substrate of information science. *Journal of the American Society for Information Science, 50*(12), 1043–1050. https://doi.org/10.1002/(SICI)1097-4571(1999)50:12<1043::AID-ASI1>3.0.CO;2-X

Batista, D., Kim, H., Lemieux, V. L., Stancic, H., & Unnithan, C. (2021). Blockchains and provenance: How a technical system for tracing origins, ownership and authenticity can transform social trust. In V. L. Lemieux & C. Feng (Eds.), *Building decentralized trust* (pp. 111–128). Springer.

Baumgaertner, B., Carlisle, J. E., & Justwan, F. (2018) The influence of political ideology and trust on willingness to vaccinate. *PLoS ONE, 13*(1). https://doi.org/10.1371/journal.pone.019172

Baycara, Y. (2014, December 2). "Business records" exception to hearsay in the Ontario Evidence Act. *CanLII Connects*. https://canliiconnects.org/en/commentaries/34810#_ftn2

Baydakova, A. (2021, January 28). Inside Iran's onslaught on bitcoin mining. *Coindesk*. www.coindesk.com/inside-irans-onslaught-on-bitcoin-mining

BBC. (2021, January 22). Google threatens to withdraw search engine from Australia. *BBC News*. www.bbc.com/news/world-australia-55760673

Beal, P. (2011). Diplomatic. In P. Beal, *A dictionary of English manuscript terminology, 1450–2000*. Oxford University Press. Online ed.

Beatty, P., Reay, I., Dick, S., & Miller, J. (2011). Consumer trust in e-commerce web sites: A meta-study. *ACM Computing Surveys, 43*(3), 1–46. https://doi.org/10.1145/1922649.1922651

Becker, L. C. (1996). Trust as noncognitive security about motives. *Ethics, 107*(1), 43–61. www.jstor.org/stable/2382243

Berger, P. L., & Luckmann, T. (1966). *The social construction of reality: A treatise in the sociology of knowledge*. Anchor Books.

Berman, E. M. (1997). Dealing with cynical citizens. *Public Administration Review, 57*(2), 105–112. https://doi.org/10.2307/977058

Berti-Equille, L., & Ba, M. L. (2016). Veracity of big data: Challenges of cross-modal truth discovery. *Journal of Data and Information Quality, 7*(3), 1–3. https://doi.org/10.1145/2935753

Berti-Équille, L., & Borge-Holthoefer, J. (2015). Veracity of data: From truth discovery computation algorithms to models of misinformation dynamics. *Synthesis Lectures on Data Management, 7*(3), 1–155. https://doi.org/10.2200/S00676ED1V01Y201509DTM042

Bhattacharjee, A., Badsha, S., Shahid, A. R., Livani, H., & Sengupta, S. (2020). Block-phasor: A decentralized blockchain framework to enhance security of synchrophasor. In *Proceedings of the 2020 IEEE Kansas Power and Energy Conference (KPEC), Manhattan, KS, USA, July 13–14, 2020* (pp. 290–295). IEEE. https://doi.org/10.1109/KPEC47870.2020.9167676

Bheemaiah, K. (2015). Why business schools need to teach about the blockchain. http://dx.doi.org/10.2139/ssrn.2596465

BIP-0009. (2020, September 2). In *GitHub*. https://github.com/bitcoin/bips/blob/master/bip-0009.mediawiki

BIPs. (2021, March 15). In *GitHub*. https://github.com/bitcoin/bips/blob/master/README.mediawiki

Bitcoin. (2015a, June 26). Implementation of BIP 101: Maximum block size increase#6341. *GitHub*. https://github.com/bitcoin/bitcoin/pull/6341

Bitcoin. (2015b, August 6). Implement hard fork to allow bigger blocks. *GitHub*. https://github.com/bitcoinxt/bitcoinxt/commit/946e3ba8c7806a66c2b834d3817ff0c986c0811b

Bitcoin. (2021). *BitcoinCore: Bitcoin development*. Bitcoin. https://bitcoin.org/en/development#dev-communities

Bitcoin improvement proposals. (2020, May 13). In *Bitcoin Wiki*. https://en.bitcoin.it/wiki/Bitcoin_Improvement_Proposals

Bitcoin SV. (2019, May 23). Bitcoin creator Craig S. Wright (Satoshi Nakamoto) granted US copyright registrations for the Bitcoin white paper and code. *Cision PR Newswire*. www.prnewswire.com/news-releases/bitcoin-creator-craig-s-wright-satoshi-nakamoto-granted-us-copyright-registrations-for-the-bitcoin-white-paper-and-code-300855914.html

Bitcoin Wiki. (2018). How many confirmations is enough? *Bitcoin Wiki*. https://en.bitcoin.it/wiki/Confirmation#How_Many_Confirmations_Is_Enough

Bitcoin XT. (2020, June 30). In *Bitcoin Wiki*. https://en.bitcoin.it/wiki/Bitcoin_XT

Bitnation. (2019). *Enter Pangea: The internet of sovereignty*. Bitnation. https://tse.bitnation.co

Bjarnason, E. (2019, April 15). Iceland is a bitcoin miner's haven, but not everyone is happy. *Al Jazeera*. www.aljazeera.com/features/2019/4/15/iceland-is-a-bitcoin-miners-haven-but-not-everyone-is-happy

Blind, P. K. (2007, June 26–29). *Building trust in government in the twenty-first century: Review of the literature and emerging issues* [Paper presentation]. 7th Global Forum on Reinventing Government, Building Trust in Government, Vienna, Austria.

Blumler, J. G. (2016). The fourth age of political communication. *Politiques de Communication*, *1*(6), 19–30. https://doi.org/10.3917/pdc.006.0019

Bodó, B. (2020, July). Mediated trust: A theoretical framework to address the trustworthiness of technological trust mediators. *New Media & Society*. https://doi.org/10.1177/1461444820939922

Borgman, C. L. (2016). *Big data, little data, no data: Scholarship in the networked world*. MIT Press.

Borkowski, M., Sigwart, M., Frauenthaler, P., Hukkinen, T., & Schulte, S. (2019). DeXTT: Deterministic cross-blockchain token transfers. *IEEE Access*, *7*, 111030–111042. https://doi.org/10.1109/ACCESS.2019.2934707

Bosri, R., Uzzal, A. R., Omar, A. A., Hasan, A. S. M. T., & Bhuiyan, M. Z. A. (2019). Towards a privacy-preserving voting system through blockchain technologies. In *Proceedings of the IEEE 17th International Conference on Dependable, Autonomic and Secure Computing, IEEE 17th International Conference on Pervasive Intelligence and Computing, IEEE 5th International Conference on Cloud and Big Data Computing, IEEE 4th Cyber Science and Technology Congress (DASC/PICom/CBDCom/CyberSciTech 2019), Fukuoka, Japan, August 5–8, 2019* (pp. 602–608). IEEE. https://doi.org/10.1109/DASC/PiCom/CBDCom/CyberSciTech.2019.00116

Boynton, J. (2021, February 4). Note to readers: Our disappearing headlines. *Toronto Star*. www.thestar.com/business/opinion/2021/02/04/note-to-readers-our-disappearing-headlines.html

Bradbury, D. (2013, October 24). Bitcoin core development update #5 brings better transaction fees and embedded data. *Coindesk*. www.coindesk.com/bitcoin-core-dev-update-5-transaction-fees-embedded-data

Brandtzaeg, P. B., & Følstad, A. (2017). Trust and distrust in online fact-checking services. *Communications of the ACM*, *60*(9), 65–71. https://doi.org/10.1145/3122803

Bratspies, R. M. (2018). Cryptocurrency and the myth of the trustless transaction. *Michigan Technology Law Review*, *25*(1). https://repository.law.umich.edu/mttlr/vol25/iss1/2

Brenneke, A. (1953). *Archivkunde. Ein beitrag zur theorie und geschichte des Europäischen archivwesens*. Koehler & Amelang.

Briet, S. (2006). *What is documentation? English translation of the classic French text* (R. E. Day, L. Martinet, & H. G. B. Anghelescu, Trans. & Eds.). Scarecrow Press. Original work published in 1951.

Broad, C. D. (1925). *The mind and its place in nature*. Routledge & Kegan Paul.

Brooke, C. N. I. (1970). The teaching of diplomatic. *Journal of the Society of Archivists*, *4*(1), 1–9. https://doi.org/10.1080/00379817009513930

Brown, J. S., & Duguid, P. (1996). The social life of documents; introduction by Esther Dyson. *First Monday*, *1*(1). https://doi.org/10.5210/fm.v1i1.466

Brunton, F. (2019). *Digital cash: A cultural history*. Princeton University Press.

Bui, T., Cooper, D., Collomosse, J., Bell, M., Green, A., Sheridan, J., Higgins, J., Das, A., Keller, J., Thereaux, O., & Brown, A. (2019). ARCHANGEL: Tamper-proofing video archives using temporal content hashes on the blockchain. In *Proceedings of the 2019 IEEE/CVF Conference on Computer Vision and Pattern Recognition Workshops (CVPRW), Long Beach, CA, USA, June 16–17, 2019* (pp. 2793–2801). https://doi.org/10.1109/CVPRW.2019.00338

Bui, T., Cooper, D., Collomosse, J., Bell, M., Green, A., Sheridan, J., Higgins, J., Das, A., Keller, J. R., & Thereaux, O. (2020). Tamper-proofing video with hierarchical attention autoencoder hashing on blockchain. *IEEE Transactions on Multimedia*, *22*(11), 2858–2872. https://doi.org/10.1109/TMM.2020.2967640

Bumblauskas, D., Mann, A., Dugan, B., & Rittmer, J. (2020). A blockchain use case in food distribution: Do you know where your food has been? *International Journal of Information Management*, *52*. https://doi.org/10.1016/j.ijinfomgt.2019.09.004

Buneman, P., & Tan, W. C. (2007). Provenance in databases. In *SIMGOD '07: Proceedings of the 2007 ACM SIGMOD International Conference on Management of Data, Beijing, China, June 12–14, 2007* (pp. 1171–1173). Association for Computing Machinery. https://doi.org/10.1145/1247480.1247646

Bureau of Canadian Archivists. (2008). *Rules for archival description: Appendix D: Glossary*. Bureau of Canadian Archivists – Planning Committee on Descriptive Standards.

Buterin, V. (2013). *Ethereum white paper*. Ethereum. https://ethereum.org/en/whitepaper

Butijn, B-J., Tamburi, D. A., & van den Heuvel, W. J. (2020). Blockchains: A systematic multivocal literature review. *ACM Computing Surveys*, *53*(3), 1–37. https://doi.org/10.1145/3369052

Butterfield, A., Ngondi, G. E., & Kerr, A. (Eds.). (2016). Abstraction. In *A dictionary of computer science* (7th ed.). Oxford University Press. Online ed. https://doi.org/10.1093/acref/9780199688975.001.0001

Cahlan, S. (2020, February 13). How misinformation helped spark an attempted coup in Gabon. *Washington Post*. www.washingtonpost.com/politics/2020/02/13/how-sick-president-suspect-video-helped-sparked-an-attempted-coup-gabon

Cai, L., & Zhu, Y. (2015). The challenges of data quality and data quality assessment in the big data era. *Data Science Journal, 14*. http://doi.org/10.5334/dsj-2015-002

Caplan, R., Hanson, L., & Donovan, J. (2018, February 21). *Dead reckoning: Navigating content moderation after "fake news."* Data & Society Research Institute. https://datasociety.net/library/dead-reckoning

Carmen, A. (2016, September 13). The World Anti-Doping Agency says it was hacked by Russia. *The Verge*. www.theverge.com/2016/9/13/12903546/wada-attack-cyber-russia-anti-doping

Carter, D. (2016). Hustle and brand: The sociotechnical shaping of influence. *Social Media + Society, 2*(3). https://doi.org/10.1177/2056305116666305

Carter, R. G. S. (2006). Of things said and unsaid: Power, archival silences, and power in silence. *Archivaria, 61*, 215–233. https://archivaria.ca/index.php/archivaria/article/view/12541

Casey, E. (2019). The chequered past and risky future of digital forensics. *Australian Journal of Forensic Sciences, 51*(6), 649–664. https://doi.org/10.1080/00450618.2018.1554090

Casey, M. J. (2021, February 26). Funding culture and empowering artists with NFTs, featuring Lethabo Huma and Cuy Sheffield [Audio podcast episode]. In *Money Reimagined*. CoinDesk. www.coindesk.com/podcasts/coindesks-money-reimagined/nfts-culture-art-power-podcast

Castaldo, S., Premazzi, K., & Zerbini, F. (2010). The meaning (s) of trust: A content analysis on the diverse conceptualizations of trust in scholarly research on business relationships. *Journal of Business Ethics, 96*(4), 657–668. https://doi.org/10.1007/s10551-010-0491-4

Castells, M. (2009). *The rise of the network society: The information age: Economy, society and culture*, vol. 1 (2nd ed.). Wiley-Blackwell.

Ceci, S. J., & Williams, W. M. (2020, October 25). The psychology of fact-checking. *Scientific American*. www.scientificamerican.com/article/the-psychology-of-fact-checking1

Cencetti, G. (1939). Il fondamento teorico della dottrina archivistica. *Archivi* 6, pp. 7–13 (reprinted in 1970 in *Scritti archivistici*, pp. 38–46).

Chan, C. C. K., Kumar, V., Delaney, S., & Gochoo, M. (2020). Combating deepfakes: Multi-LSTM and blockchain as proof of authenticity for digital media. In *Proceedings of 2020 IEEE/ITU International Conference on Artificial Intelligence for Good (AI4 G), Geneva, Switzerland, September 21–25, 2020* (pp. 55–62). IEEE. https://doi.org/10.1109/AI4G50087.2020.9311067

Charikar, M., Steinhardt, J., & Valiant, G. (2017). Learning from untrusted data. In *STOC 2017: Proceedings of the 49th Annual ACM SIGACT Symposium on Theory of Computing, Montreal, Canada, June 2017* (pp. 47–60). Association of Computing Machinery. https://doi.org/10.1145/3055399.3055491

Charles, W., Marler, N., Long, L., & Manion, S. (2019). Blockchain compliance by design: Regulatory considerations for blockchain in clinical research. *Frontiers in Blockchain, 2*. https://doi.org/10.3389/fbloc.2019.00018

Chavez-Dreyfuss, G. (2015, May 15). Honduras to build land title registry using bitcoin technology. *Reuters*. www.reuters.com/article/usa-honduras-technology-idINKBN0OO1V720150515

Cheema, G. S. (2010). Building trust in government: An introduction. In G. S. Cheema & V. Popovski (Eds.), *Building trust in government: Innovations in governance reform in Asia* (pp. 1–21). United Nations University Press. https://collections.unu.edu/eserv/UNU:2502/ebrary9789280811896.pdf

Choi, W., & Haigh, M. (2019). Analyzing divergent methodologies for political fact checking: United States and South Korea. *Proceedings of the Association for Information Science and Technology, 56*(1), 627–628. https://doi.org/10.1002/pra2.112

Choy, W. L., & Teng, P. (2017). When smart contracts are outsmarted: The parity wallet "freeze" and software liability in the Internet of value. *National Law Review, 11*(77). www.natlawreview.com/article/when-smart-contracts-are-outsmarted-parity-wallet-freeze-and-software-liability

Christensen, D. (2007). Epistemology of disagreement: The good news. *Philosophical Review, 116*(2), 187–217. https://doi.org/10.1215/00318108-2006-035

Christensen, D. (2009). Disagreement as evidence: The epistemology of controversy. *Philosophy Compass, 4*(5), 756–767. https://doi.org/10.1111/j.1747-9991.2009.00237.x

Christensen, D. (2013). Epistemic modesty defended. In D. Christensen & J. Lackey (Eds.), *The epistemology of disagreement: New essays* (pp. 1–25). Oxford University Press.

Christidis, K., & Devetsikiotis, M. (2016). Blockchains and smart contracts for the internet of things. *IEEE Access, 4*, 2292–2303. https://doi.org/10.1109/ACCESS.2016.2566339

Clanchy, M. T. (1980). "Tenacious letters": Archives and memory in the Middle Ages. *Archivaria, 11*, 115–125. https://archivaria.ca/index.php/archivaria/article/view/1084

Clanchy, M. T. (2012). *From memory to written record: England 1066–1307* (3rd ed.). Wiley-Blackwell.

Clark, J. (2016). The long road to Bitcoin. In A. Narayanan et al. *Bitcoin and cryptocurrency technologies: A comprehensive introduction* (pp. ix–xxvii). Princeton University Press.

Cobain, I. (2016). *The history thieves: Secrets, lies and the shaping of a modern nation*. Portobello Books.

Coeckelbergh, M., & Reijers, W. (2016). Cryptocurrencies as narrative technologies. *ACM SIGCAS Computers and Society, 45*(3), 172–178. https://doi.org/10.1145/2874239.2874264

Cohen, F. (2015). A tale of two traces – Diplomatics and forensics. In G. Peterson & S. Shenoi (Eds.), *IFIP advances in information and communication technology*, vol. 462. *Advances in Digital Forensics XI, DigitalForensics 2015, Orlando, FL, USA, January 26–28, 2015* (pp. 3–27). Springer. https://doi.org/10.1007/978-3-319-24123-4_1

Coleman, J. S. (1990). *Foundations of social theory*. Harvard University Press.

Collomosse, J., Bui, T., Brown, A., Sheridan, J., Green, A., Bell, M., Fawcett, J., Higgins, J., & Thereaux, O. (2018). ARCHANGEL: Trusted archives of digital public documents. In *Proceedings of DocEng '18: 18th ACM Symposium on Document*

Engineering, Halifax, NS, Canada, August 28–31, 2018 (pp. 1–4). Association for Computing Machinery. https://doi.org/10.1145/3209280.3229120

Computer History Museum. (2003). *The origins and impact of VisiCalc*. Computer History Museum. https://computerhistory.org/events/origins-impact-visicalc/

Computer History Museum. (2021). *Timeline of computer history: Software & languages*. Computer History Museum. www.computerhistory.org/timeline/software-languages/

Conway, P. (2010). Modes of seeing: Digitized photographic archives and the experienced user. *American Archivist, 73*(2), 425–462. www.jstor.org/stable/23290754

Cook, J., Lewandowsky, S., & Ecker, U. K. H. (2017). Neutralizing misinformation through inoculation: Exposing misleading argumentation techniques reduces their influence. *PloS one, 12*(5), e0175799. https://doi.org/10.1371/journal.pone.0175799

Cook, T. (2009). CHR forum: The archive(s) is a foreign country: Historians, archivists, and the changing archival landscape. *Canadian Historical Review, 90*(3), 497–534. https://doi.org/10.3138/chr.90.3.497

Cornelius, K. B. (2018). Standard form contracts and a smart contract future. *Internet Policy Review, 7*(2). https://doi.org/10.14763/2018.2.790

Cornelius, K. B. (2020). Smart contracts as evidence: Trust, records, and the future of decentralized transactions. In J. Hunsinger, M. M. Allen & L. Klastrup (Eds.), *Second international handbook of internet research* (pp. 627–646). Springer. https://doi.org/10.1007/978-94-024-1555-1_28

Cosmides, L., & Tooby, J. (1992). Cognitive adaptations for social exchange. In J. H. Barkow, J. Tooby & L. Cosmides (Eds.), *The adapted mind: Evolutionary psychology and the generation of culture* (pp. 163–228). Oxford University Press.

Cramer, M. (2020, January 18). National Archives apologizes for altering image of 2017 Women's March. *New York Times*. www.nytimes.com/2020/01/18/us/national-archives-womens-march-images.html

Cukier, K., & Mayer-Schoenberger, V. (2013). The rise of big data: How it's changing the way we think about the world. *Foreign Affairs, 92*(3), 28–40. www.jstor.org/stable/23526834

Daian, P. (2016, June 18). Analysis of the DAO exploit. *Hacking, Distributed*. https://hackingdistributed.com/2016/06/18/analysis-of-the-dao-exploit/

Dale, K., Sunkavalli, K., Johnson, M. K., Vlasic, D., Matusik, W. & Pfister, H. (2011). Video face replacement. In *Proceedings of ACM SIGGRAPH Asia 2011 Conference (SA '11), Hong Kong, China, December 13–15, 2011* (Article 130). Association of Computing Machinery. https://doi.org/10.1145/2024156.2024164

Dalesio, E. (2012, March 14). NC county sues banks over mortgage robo-signing. *Yahoo! News*. https://news.yahoo.com/news/nc-county-sues-banks-over-212905726.html

Daniels, M. F, & Walch, T. (1984). *A modern archives reader*. National Archives and Records Service, US General Services Administration.

Das, D., & Dutta, A. (2020). Bitcoin's energy consumption: Is it the Achilles heel to miner's revenue? *Economics Letters, 186*. https://doi.org/10.1016/j.econlet.2019.108530

Dasgupta, P. (1988). Trust as a commodity. In D. Gambetta (Ed.), *Trust: Making and breaking cooperative relations* (pp. 49–72). Basil Blackwell.

Dasgupta, S. (2014). *It began with Babbage: The genesis of computer science*. Oxford University Press.

Dasgupta, S. (2016). *Computer science: A very short introduction*. Oxford University Press.

Decred. (n.d.). *History*. Decred. www.decred.org/history

Decred. (2020). *Decred constitution*. Decred. https://docs.decred.org/governance/decred-constitution

Decred. (2021, April 8). *Decred's proposal platform politeia: The decision-making force behind the ~$125 M Decred DAO*. [Video]. YouTube. www.youtube.com/watch?v=dfpUgwXBUmM

De Filippi, P. F., & Wright, A. (2018). *Blockchain and the law: The rule of code*. Harvard University Press.

De Filippi, P. F., Mannan, M., & Reijers, W. (2020). Blockchain as a confidence machine: The problem of trust & challenges of governance. *Technology in Society, 62*. https://doi.org/10.1016/j.techsoc.2020.101284

Delmolino, K., Arnett, M., Kosba, A., Miller, A., & Shi, E. (2016). Step by step towards creating a safe smart contract: Lessons and insights from a cryptocurrency lab. In J. Clark, S. Meiklejohn, P. Y. A. Ryan, D. Wallach, M. Brenner & K. Rohloff (Eds.), *Lecture notes in computer science*, vol. 9604: *FC 2016 International Workshops, BITCOIN, VOTING, and WAHC, Christ Church, Barbados, February 26, 2016, Revised selected papers* (pp. 79–94). Springer. https://doi.org/10.1007/978-3-662-53357-4_6

Derakhshan, H., & Wardle, C. (2017). Information disorder: Definitions. In *Understanding and addressing the disinformation ecosystem* [Papers from the workshop held at the Annenberg School for Communication, December 15–16, 2017], (pp. 5–12). Annenberg School for Communication (University of Pennsylvania), First Draft, & Knight Foundation. https://firstdraftnews.org/wp-content/uploads/2018/03/The-Disinformation-Ecosystem-20180207-v4.pdf?x67996

Derrida, J. (1996). *Archive fever: A Freudian impression*. University of Chicago Press.

de Soto, H. (2000). *The mystery of capital: Why capitalism triumphs in the West and fails everywhere else*. Basic Books.

Deutch, J. (2020). Challenges in codifying events within large and diverse data sets of human rights documentation: Memory, intent, and bias. *International Journal of Communication 14*, 5055–5071. https://web.b.ebscohost.com/ehost/pdfviewer/pdfviewer?vid=0&sid=adf7998a-49eb-4c56-b683-aff7f3e7d317%40sessionmgr103

Deutsch, M., & Gerard, H. B. (1955). A study of normative and informational social influences upon individual judgment. *Journal of Abnormal and Social Psychology, 51*(3), 629–636. https://doi.org/10.1037/h0046408

de Vries, A. (2018). Bitcoin's growing energy problem. *Joule, 2*(5), 801–805. https://doi.org/10.1016/j.joule.2018.04.016

Diffie, W. (1988). The first ten years of public-key cryptography. *Proceedings of the IEEE, 76*(5), 560–577. https://doi.org/10.1109/5.4442

Digiconomist. (2021). Bitcoin energy consumption index. *Digiconomist*. https://digiconomist.net/bitcoin-energy-consumption

Digital Currency Initiative. (n.d.). *Bitcoin Core development*. MIT Media Lab. https://dci.mit.edu/bitcoin-core-development

Directorate-General for Communication Networks, Content and Technology. (2018). *A multi-dimensional approach to disinformation: Report of the independent high level group on fake news and online disinformation*. European Commission. http://ec .europa.eu/newsroom/dae/document.cfm?doc_id=50271

DiResta, R. (2019, December 30). Year in review: "Journalists need to recognise they are a target of influence operations." *First Draft*. https://firstdraftnews.org/latest/year-in-review-journalists-need-to-recognise-they-are-a-target-of-influence-operations/

DiResta, R. (2020, July 31). AI-generated text is the scariest deepfake of all. *Wired*. www.wired.com/story/ai-generated-text-is-the-scariest-deepfake-of-all/

Dixit, A., & Norta, A. (2018). A self-aware contract for decentralized peer-to-peer (P2P) commerce. In *Proceedings: 2018 IEEE 3rd International Workshops on Foundations and Applications of Self* Systems (FAS* W), Trento, Italy, September 3–7, 2018* (pp. 17–19). IEEE. https://doi.org/10.1109/FAS-W.2018.00018

Donaldson, D. R. (2019). Trust in archives – Trust in digital archival content framework. *Archivaria, 88*, 50–83. https://archivaria.ca/index.php/archivaria/article/view/13697

Donaldson, D. R., & Bell, L. (2019). Security, archivists, and digital collections. *Journal of Archival Organization, 15*(1–2), 1–19. https://doi.org/10.1080/15332748 .2019.1609311

Dooley, J. F. (2018). *History of cryptography and cryptanalysis: Codes, Ciphers, and their algorithms*. Springer.

Dotan, J. (2021, June 10). *Trustless truth: How private and public ledgers can take on misinformation and win* [Keynote presentation]. Hyperledger Global Forum 2021, Virtual. www.youtube.com/watch?v=w1r3Fsjaw0s

Dretske, F. I. (1982). A cognitive cul-de-sac. *Mind, 91*(361), 109–111. www.jstor.org /stable/i313351

Du, M., Chen, Q., Chen, J., & Ma, X. (2020). An optimized consortium blockchain for medical information sharing. *IEEE Transactions on Engineering Management (early access)*. https://doi.org/10.1109/TEM.2020.2966832

Duddu, V. (2018). A survey of adversarial machine learning in cyber warfare. *Defence Science Journal, 68*(4), 356–366. https://doi.org/10.14429/dsj.68.12371

Dunn, J. (1988). Trust and political agency. In D. Gambetta (Ed.), *Trust: Making and breaking cooperative relations* (pp. 73–93). Basil Blackwell.

Dupont, Q. (2019). *Cryptocurrencies and blockchains*. Polity Press.

Duranti, L. (1989). The odyssey of records managers. Part II: From the Middle Ages to modern times. *Records Management Quarterly, 23*(4), 3–10.

Duranti, L. (1995). Reliability and authenticity: The concepts and their implications. *Archivaria, 39*, 5–10. https://archivaria.ca/index.php/archivaria/article/view/12063/ 13035

Duranti, L. (1996). Archives as place. *Archives and Manuscripts, 24*(2), 242–255. https://publications.archivists.org.au/index.php/asa/article/view/8579

Duranti, L. (1998). *Diplomatics: New uses for an old science*. Scarecrow Press.

Duranti, L. (1999). Concepts and principles for the management of electronic records, or records management theory is archival diplomatics. *Records Management Journal, 9* (3), 149–171. https://doi.org/10.1108/EUM0000000007248

Duranti, L. (2009). From digital diplomatics to digital records forensics. *Archivaria, 68*, 39–66. https://archivaria.ca/index.php/archivaria/article/view/13229

Duranti, L. (2018). Whose truth? Records and archives as evidence in the era of post-truth and disinformation. In C. Brown (Ed.), *Archival futures* (pp. 19–32). Facet.

Duranti L., & Michetti, G. (2016). The archival method. In A. Gilliland, S. McKemmish & A. J. Lau (Eds.), *Research in the archival multiverse* (pp. 75–95). Monash University Publishing.

Duranti, L., & Preston, R. (Eds.) (2008). *International research on permanent authentic records in electronic systems (InterPARES) 2: Experiential, interactive and dynamic records.* Associazione Nazionale Archivistica Italiana. www.interpares.org/ip2/dis play_file.cfm?doc=ip2_book_complete.pdf

Duranti, L., & Rogers, C. (2012). Trust in digital records: An increasingly cloudy legal area. *Computer Law & Security Review, 28*(5), 522–531. https://doi.org/10.1016/j .clsr.2012.07.009

Duranti, L., & Rogers, C. (2019). *Trusting records in the cloud.* Facet Publishing.

Duranti, L., & Thibodeau, K. (2006). The concept of record in interactive, experiential and dynamic environments: The view of InterPARES. *Archival Science, 6*(1), 13–68. https://doi.org/10.1007/s10502-006-9021-7

Dutton, W. H., Reisdorf, B., Dubois, E., & Blank, G. (2017). *Social shaping of the politics of internet search and networking: Moving beyond filter bubbles, echo chambers, and fake news* (Working Paper No. 2944191). Quello Center. http://dx .doi.org/10.2139/ssrn.2944191

Dwyer, C. (2017, February 3). Is blockchain a "future of work gamechanger"? *CPO Rising.* https://cporising.com/2017/02/03/is-blockchain-a-future-of-work-gamechan ger-2/

Economist. (2015a, October 31). Blockchains: The great chain of being sure about things. *Economist,* (417), 21–24. www.economist.com/briefing/2015/10/31/the-great -chain-of-being-sure-about-things

Economist. (2015b, October 31). The promise of the blockchain: The trust machine. *Economist,* (417), 13. www.economist.com/leaders/2015/10/31/the-trust-machine

Economist. (2017, May 6). The world's most valuable resource is no longer oil, but data. *Economist.* www.economist.com/leaders/2017/05/06/the-worlds-most-valuable- resource-is-no-longer-oil-but-data

Edelman. (2015). *2015 Edelman trust barometer: Executive summary.* www .edelman.com/trust/2015-trust-barometer

Edelman. (2016). *2016 Edelman trust barometer: Executive summary.* www .edelman.com/trust/2016-trust-barometer

Edelman. (2017). *2017 Edelman trust barometer.* www.edelman.com/trust/2017-trust- barometer

Edelman. (2020). *2020 Edelman trust barometer.* www.edelman.com/trust/2020-trust- barometer

Edwards, M. (2015, April 20). *The trust deficit – concepts and causes of low public trust in governments* (E/C.16/2015/CRP.3/Rev.1) [Paper presentation]. 14th Session of the United Nations Committee of Experts on Public Administration, New York. https:// publicadministration.un.org/en/cepa/session14

Elga, A. (2007). Reflection and disagreement. *Noûs, 41*(3), 478–502. https://doi.org/10 .1111/j.1468-0068.2007.00656.x

Elghawaby, A. (2018, August 2). Social media's self-regulation isn't enough. *Centre for International Governance Innovation*. www.cigionline.org/articles/social-medias-self-regulation-isnt-enough

EMA [European Medicines Agency]. (2021, January 25). Cyberattack on EMA – update 6. www.ema.europa.eu/en/news/cyberattack-ema-update-6

Enders, A. M., Uscinski, J. E., Klofstad, C., & Stoler, J. (2020). The different forms of COVID-19 misinformation and their consequences. *Harvard Kennedy School (HKS) Misinformation Review*. https://doi.org/10.37016/mr-2020-48

Eppard, P. (2008). Appendix 20: Creator guidelines: Making and maintaining digital materials: Guidelines for individuals. In L. Duranti & R. Preston (Eds.), *International research on permanent authentic records in electronic systems (InterPARES) 2: Experiential, interactive and dynamic records* (pp. 684–697). Associazione Nazionale Archivistica Italiana. www.interpares.org/ip2/display_file.cfm?doc=ip2_book_appendix_20.pdf

Eskandari, S., Clark, J., Barrera, D., & Stobert, E. (2015, February 7). *A first look at the usability of bitcoin key management* [Paper presentation]. 2015 Network and Distributed System Security (NDSS) Symposium, San Diego, CA, United States. www.ndss-symposium.org/wp-content/uploads/2017/09/05_3_3.pdf

Espinal, R., Hartlyn, J., & Kelly, J. M. (2006). Performance still matters: Explaining trust in government in the Dominican Republic. *Comparative Political Studies, 39*(2), 200–223. https://doi.org/10.1177/0010414005281933

Ess, C. M. (2020). Trust and information communications technologies. In J. Simon (Ed.), *The Routledge handbook of trust and philosophy*. Routledge.

Ethereum. (2020). *Proof-of-stake (POS)*. Ethereum. https://ethereum.org/en/developers/docs/consensus-mechanisms/pos

Ethereum. (2021a). *Glossary*. Ethereum. https://ethereum.org/en/glossary

Ethereum. (2021b, March 12). *ERC 721 Non-fungible token standard*. Ethereum. https://ethereum.org/en/developers/docs/standards/tokens/erc-721

Ethos.dev. (2020, May 23). The Beacon Chain Ethereum 2.0 explainer you need to read first. *ethos.dev*. https://ethos.dev/beacon-chain

European Commission (2018, March). *A multi-dimensional approach to disinformation: Report of the independent high level group on fake news and online disinformation*. European Union. https://op.europa.eu/en/publication-detail/-/publication/6ef4df8b-4cea-11e8-be1d-01aa75ed71a1/language-en

Eyal, I., & Sirer, E. G. (2014). Majority is not enough: Bitcoin mining is vulnerable. In N. Christin & R. Safavi-Naini (Eds.), *Lecture notes in computer science*, vol. 8437: *Financial Cryptography and Data Security: 18th International Conference, FC2014, Christ Church, Barbados, March 3–7, 2014, revised selected papers* (pp. 436–454). Springer.

Faller, M. T. (2002). *Semantics and pragmatics of evidentials in Cuzco Quechua* [Doctoral dissertation, Stanford University].

Fallis, D. (2006). Social epistemology and information science. *Annual Review of Information Science and Technology, 40*(1), 475–519. https://doi.org/10.1002/aris.1440400119

Faulkner, P. (2007a). A genealogy of trust. *Episteme, 4*(3), 305–321. https://doi.org/10.3366/E174236000700010X

Faulkner, P. (2007b). On telling and trusting. *Mind, 116*(464), 875–902. https://doi.org /10.1093/mind/fzm875

FBI. (2019). *2019 Internet crime report.* Federal Bureau of Investigation. https://ic3pdfs .blob.core.usgovcloudapi.net/docs/2019_IC3Report.pdf

Federal Republic of Germany. (2017, September 1). Gesetz zur Verbesserung der Rechtsdurchsetzung in sozialen Netzwerken (Netzwerksdurchsetzungsgesetz – NetzDG). Bundesgesetzblatt [BGBl.] [Federal Law Gazette] I at 3352. https://perma .cc/4LPN-WS7Z (original), http://perma.cc/J86H-GTY4 (unofficial English translation).

Federal Trade Commission. (2019). *Consumer information: How to recognize and avoid phishing scams.* www.consumer.ftc.gov/articles/how-recognize-and-avoid-phishing-scams

Feldman, R. (2006). Epistemological puzzles about disagreement. In S. Hetherington (Ed.), *Epistemic futures* (pp. 216–236). Oxford University Press.

Feldman, R. (2007). Reasonable religious disagreement. In L. Antony (Ed.), *Philosophers without gods: Meditations on atheism and the secular life* (pp. 194–214). Oxford University Press.

Ferguson, M. C. (1960–1). A day in court in Justinian's Rome: Some problems of evidence, proof, and justice in Roman law. *Iowa Law Review, 46.*

Fernández-Caramès, T. M., & Fraga-Lamas, P. (2020). Towards post-quantum blockchain: A review on blockchain cryptography resistant to quantum computing attacks. *IEEE Access, 8,* 21091–21116. https://doi.org/10.1109/ACCESS.2020.2968985

Ferrara, E., Varol, O., Davis, C., Menczer, F., & Flammini, A. (2016). The rise of social bots. *Communications of the ACM, 59*(7), 96–104. https://doi.org/10.1145/2818717

Filippova, E., Scharl, A., & Filippov P. (2019). Blockchain: An empirical investigation of its scope for improvement. In J. Joshi, S. Nepal, Q. Zhang & L. J. Zhang. (Eds.), *Lecture notes in computer science,* vol. 11521: *Blockchain – ICBC 2019: Second international conference, held as part of the Services Conference Federation, SCF 2019, San Diego, CA, USA, June 25–30, 2019, proceedings* (pp. 1–17). Springer.

Finck, M. (2018). Blockchains and data protection in the European Union. *European Data Protection Law Review, 4*(1), 17–35. https://doi.org/10.21552/edpl/2018/1/6

Finney, H. (2008, November 8). Bitcoin P2P e-cash paper. *Cryptography Mailing List.* https://satoshi.nakamotoinstitute.org/emails/cryptography/6

Fiorina, M. P. (1978). Economic retrospective voting in American national elections: A micro-analysis. *American Journal of Political Science, 22*(2), 426–443. https://doi .org/10.2307/2110623

Fisher, M., Cox, J. W., & Hermann, P. (2016, December 6). Pizzagate: From rumor, to hashtag, to gunfire in DC. *Washington Post.* www.washingtonpost.com/local/pizza gate-from-rumor-to-hashtag-to-gunfire-in-dc/2016/12/06/4c7def50-bbd4-11e6-94ac-3d324840106c_story.html

Flores, D., Lacombe, C., & Lemieux, V. (2018). *Real estate transaction recording in the blockchain in Brazil* (RCPLAC-01 Case study 1). https://blogs.ubc.ca/record sinthechain/2018/01/26/real-estate-transaction-recording-in-the-blockchain-in-brazil/

Flynn, L. R., Goldsmith, R. E., & Eastman, J. K. (1996). Opinion leaders and opinion seekers: Two new measurement scales. *Journal of the Academy of Marketing Science, 24*(2), 137–147. https://doi.org/10.1177/0092070396242004

Force, D. C. (2010). From Peruvian guano to electronic records: Canadian e-discovery and records professionals. *Archivaria*, *69*, 49–75. https://archivaria.ca/index.php/archivaria/article/view/13261

Foucault, M. (1973). *The order of things: An archaeology of the human sciences.* Vintage.

Foucault, M. (1980). *Power/knowledge: Selected interviews and other writings, 1972–1977.* Vintage.

Frenda, S. J., Knowles, E. D., Saletan, W., & Loftus, E. F. (2013). False memories of fabricated political events. *Journal of Experimental Social Psychology*, *49*(2), 280–286. https://doi.org/10.1016/j.jesp.2012.10.013

Froehlich, T. J. (2020). Ten lessons for the age of disinformation. In K. Dalkir & R. Katz (Eds.), *Navigating fake news, alternative facts, and misinformation in a post-truth world* (pp. 36–88). IGI Global.

Fukuyama, F. (1995). *Trust: The social virtues and the creation of prosperity.* Free Press.

Gambetta, D. (Ed.) (1988). *Trust: Making and breaking cooperative relations.* Basil Blackwell.

Gani, Y., & Aşkaroğlu, M. M. (2019). A voting application which provides data security via blockchain technology. In *Proceedings of the 2019 4th International Conference on Computer Science and Engineering (UBMK), Samsun, Turkey, September 11–15, 2019* (pp. 773–777). IEEE. https://doi.org/10.1109/UBMK.2019.8907111

Gao, X., Clark, G. D., & Lindqvist, J. (2016). Of two minds, multiple addresses, and one ledger: Characterizing opinions, knowledge, and perceptions of Bitcoin across users and non-users. In *Proceedings of the 34th Annual CHI Conference on Human Factors in Computing Systems, CHI'16, San Jose, CA, USA, May 7–12, 2016* (pp. 1656–1668). Association for Computing Machinery.

Garfinkel, H. (Ed.). (2017). *Routledge revivals: Ethnomethodological studies of work.* Routledge. Original work published in 1986.

Gerard, D. (2017). *Attack of the 50 foot blockchain: Bitcoin, blockchain, Ethereum & smart contracts.* David Gerard.

Gettier, E. L. (1963). Is justified true belief knowledge? *Analysis*, *23*(6), 121–123. https://doi.org/10.1093/analys/23.6.121

Ghanem, B., Rosso P., & Rangel, F. (2020). An emotional analysis of false information in social media and news articles. *ACM Transactions on Internet Technology*, *20*(2). https://doi.org/10.1145/3381750

Giddens, A. (1990). *The consequences of modernity.* Stanford University Press.

Gilliland, A. J., McKemmish, S., & Lau, A. J. (Eds.) (2016). *Research in the archival multiverse.* Monash University Publishing.

Gingras, R. (2016, October 13). Labeling fact-check articles in Google News. *Google: The Keyword.* https://blog.google/outreach-initiatives/google-news-initiative/labeling-fact-check-articles-google-news

Goldman, A. I. (1986). *Epistemology and cognition.* Harvard University Press.

Goldman, A. I. (1999). *Knowledge in a social world.* Clarendon Press.

Goldman, A. & Beddor, B. (2016). Reliabilist epistemology. In E. N. Zalta (Ed.), *The Stanford encyclopedia of philosophy* (Winter ed.). Stanford University. https://plato.stanford.edu/archives/win2016/entries/reliabilism

Goldman, A., & O'Connor, C. (2021). Social epistemology. In E. N. Zalta (Ed.), *The Stanford encyclopedia of philosophy* (Spring ed.). Stanford University. https://plato .stanford.edu/archives/spr2021/entries/epistemology-social

Goldthorpe, J. H. (1991). The uses of history in sociology: Reflections on some recent tendencies. *British Journal of Sociology, 42*(2), 211–230. https://doi.org/10.2307/590368

Goldwasser, S., Micali, S., & Rackoff, C. (1989). The knowledge complexity of interactive proof systems. *SIAM Journal on Computing, 18*(1), 186–208. https://doi .org/10.1137/0218012

Golumbia, D. (2016). *The politics of Bitcoin: Software as right-wing extremism.* University of Minnesota Press.

Goodyear, S. (2021, January 15). This man owns $321 M in bitcoin – but he can't access it because he lost his password. *CBC Radio: As It Happens.* www.cbc.ca/radio/asithap pens/as-it-happens-friday-edition-1.5875363/this-man-owns-321m-in-bitcoin-but-he-can-t-access-it-because-he-lost-his-password-1.5875366

Gorwa, R. (2019). What is platform governance? *Information, Communication & Society, 22*(6), 854–871. https://doi.org/10.1080/1369118X.2019.1573914

Graham, P., & Bachman, Z. (2019). Counterexamples to testimonial transmission. In M. Fricker, P. J. Graham, D. Henderson, & N. J. L. L. Pedersen (Eds.), *The Routledge handbook of social epistemology* (pp. 61–78). Routledge.

Graves, L., & Cherubini, F. (2016). *The rise of fact-checking sites in Europe.* Reuters Institute.

Green, A., Bell, M., Sheridan, J., Collomosse, J. P., Bui, T., Brown, A., Fawcett, J., Thereaux, O., & Tennison, J. (2018). Using blockchain to engender trust in public digital archives. In *Proceedings of iPRES 2018, 15th International Conference on Digital Preservation, Boston, MA, USA, September 24–28, 2018.* iPRES. https://osf .io/kefj8

Greenspan, G. (2015, November 2). Smart contracts: The good, the bad and the lazy. *Multichain.* www.multichain.com/blog/2015/11/smart-contracts-good-bad-lazy

Greenspan, G. (2017, May 9). The Blockchain immutability myth. *Coindesk.* www .coindesk.com/blockchain-immutability-myth

Gregor, S. (2006). The nature of theory in information systems. *MIS Quarterly, 30*(3), 611–642. https://aisel.aisnet.org/misq/vol30/iss3/5/

Grönlund, Å., & Horan, T. A. (2005). Introducing e-gov: history, definitions, and issues. *Communications of the Association for Information Systems, 15*(1). https://doi.org/10 .17705/1CAIS.01539

Guess, A. M., Lerner, M., Lyons, B., Montgomery, J. M., Nyhan, B., Reifler, J., & Sircar, N. (2020). A digital media literacy intervention increases discernment between mainstream and false news in the United States and India. *Proceedings of the National Academy of Sciences, 117*(27), 15536–15545. https://doi.org/10.1073 /pnas.1920498117

Habermas, J., McCarthy, T., & McCarthy, T. (1984). *The theory of communicative action,* vol. 1. Beacon Press.

Haley, M. S. (2020, March 16). Arweave's permanent "library of Alexandria" on blockchain to halt censorship, empower information. *Forbes.* www.forbes.com /sites/michaelhaley/2020/03/16/arweaves-permanent-library-of-alexandria-on-blockchain-to-halt-censorship-empower-information/

Hamouda, H., Bushey, J., Lemieux, V., Stewart, J., Rogers, C., Cameron, J., Thibodeau, K., & Feng, C. (2019). Extending the scope of computational archival science: A case study on leveraging archival and engineering approaches to develop a framework to detect and prevent "fake video." In *2019 IEEE International Conference on Big Data (Big Data), Los Angeles, CA, USA, 2019* (pp. 3087–3097). IEEE. https://doi.org/10.1109/BigData47090.2019.9006170

Hannam, K. (2017). This emerging tech company has put Asia's tuna on the blockchain. *Forbes*. www.forbes.com/sites/keshiahannam/2016/09/30/this-emerging-tech-company-has-put-asias-tuna-on-the-blockchain

Hardin, R. (2002). *Trust and trustworthiness*. Russell Sage Foundation.

Hardwig, J. (1991). The role of trust in knowledge. *Journal of Philosophy, 88*(12), 693–708. https://doi.org/10.2307/2027007

Harsin, J. (2018a). A critical guide to fake news: From comedy to tragedy. *Pouvoirs, 164* (1), 99–119. https://doi.org/10.3917/pouv.164.0099

Harsin, J. (2018b). Post-truth and critical communication studies. In *Oxford research encyclopedia of communication*. Oxford University Press. https://doi.org/10.1093 /acrefore/9780190228613.013.757

Harsin, J. (2019). Post-truth and critical communication. In D. L. Cloud (Ed.), *The Oxford encyclopedia of communication and critical cultural studies*. Oxford University Press. https://doi.org/10.1093/acref/9780190459611.001.0001

Harwell, D. (2019, June 13). Scramble is on to detect, stop "deepfake" videos. *Washington Post*.

Hasher, L., Goldstein, D., & Toppino, T. (1977). Frequency and the conference of referential validity. *Journal of Verbal Learning and Verbal Behavior, 16*(1), 107–112. https://doi.org/10.1016/S0022-5371(77)80012-1

Hayes, P. J. (2011). Bollandists. In G. T. Kurian (Ed.), *The encyclopedia of Christian civilization*. Wiley Online. https://doi.org/10.1002/9780470670606.wbecc0173

Hazlett, A. (2015). The maturation of the Gettier problem. *Philosophical Studies, 172* (1), 1–6. https://doi.org/10.1007/s11098-014-0385-x

Hearn, M. (2015a, August 15). Why is Bitcoin forking? *Medium*. https://medium.com /faith-and-future/why-is-bitcoin-forking-d647312d22c1

Hearn, M. (2015b, August 27). An XT FAQ. *Medium*. https://medium.com/@octsky ward/an-xt-faq-38e78aa32ff0

Hearn, M. (2016, January 14). The resolution of the Bitcoin experiment. *Mike's Blog*. https:// blog.plan99.net/the-resolution-of-the-bitcoin-experiment-dabb30201f7#.fn9ngkl1p

Hearn, M. (2020, December 12). The philosophical origins of Bitcoin's civil war. *Mike's Blog*. https://blog.plan99.net/the-philosophical-origins-of-bitcoins-civil-war -400468335377

Heeks, R. (1998). *Information systems and public sector accountability* (Information Systems for Public Sector Management Working Paper no. 1). Institute for Development Policy and Management. https://dx.doi.org/10.2139/ssrn.3540081

Heeks, R. (2006). *Implementing and managing eGovernment: An international text*. Sage.

Heintze, T., & Bretschneider, S. (2000). Information technology and restructuring in public organizations: Does adoption of information technology affect organizational structures, communications, and decision making? *Journal of Public Administration*

Research and Theory, 10(4), 801–830. https://doi.org/10.1093/oxfordjournals .jpart.a024292

Heintzman, R. (2007, May 14). *Toward a new moral contract: Reclaiming trust in public service* [Lecture]. The Vanier Lecture, Regina, SK, Canada.

Held, V. (1984). *Rights and goods: Justifying social action.* Free Press, Collier Macmillan.

Helm, J. (2020, Jan. 17). National Archives exhibit blurs images critical of President Trump. *Washington Post.* www.washingtonpost.com/local/national-archives-exhibit-blurs-images-critical-of-president-trump/2020/01/17/71d8e80c-37e3-11ea-9541-9107303481a4_story.html

Henderson, M. T., & Churi, S. (2019). *The trust revolution: How the digitization of trust will revolutionize business and government.* Cambridge University Press.

Herlihy, M. (2018). Atomic cross-chain swaps. In *PODC '18: Proceedings of the 2018 ACM Symposium on Principles of Distributed Computing, Egham, United Kingdom, July 23–27, 2018* (pp. 245–254). Association for Computing Machinery. https://doi .org/10.1145/3212734.3212736

Hermida, A. (2013). #Journalism: Reconfiguring journalism research about Twitter, one tweet at a time. *Digital Journalism, 1*(3), 295–313. https://doi.org/10.1080/21670811 .2013.808456

Hern, A. (2016, July 7). Blockchain: The answer to life, the universe and everything? *Guardian.* www.theguardian.com/world/2016/jul/07/blockchain-answer-life-universe-everything-bitcoin-technology

Hetherington, M. J. (2005). *Why trust matters: Declining political trust and the demise of American liberalism.* Princeton University Press.

Hetherington, M. J., & Rudolph, T. J. (2008). Priming, performance, and the dynamics of political trust. *Journal of Politics, 70*(2), 498–512. https://doi.org/10.1017 /S0022381608080468

Hevner, A. R., & Berndt, D. J. (2000). Eras of business computing. *Advances in Computers, 52,* 1–90. https://doi.org/10.1016/S0065-2458(00)80016-9

Hey, J. (2004). The data, information, knowledge, wisdom chain: The metaphorical link. In *Ocean teacher: A training system for ocean data and information management.* Intergovernmental Oceanographic Commission. www.dataschemata.com/uploads/7/ 4/8/7/7487334/dikwchain.pdf

Hiatt, A. (2004). *The making of medieval forgeries: False documents in fifteenth-century England.* University of Toronto Press.

Hieronymi, P. (2008). The reasons of trust. *Australasian Journal of Philosophy, 86*(2), 213–236. https://doi.org/10.1080/00048400801886496

Higgins, S. (2014, November 19). Factom outlines record-keeping network that utilises Bitcoin's blockchain. *Coindesk.* www.coindesk.com/factom-white-paper-outlines-record-keeping-layer-bitcoin

Hill Collins, P. (2015). *Black feminist thought: Knowledge, consciousness, and the politics of empowerment* (2nd ed.). Routledge.

Hinchman, E. S. (2005). Telling as inviting to trust. *Philosophy and Phenomenological Research, 70*(3), 562–587. https://doi.org/10.1111/j.1933-1592.2005.tb00415.x

Hirsch, D. D. (2013). The glass house effect: Big data, the new oil, and the power of analogy. *Maine Law Review, 66*(2), article 3. https://digitalcommons.mainelaw.maine .edu/mlr/vol66/iss2/3

Hirschman, A. O. (1978). Exit, voice, and the state. *World Politics, 31*(1), 90–107. https://doi.org/10.2307/2009968

Hoffman, R. (2014, November 17). The future of the Bitcoin ecosystem and "trustless trust" – Why I invested in Blockstream. *LinkedIn.* www.linkedin.com /pulse/20141117154558–1213-the-future-of-the-bitcoin-ecosystem-and-trustless-trust-why-i-invested-in-blockstream

Hofman, D., Lemieux, V. L., Joo, A., & Batista, D. A. (2019). "The margin between the edge of the world and infinite possibility": Blockchain, GDPR and information governance. *Records Management Journal, 29*(1/2), 249–257. https://doi.org/10 .1108/RMJ-12-2018-0045

Horsburgh, H. J. N. (1961). Trust and social objectives. *Ethics, 72*(1), 28–40. https://doi .org/10.1086/291373

Hsu, S. S. (2017, March 24). Comet Pizza gunman pleads guilty to federal and local charges. *Washington Post.* www.washingtonpost.com/local/public-safety/comet-pizza-gunman-to-appear-at-plea-deal-hearing-friday-morning/2017/03/23/ e12c91ba-0986-11e7-b77c-0047d15a24e0_story.html

Huguet, A., Baker, G., Hamilton, L. S., & Pane, J. F. (2021). *Media literacy standards to counter truth decay* (RR-A112-12). RAND Corporation. https://doi.org/10.7249 /RRA112-12

Hui, Y. (2012). What is a digital object? *Metaphilosophy, 43*(4), 380–395. https://doi.org /10.1111/j.1467-9973.2012.01761.x

Humphreys, R. (2021, January 19) Is bitcoin a scam? [Audio podcast episode]. *Guardian.* www.theguardian.com/news/audio/2021/jan/19/is-bitcoin-a-scam

Husain, S. O., Franklin, A., & Roep, D. (2020). The political imaginaries of blockchain projects: Discerning the expressions of an emerging ecosystem. *Sustainability Science, 15*, 379–394. https://doi.org/10.1007/s11625-020-00786-x

Husserl, E. (1970). *The crisis of European sciences and transcendental phenomenology: An introduction to phenomenological philosophy* (D. Carr, Trans.). Northwestern University Press. Original work published in 1954.

Hyperledger. (2019). *Hyperledger membership overview: January 2019.* Hyperledger. www.hyperledger.org/wp-content/uploads/2019/01/Membership-Benefits.pdf

Hyperledger. (2020). *Contributions welcome!* Hyperledger. https://hyperledger-fabric.readthedocs.io/en/latest/CONTRIBUTING.html#maintainers

Hyperledger / fabric-rfcs. (2021). In *GitHub.* https://github.com/hyperledger/fabric-rfcs

IBM. (n.d.). *IBM Food Trust: A new era for the world's food supply.* IBM. www .ibm.com/blockchain/solutions/food-trust

IBM. (2019). *About IBM Food Trust.* IBM. www.ibm.com/downloads/cas/ 8QABQBDR

Ijiri, Y. (1975). *Theory of accounting measurement: Studies in accounting research # 10.* American Accounting Association.

Imbert, F. (2017, September 12). JP Morgan CEO Jamie Dimon says bitcoin is a "fraud" that will eventually blow up. *CNBC.* www.cnbc.com/2017/09/12/jpmorgan-ceo-jamie-dimon-raises-flag-on-trading-revenue-sees-20-percent-fall-for-the-third-quar ter.html

Internet Archive. (n.d.). *Wayback machine.* Internet Archive. https://archive.org

InterPARES 2 Project. (2021a). Document. In *The InterPARES 2 project glossary.* www .interpares.org/ip2/display_file.cfm?doc=ip2_glossary.pdf

InterPARES 2 Project. (2021b). *The InterPARES 2 project glossary.* www.interpares.org /ip2/display_file.cfm?doc=ip2_glossary.pdf

InterPARES 2 Project. (2021c). Juridical system. In *The InterPARES 2 project glossary.* www.interpares.org/ip2/display_file.cfm?doc=ip2_glossary.pdf

InterPARES 2 Project, Terminology Cross-domain Task Force. (2008). Ontology C: Trustworthiness of a record. In L. Duranti & R. Preston (Eds.), *International research on permanent authentic records in electronic systems (InterPARES) 2: Experiential, interactive and dynamic records* (p. 731). Associazione Nazionale Archivistica Italiana. www.interpares.org/ip2/display_file.cfm?doc=ip2_ontology_c.pdf

Ireton, C., & Posetti, J. (Eds.) (2018). *Journalism, fake news and disinformation. Handbook for journalism education and training.* UNESCO. https://en.unesco.org /sites/default/files/journalism_fake_news_disinformation_print_friendly_0.pdf

ISO [International Organization for Standardization]. (2016). *Information and documentation – Records management – Part I: Concepts and principles.* (ISO Standard No. 15489: 2016). www.iso.org/standard/62542.html

ISO [International Organization for Standardization]. (2017). *Electronic fee collection – Guidelines for security protection profiles.* (ISO Standard No. 17574:2017). www .iso.org/standard/70051.html

ISO [International Organization for Standardization]. (2018a). *Information technology – Security techniques – Information security management systems – Overview and vocabulary.* (ISO Standard No. 27000:2018). www.iso.org/standard/73906 .html

ISO [International Organization for Standardization]. (2018b). *Risk management – Guidelines.* (ISO Standard No. 31000:2018). www.iso.org/standard/65694.html

ISO [International Organization for Standardization]. (2020a). *Blockchain and distributed ledger technologies – Vocabulary.* (ISO Standard No. 22739:2020). www.iso.org /standard/73771.html

ISO [International Organization for Standardization]. (2020b). *Information and documentation – Records management – Core concepts & vocabulary.* (ISO Standard No. 30300:2020). www.iso.org/standard/74291.html

ISO [International Organization for Standardization]. (2021). *Blockchain and distributed ledger technologies – Reference architecture.* (ISO Standard No. 23257:2021 [under development]). www.iso.org/standard/75093.html

ITV News (2014, February 26). 30 facts for 30 years – The truth about "Spitting Image." *ITV News.* www.itv.com/news/central/2014-02-26/30-facts-for-30-years-the-truth-about-spitting-image

Jamieson, K. H., & Cappella, J. N. (2008). *Echo chamber: Rush Limbaugh and the conservative media establishment.* Oxford University Press.

Jeffries, A. (2018, March 7). "Blockchain" is meaningless. *The Verge.* www.theverge.com /2018/3/7/17091766/blockchain-bitcoin-ethereum-cryptocurrency-meaning

Jenkinson, H. (1922). *A manual of archive administration including the problems of war archives and archive making,* vol. 4. Clarendon Press.

Jenkinson, H. (1937). *A manual of archive administration.* (New and revised edition.) P. Lund, Humphries.

Jenkinson, H. (1944). Reflections of an archivist. *Contemporary Review, 165,* 355–361.

Jo, E. S., & Gebru, T. (2020). Lessons from archives: Strategies for collecting sociocultural data in machine learning. In *FAT* '20: Proceedings of the 2020 Conference on Fairness, Accountability, and Transparency, Barcelona, Spain, January 27–30, 2020* (pp. 306–316). Association for Computing machinery. https://doi.org/10.1145/3351095.3372829

Job, J. (2005). How is trust in government created? It begins at home, but ends in the parliament. *Australian Review of Public Affairs*, *6*(1), 1–23. www.australianreview.net/journal/v6/n1/job.html

Johnson, J. (2019, October 25). The Filipino anti-false content bill: Fake news and free expression. *Oxford Human Rights Hub*. https://ohrh.law.ox.ac.uk/the-filipino-anti-false-content-bill-fake-news-and-free-expression

Jones, K. (1996). Trust as an affective attitude. *Ethics*, *107*(1), 4–25. https://doi.org/10.1086/233694

Kahneman, D. (2011). *Thinking fast and slow*. Farrar, Strauss & Giroux.

Kaminska, I. (2017). A module in fake news from the info-wars of ancient Rome. *Financial Times*. www.ft.com/content/aaf2bb08-dca2-11e6-86ac-f253db7791c6

Kandel, S., Paepcke, A., Hellerstein, J. M., & Heer, J. (2012). Enterprise data analysis and visualization: An interview study. *IEEE Transactions on Visualization and Computer Graphics*, *18*(12), 2917–2926. https://doi.org/10.1109/TVCG.2012.219

Kandukuri, B. R., Paturi V. R., & Rakshit, A. (2009). Cloud security issues. In *2009 IEEE International Conference on Services Computing, Bangalore, India, September 21–25, 2009* (pp. 517–520). IEEE. https://doi.org/10.1109/SCC.2009.84

Kapantai, E., Christopoulou, A., Berberidis, C., & Peristeras, V. (2020). A systematic literature review on disinformation: Toward a unified taxonomical framework. *New Media & Society*, *23*(5), 1301–1326. https://doi.org/10.1177/1461444820959296

Karataş A., & Şahin, S. (2017). A review on social bot detection techniques and research directions. In Ş. Sağıroğlu, M. Alkan, & S. Akleylek (Eds). *Proceedings of the 10th International Conference on Information Security & Cryptology (ISCTURKEY 2017), Ankara, Turkey, October 20–21, 2017* (pp. 156–161). ISC Turkey. www.iscturkey.org/assets/files/ISC_Turkey_2017_Bildiriler_Kitabi.pdf

Kastrenakes, J. (2021, March 25). Your million-dollar NFT can break tomorrow if you're not careful. *The Verge*. www.theverge.com/2021/3/25/22349242/nft-metadata-explained-art-crypto-urls-links-ipfs

Keim, D. Kohlhammer, J., Ellis, G., & Mansmann, F. (Eds.). (2010). *Mastering the information age: Solving problems with visual analytics*. Eurographics Association.

Kelley, D. R. (2012). Philology and history. In J. Rabasa, M. Sato, E. Tortarolo, & D. Woolf (Eds.) *The Oxford history of historical writing*, vol. 3: *1400–1800* (pp. 233–243). Oxford University Press.

Kelly, B. (2016, September 30). The case against editable blockchains. *Coindesk*. www.coindesk.com/sorry-accenture-bitcoins-un-editable-blockchain-feature-not-flaw

Kelly, T. (2010). Peer disagreement and higher order evidence. In R. Feldman & T. Warfield (Eds.), *Disagreement* (pp. 111–174). Oxford University Press.

Kent, K. S. (2013). Propaganda, public opinion, and the second South African Boer War. *Inquiries Journal*, *5*(10). www.inquiriesjournal.com/a?id=781

Kenton, W. (2020). Block time. *Investopedia*. www.investopedia.com/terms/b/block-time-cryptocurrency.asp

Keren, A. (2014). Trust and belief: A preemptive reasons account. *Synthese, 191*(12), 2593–2615. https://doi.org/10.1007/s11229-014-0416-3

Kietzmann, J., Lee, L. W., McCarthy, I. P., & Kietzmann, T. C. (2020). Deepfakes: Trick or treat? *Business Horizons, 63*(2), 135–146. https://doi.org/10.1016/j.bushor.2019.11.006

King, S., & Nadal, S. (2012). *PPCoin: Peer-to-peer crypto-currency with proof-of-stak* e [White paper]. Decred. https://decred.org/research/king2012.pdf

Klonick, K. (2017). The new governors: The people, rules, and processes governing online speech. *Harvard Law Review, 131*, 1598–1670. https://harvardlawreview.org /2018/04/the-new-governors-the-people-rules-and-processes-governing-online-speech

Knight, W. (2018, May 23). The US military is funding an effort to catch deepfakes and other AI trickery. *MIT Technology Review*. www.technologyreview.com/2018/05/23/ 142770/the-us-military-is-funding-an-effort-to-catch-deepfakes-and-other-ai-trickery

Knowles, D. (1959). Jean Mabillon. *Journal of Ecclesiastical History, 10*(2), 153–173. https://doi.org/10.1017/S0022046900062308

Koenig, M. A., & McMyler, B. (2019). Understanding the evidential, uncovering the interpersonal. In M. Fricker, P. J. Graham, D. Henderson, & N. J. L. L. Pedersen (Eds.), *The Routledge handbook of social epistemology* (pp. 103–114). Routledge.

Koens, T., & Poll, E. (2019). Assessing interoperability solutions for distributed ledgers. *Pervasive and Mobile Computing, 59*. https://doi.org/10.1016/j .pmcj.2019.101079

Konstantinov, N., & Lampert, C. (2019). Robust learning from untrusted sources. In K. Chaudhuri & R. Salakhutdinov (Eds.), *Proceedings of the 36th International Conference on Machine Learning, PMLR 97, Long Beach, CA, USA, June 9–15, 2019* (pp. 3488–3498). PMLR. http://proceedings.mlr.press/v97/konstantinov19a .html

Korotkova, N. (2016). Disagreement with evidentials: A call for subjectivity. In J. Hunter, M. Simons, & M. Stone (Eds.), *JerSem: The 20th Workshop on the Semantics and Pragmatics of Dialogue, New Brunswick, NJ, USA, July 16–18, 2016* (pp. 65–75). SemDial.

Korte, N. E. (2005). Procopius' portrayal of Theodora in the Secret History. *Hirundo: The McGill Journal of Classical Studies, 3*, 109–130. www.mcgill.ca/classics/files/ classics/2004-09.pdf

Krombholz, K., Judmayer, A., Gusenbauer, M., & Weippl, E. (2016). The other side of the coin: User experiences with bitcoin security and privacy. In J. Grossklags & B. Preneel (Eds.), *Lecture notes in computer science*, vol. 9603: *Financial Cryptography and Data Security, 20th International Conference, FC 2016, Christ Church, Barbados, February 22–26, 2016, revised selected papers* (pp. 555–580). Springer.

Kshetri, N. (2018). 1 Blockchain's roles in meeting key supply chain management objectives. *International Journal of Information Management, 39*, 80–89. https://doi .org/10.1016/j.ijinfomgt.2017.12.005

Kumar A., & Kumar, S. (2020). A systematic review of the research on disruptive technology – Blockchain. In *2020 5th International Conference on Communication and Electronics System (ICCES 2020), Coimbatore, India, June 10–12, 2020, proceedings* (pp. 900–905). IEEE.

Kuran, T., & Sunstein, C. R. (1999). Availability cascades and risk regulation. *Stanford Law Review*, *51*(4), 683. https://ssrn.com/abstract=138144

Lackey, J. (2006). Knowing from testimony. *Philosophy Compass*, *1*(5), 432–448. https://doi.org/10.1111/j.1747-9991.2006.00035.x

Lackey, J. (2008). *Learning from words: Testimony as a source of knowledge*. Oxford University Press.

Lafourcade, P., & Lombard-Platet, M. (2020). About blockchain interoperability. *Information Processing Letters*, *161*, 105976. https://doi.org/10.1016/j.ipl.2020.105976

Lahno, B. (2001). Institutional trust: A less demanding form of trust? *RELEA: Revista Latinoamerica de Estudios Avanzados*, *15*, 19–58.

Lahno, B. (2020). Trust and emotion. In J. Simon (Ed.), *The Routledge handbook of trust and philosophy* (pp. 147–159). Taylor & Francis.

Lamport, L., Shostak, R., & Pease, M. (1982). The Byzantine generals problem. *ACM Transactions on Programming Languages and Systems*, *4*(3), 382–401. https://doi.org/10.1145/357172.357176

Laney, D. (2001). *3D Data management: Controlling data volume, velocity, and variety*. META Group.

Laslett, P. (Ed.) (1988). *Locke: Two treatises of government*. Cambridge University Press.

Latour, B. (1986). Visualization and cognition. In H. Kulick (Ed.), *Knowledge and society studies in the sociology of culture past and present* (pp. 1–40). Jai Press.

Latour, B. (1987). *Science in action: How to follow scientists and engineers through society*. Harvard University Press.

Latour, B. (1992). Where are the missing masses? The sociology of a few mundane artifacts. In W. E. Bijker & J. Law (Eds.), *Shaping technology/building society: Studies in sociotechnical change* (pp. 225–258). MIT Press.

Latour, B., & Venn, C. (2002). Morality and technology. *Theory, Culture & Society*, *19*(5–6), 247–260. https://doi.org/10.1177/026327602761899246

Latour, B., & Woolgar, S. (1979). *Laboratory life: The social construction of scientific facts*. Sage.

Laudon, K. C., & Laudon, J. P. (2015). *Management information systems: Managing the digital firm* (14th ed.). Pearson.

The Law Dictionary. (n.d.). What is business record exception? In *The law dictionary: Featuring Black's law dictionary free online legal dictionary* (2nd ed.). https://thelawdictionary.org/business-record-exception

Lazarenko, A., & Avdoshin, S. (2018). Financial risks of the blockchain industry: A survey of cyberattacks. In K. Arai, R. Bhatia, & S. Kapoor (Eds.), *Advances in intelligent systems and computing*, vol. 881: *Proceedings of the Future Technologies Conference (FTC) 2018, FTC 2018, Vancouver, BC, Canada, November 13–14, 2018* (pp. 368–384). Springer. https://doi.org/10.1007/978-3-030-02683-7_26

Lazer, D., Baum, M., Grinberg, N., Friedland, L., Joseph, K., Hobbs, W., & Mattsson C. (2017). *Combating fake news: An agenda for research and action*. Harvard Kennedy School Shorenstein Center on Media, Politics and Public Policy. https://shorensteincenter.org/combating-fake-news-agenda-for-research

Lazer, D. M. J., Baum, M. A., Benkler, Y., Berinsky, A. J., Greenhill, K. M., Menczer, F., Metzger, M. J., Nyhan, B., Pennycook, G., Rothschild, D., Schudson, M.,

Sloman, S. A., Sunstein, C. R., Thorson, E. A., Watts, D. J., & Zittrain, J. L. (2018). The science of fake news. *Science, 359*(6380), 1094–1096. https://doi.org/10.1126 /science.aao2998

LeCun, Y., Bengio, Y., & Hinton, G. (2015). Deep learning. *Nature, 521*(7553), 436–444. https://doi.org/10.1038/nature14539

Lee, C., & Woods, K. (2014). *Enabling digital forensics practices in libraries, archives and museums: The BitCurator experience* [Conference presentation]. Digital Forensics Research Workshop, The Digital Forensic Research Conference, DFRWS 2014 USA, Denver, CO, USA, August 3–6,2014. https://dfrws.org/presentation/enab ling-digital-forensics-practices-in-libraries-archives-and-museums-the-bitcurator-experience

Lee, G., & Perry, J. L. (2002). Are computers boosting productivity? A test of the paradox in state governments. *Journal of Public Administration Research and Theory, 12*(1), 77–102. www.jstor.org/stable/3525740

Leibenstein, H. (1950). Bandwagon, snob, and Veblen effects in the theory of consumers' demand. *Quarterly Journal of Economics, 64*(2), 183–207. https://doi.org/10 .2307/1882692

Leigh, A. (2006). Trust, inequality and ethnic heterogeneity. *Economic Record, 82*(258), 268–280. https://doi.org/10.1111/j.1475-4932.2006.00339.x

Lemieux, V. L. (1993). Archival solitudes: The impact on appraisal and acquisition of legislative concepts of records and archives. *Archivaria, 35*, 153–161. https://archi varia.ca/index.php/archivaria/article/view/11894

Lemieux, V. L. (Ed.). (2012). *Financial analysis and risk management: Data governance, analytics and life cycle management.* Springer.

Lemieux, V. L. (2014). Toward a "third order" archival interface: Research notes on some theoretical and practical implications of visual explorations in the Canadian context of financial electronic records. *Archivaria, 78*, 53–93. https://archivaria.ca /index.php/archivaria/article/view/13721

Lemieux, V. L. (2016a). *One step forward, two steps backward? Does e-government make governments in developing countries more transparent and accountable?* (WDR 2016 Background Paper). World Bank. https://openknowledge .worldbank.org/handle/10986/23647

Lemieux, V. L. (2016b). Provenance: Past, present and future in interdisciplinary and multidisciplinary perspective. In V. L. Lemieux (Ed.), *Building trust in information* (pp. 3–45). Springer.

Lemieux, V. L. (2016c). Trusting records: Is blockchain technology the answer? *Records Management Journal, 26*(2), 110–139. https://doi.org/10.1108/RMJ-12-2015-0042

Lemieux, V. L. (2017a). Evaluating the use of blockchain in land transactions: An archival science perspective. *European Property Law Journal, 6*(3), 392–440. https:// doi.org/10.1515/eplj-2017-0019

Lemieux, V. L. (2017b). A typology of blockchain recordkeeping solutions and some reflections on their implications for the future of archival preservation. In J-Y Nie, Z, Obradovic, T. Suzumura, R. Ghosh, R. Nambiar, C. Wang, H. Zang, R. Baeza-Yates, X. Hu, J. Kepner, A. Cuzzocrea, J. Tang, & M. Toyoda (Eds.), *Proceedings: 2017 IEEE International Conference on Big Data, Boston, MA, USA, December 11–14, 2017* (pp. 2271–2278). IEEE. https://doi.org/10.1109/BigData.2017.8258180

Lemieux, V. L. (2019). Blockchain and public recordkeeping: Of temples, prisons and the (re) configuration of power. *Frontiers in Blockchain, 2.* https://doi.org/10.3389/fbloc.2019.00005

Lemieux, V. L., & Feng, C. (2021). Theorizing from multidisciplinary perspectives on the design of blockchains and distributed ledger systems (part 2). In V. L. Lemieux & C. Feng (Eds.), *Building decentralized trust: Multidisciplinary perspectives on the design of blockchains and distributed ledgers.* Springer.

Lemieux, V., & Limonad, L. (2011). What "good" looks like: Understanding records ontologically in the context of the global financial crisis. *Journal of Information Science, 37*(1), 29–39. https://doi.org/10.1177/0165551510391359

Lemieux, V. L., & Trapnell, S. E. (2016). *Public access to information for development: A guide to the effective implementation of right to information laws.* World Bank. https://elibrary.worldbank.org/doi/abs/10.1596/978-1-4648-0879-1

Lemieux, V. L., Hoffman, D., Batista, D., & Joo, A. (2019). *Blockchain technology & recordkeeping.* ARMA International Education Foundation. http://armaedfoundation.org/wp-content/uploads/2019/06/AIEF-Research-Paper-Blockchain-Technology-Recordkeeping.pdf

Lemieux, V. L., Voskobojnikov, A., & Meng, K. (2021). *Addressing audit and accountability issues in self-sovereign identity blockchain systems using archival science principles* [Conference paper]. IEEE COMPSAC '21: Intelligent and Resilient Computing for a Collaborative World, 45th Anniversary Conference, virtual, July 12–16, 2021.

Lévi-Strauss, C. (1985). Structural analysis in linguistics and in anthropology. In R. E. Innis (Ed.), *Semiotics: An introductory anthology* (pp. 110–128). Indiana University Press. Originally published in 1963 in C. Lévi-Strauss, *Structural anthropology.* Basic Books.

Lewandowsky, S. (2020). The "post-truth" world, misinformation, and information literacy: A perspective from cognitive science. In S. Goldstein (Ed.), *Informed societies: Why information literacy matters for citizenship, participation and democracy* (pp. 69–88). Facet.

Lewandowsky, S., & van der Linden, S. (2021). Countering misinformation and fake news through inoculation and prebunking. *European Review of Social Psychology,* 1–38. https://doi.org/10.1080/10463283.2021.1876983

Lexico. (2021). Usability. *Lexico.* www.lexico.com/definition/usability

Li, J., Li, N., Peng, J., Cui, H., & Wu, Z. (2019). Energy consumption of cryptocurrency mining: A study of electricity consumption in mining cryptocurrencies. *Energy, 168,* 160–168. https://doi.org/10.1016/j.energy.2018.11.046

Liberman, E. (2017, June 20). The age of disinformation. *Quadangles Online, URI Alumni Magazine.* https://web.uri.edu/quadangles/020-the-age-of-disinformation

Library of Congress. (n.d.). The deterioration and preservation of paper: Some essential facts. *Library of Congress.* www.loc.gov/preservation/care/deterioratebrochure.html

Ling, R. (2012). *Taken for grantedness: The embedding of mobile communication into society.* MIT Press.

Lipset, S. M., & Schneider, W. (1983). *The confidence gap: Business, labor, and government in the public mind.* Free Press.

Liu, L., & Özsu, M. T. (Eds.). (2009). *Encyclopedia of database systems.* Springer.

Liu, S., Mohsin, F., Xia, L., & Seneviratne, O. (2019). Strengthening smart contracts to handle unexpected situations. In *Proceedings: 2019 IEEE International Conference on Decentralized Applications and Infrastructures (DAPPCON), Newark, CA, USA, April 4–9, 2019* (pp. 182–187). IEEE. https://doi.org/10.1109/DAPPCON.2019.00034

Liv, N., & Greenbaum, D. (2020). Deep fakes and memory malleability: False memories in the service of fake news. *AJOB Neuroscience, 11*(2), 96–104. https://doi.org/10.1080/21507740.2020.1740351

Locke, J. (1689). *Two treatises of government: In the former, the false principles, and foundation of Sir Robert Filmer, and his followers, are detected and overthrown. The latter is an essay concerning the true original, extent, and end of civil government.* Awnsham Churchill.

Lockl, J., Schlatt, V., Schweizer, A., Urbach, N., & Harth, N. (2020). Toward trust in Internet of Things ecosystems: Design principles for blockchain-based IoT applications. *IEEE Transactions on Engineering Management, 67*(4), 1256–1270. https://doi.org/10.1109/TEM.2020.2978014

Lopp, J. (2018). Who controls Bitcoin Core? *Cypherpunk Cogitations.* https://blog.lopp.net/who-controls-bitcoin-core-/

Lorenz, C. (2001). History: Theories and methods. In N. J. Smelser & P. B. Baltes (Eds.), *International encyclopedia of the social & behavioral sciences* (pp. 6869–6876). Pergamon.

Lu, C., Batista, D., Hamouda, H., & Lemieux, V. (2020). Consumers' intentions to adopt blockchain-based personal health records and data sharing: Focus group study. *JMIR Formative Research, 4*(11). https://doi.org/10.2196/21995

Lu, Q., Staples, M., O'Connor, H., Chen, S., & Guabtni, A. (2020). Software architecture for blockchain-based trade certificate systems. In *Proceedings of the 2020 IEEE International Conference on Blockchain and Cryptocurrency (ICBC), Toronto, ON, Canada, May 2–6, 2020* (pp. 1–3). IEEE. https://doi.org/10.1109/ICBC48266.2020.9169390

Ludäscher, B. (2016). A brief tour through provenance in scientific workflows and databases. In V. L. Lemieux (Ed.), *Building trust in information* (pp. 103–126). Springer.

Luhmann, N. (1979). *Trust and power.* Wiley & Sons.

Luhmann, N. (2000). Familiarity, confidence, trust: Problems and alternatives. In D. Gambetta (Ed.), *Trust: Making and breaking cooperative relations* (Electronic ed.) (pp. 94–107). University of Oxford.

Lund, N. W., & Skare, R. (2017). Document theory. In J. D. McDonald and M. Levine-Clark (Eds.), *Encyclopedia of library and information sciences* (4th ed.) (pp. 1372–1380). CRC Press. https://doi.org/10.1081/E-ELIS4-120053306

Lustig, J. (2020). Epistemologies of the archive: Toward a critique of archival reason. *Archival Science, 20*(1), 65–89. https://doi.org/10.1007/s10502-019-09313-z

Lynch, C. A. (2001). When documents deceive: Trust and provenance as new factors for information retrieval in a tangled web. *Journal of the American Society for Information Science and Technology, 52*(1), 12–17. https://doi.org/10.1002/1532-2890(2000)52:1<12::AID-ASI1062>3.0.CO;2-V

Lynch, C. A. (2017). Stewardship in the age of algorithms. *First Monday, 22*(12). https://doi.org/10.5210/fm.v22i12.8097

Lynch, C. A. (2018). Managing the cultural record in the information warfare era. *EDUCAUSE Review, 53*(6). https://er.educause.edu/articles/2018/10/managing-the-cultural-record-in-the-information-warfare-era

Lyons, K. (2021, January 25). Twitter launches Birdwatch, a fact-checking program intended to fight misinformation. *The Verge.* www.theverge.com/2021/1/25/22248903/twitter-birdwatch-fact-checking-misinformation

Ma, J., Gao, W., Mitra, P., Kwon, S., Jansen, B. J., Wong, K. F., & Cha, M. (2016). Detecting rumors from microblogs with recurrent neural networks. In *Proceedings of the 25th International Joint Conference on Artificial Intelligence (IJCAI 2016), New York, NY, USA, July 9–15, 2016* (pp. 3818–3824). AAAI Press. https://ink.library.smu.edu.sg/sis_research/4630

Mackenzie, A. (2014). *Memcoin$_2$: A hybrid proof of work/proof of stake cryptocurrency* [White paper]. Decred. https://decred.org/research/mackenzie2013.pdf

MacKuen, M. B., Erikson, R. S., & Stimson, J. A. (1992). Peasants or bankers? The American electorate and the US economy. *American Political Science Review, 86*(3), 597–611. https://doi.org/10.2307/1964124

MacNeil, H. (1992). *Without consent: The ethics of disclosing personal information in public archives.* Society of American Archivists and Scarecrow Press.

MacNeil, H. M. (1998). *Trusting records: The evolution of legal, historical and diplomatic methods of assessing the trustworthiness of records, from antiquity to the digital age.* [Doctoral dissertation, University of British Columbia]. http://hdl.handle.net/2429/10157

MacNeil, H. (2004). Contemporary archival diplomatics as a method of inquiry: Lessons learned from two research projects. *Archival Science, 4*(3–4), 199–232. https://doi.org/10.1007/s10502-005-2592-x

MacNeil, H. (2009). Trusting description: Authenticity, accountability, and archival description standards. *Journal of Archival Organization, 7*(3), 89–107. https://doi.org/10.1080/15332740903117693

MacNeil, H. (2013). *Trusting records: Legal, historical and diplomatic perspectives*, vol. 1. Springer.

MacNeil, H. (2016). Deciphering and interpreting an archival fonds and its parts: A comparative analysis of textual criticism and the theory of archival arrangement. In A. Gilliland, S. McKemmish., & A. J. Lau (Eds.), *Research in the archival multiverse* (pp. 161–197). Monash University Publishing.

MacNeil, H., Wei, C., Duranti, L., Gilliland-Swetland, A., Guercio, M., Hackett, Y., Hamidzadeh, B., Iacovino, L., Lee, B., McKemmish, S., Roeder, J., Ross, S., Wan, W.-K., & Xiu, Z. Z. (2001). *InterPARES 1 project book: Authenticity task force report.* InterPARES. http://interpares.org/display_file.cfm?doc=ip1_atf_report.pdf

Maddocks, S. (2020). "A deepfake porn plot intended to silence me": Exploring continuities between pornographic and "political" deep fakes. *Porn Studies, 7*(4), 415–423. https://doi.org/10.1080/23268743.2020.1757499

Maniatis, P., Roussopoulos, M., Giuli, T. J., Rosenthal, D. S. H., & Baker, M. (2005). The LOCKSS peer-to-peer digital preservation system. *ACM Transactions on Computer Systems, 23*(1), 2–50. https://doi.org/10.1145/1047915.1047917

Mannheim, K. (1954). *Ideology and utopia: An introduction to the sociology of knowledge.* (L. Wirth & E. Shils, Trans.). Harcourt Brace & Company. Original work published in 1929.

Manoff, M. (2004). Theories of the archive from across the disciplines. *Portal: Libraries and the Academy, 4*(1), 9–25. https://doi.org/10.1353/pla.2004.0015

Mansbridge, J. (1997). Social and cultural causes of dissatisfaction with US government. In J. S. Nye, Jr., P. D. Zelikow, & D. C. King (Eds.), *Why people don't trust government* (pp. 133–153). Harvard University Press.

Marciano, R., Lemieux, V., Hedges, M., Esteva, M., Underwood, W., Kurtz, M., & Conrad, M. (2018). Archival records and training in the age of big data. In J. Percell, L. C. Sarin, P. T. Jaeger, & J. C. Bertot (Eds.), *Re-envisioning the MLS: Perspectives on the future of library and information science education*. Emerald Publishing. https://doi.org/10.1108/S0065-28302018000044B010

Marciano, R., Underwood, W., Hanaee, M., Mullane, C., Singh, A., & Tethong, Z. (2018). Automating the detection of personally identifiable information (PII) in Japanese-American WWII incarceration camp records. In N. Abe, H. Liu, C. Pu, X. Hu, N. Ahmed, M. Qiao, Y. Song, D. Kossmann, B. Liu, K. Lee, J. Tang, J. He, & J. Saltz (Eds.), *Proceedings of the 2018 IEEE International Conference on Big Data (Big Data), Seattle, WA, USA, December 10–13, 2018* (pp. 2725–2732). IEEE. https://doi.org/10.1109/BigData.2018.8622634

Marino, B., & Juels, A. (2016). Setting standards for altering and undoing smart contracts. In J. Alferes, L. Bertossi, G. Governatori, P. Fodor, & D. Roman (Eds.), *Lecture notes in computer science*, vol. 9718: *Rule technologies. Research, tools, and applications. 10th International Symposium, RuleML 2016, Stony Brook, NY, USA, July 6–9, 2016, proceedings* (pp. 151–166). Springer. https://doi.org/10.1007/978-3-319-42019-6_10

Martinez-Ávila, D., & Zandonade, T. (2020). Social epistemology in information studies: A consolidation. *Brazilian Journal of Information Science, 14*(1), 7–36. https://doi.org/10.36311/1981-1640.2020.v14n1.02.p7

Martinovic, I., Kello, L., & Sluganovic, I. (2017). *Blockchains for governmental services: Design principles, applications, and case studies* (Working Paper Series – No. 7). Centre for Technology and Global Affairs, University of Oxford. www.ctga.ox.ac.uk/sites/default/files/ctga/documents/media/wp7_martinovickellosluganovic.pdf

Mashatan, A., & Heintzman, D. (2021). The complex path to quantum resistance: Is your organization prepared? *Queue,19*(2), 65–92. https://doi.org/10.1145/3466132.3466779

Mashatan, A., & Turetken, O. (2020). Preparing for the information security threat from quantum computers. *MIS Quarterly Executive, 19*(2), 157–164. https://aisel.aisnet.org/misqe/vol19/iss2/7

Matthews, A., & Posetti, J. (2020, March 25). *You cannot afford to ignore the disinformation crisis: A call to action for Canadian magazines* [White paper]. Magazines Canada. https://magazinescanada.ca/pdf/you-cannot-afford-to-ignore-the-disinformation-crisis-a-call-to-action-for-canadian-magazines

Maurer, W. M., & DuPont, Q. (2015, June 23). Ledgers and law in the blockchain. *King's Review.* www.kingsreview.co.uk/essays/ledgers-and-law-in-the-blockchain

Maxwell, G. (2017, April 5). BIP proposal: Inhibiting a covert attack on the Bitcoin POW function. *Bitcoin Dev Mailing List.* www.mail-archive.com/bitcoin-dev@lists.linuxfoundation.org/msg05055.html

Mayer-Schönberger, V., & Cukier, K. (2013). *Big data: A revolution that will transform how we live, work, and think.* Houghton Mifflin Harcourt.

McDowell, A. (2002). Trust and information: The role of trust in the social epistemology of information science, *Social Epistemology*, *16*(1), 51–63. https://doi.org/10 .1080/210132798

McKnight, D. H., Carter, M., Thatcher, J. B., & Clay, P. F. (2011). Trust in a specific technology: An investigation of its components and measures. *ACM Transactions on Management Information Systems*, *2*(2), 1–25. https://doi.org/10.1145/1985347.1985353

McKnight, D. H., Choudhury, V., & Kacmar, C. (2002). Developing and validating trust measures for e-commerce: An integrative typology. *Information Systems Research*, *13*(3), 334–359. https://doi.org/10.1287/isre.13.3.334.81

McLeod, C. (2002). *Self-trust and reproductive autonomy*. MIT Press.

Mead, G. H. (1934). *Mind, self and society: From the standpoint of a social behaviorist*. University of Chicago Press.

Meijer, A. J. (2003). Trust this document! ICTs, authentic records and accountability. *Archival Science*, *3*(3), 275–290. https://doi.org/10.1007/s10502-004-1287-z

Meyerson, D., Weick, K. E., & Kramer, R. M. (1996). Swift trust and temporary groups. In R. M. Kramer & T. R. Tyler (Eds.), *Trust in organizations: Frontiers of theory and research* (pp. 166–195). SAGE Publications. http://dx.doi.org/10.4135/9781452243610 .n9

Mickens, J. (2018, June 4). *Blockchains are a bad idea* [Video]. YouTube. www.youtube .com/watch?v=15RTC22Z2xl&list=LL1wbwzUs5xzdGUAeCMP5e6Q&index=377

Millar, L. A. (2019). *A matter of facts: The value of evidence in an information age*. ALA Neal-Schuman.

Miller, A. H., & Listhaug, O. (1984). Economic effects on the vote in Norway. *Political Behavior*, *6*(4), 301–319. https://doi.org/10.1007/BF00987069

Mirsky, Y., & Lee, W. (2021). The creation and detection of deepfakes: A survey. *ACM Computing Surveys*, *54*(1), 1–41. https://doi.org/10.1145/3425780

Mirsky, Y., Mahler, T., Shelef, I., & Elovici, Y. (2019). CT-GAN: Malicious tampering of 3D medical imagery using deep learning. In *SEC'19: Proceedings of the 28th USENIX Conference on Security Symposium, Santa Clara, CA, USA, August 14–16, 2019* (pp. 461–478). USENIX Association.

Mishler, W., & Rose, R. (2001). What are the origins of political trust? Testing institutional and cultural theories in post-communist societies. *Comparative Political Studies*, *34*(1), 30–62. https://doi.org/10.1177/0010414001034001002

Missier, P., Moreau, L., Cheney, J., Lebo, T., & Soiland-Reyes, S. (2013). *PROV-dictionary: Modeling provenance for dictionary data structures* (W3 C Working Group Note April 30, 2013). World Wide Web Consortium. www.w3.org/TR/2013/ NOTE-prov-dictionary-20130430

Mitre Corporation (MITRE). (2020). Common Attack Pattern Enumeration and Classification [database]. Mitre Corporation. https://capec.mitre.org/data/defin itions/98.html

Montgomery, B. P. (2001). The Iraqi secret police files: A documentary record of the Anfal genocide. *Archivaria*, *52*, 69–99. https://archivaria.ca/index.php/archivaria/ article/view/12815

Moreau, L. (2010). *The foundations for provenance on the web*. Now Publishers.

Morgan, R. M., & Hunt, S. D. (1994). The commitment-trust theory of relationship marketing. *Journal of Marketing*, *58*(3), 20–38. https://doi.org/10.1177 /002224299405800302

Morisander. (2018, March 23). The biggest smart contract hacks in history or how to endanger up to US $2.2 billion. *Medium*. https://medium.com/solidified/the-biggest-smartcontract-hacks-in-history-or-how-to-endanger-up-to-us-2-2-billion-d5a72961d15d

Mosseri, A. (2016, December 16). Addressing hoaxes and fake news. *Facebook*. https://about.fb.com/news/2016/12/news-feed-fyi-addressing-hoaxes-and-fake-news

Mosseri, A. (2017, April 6). Working to stop misinformation and false news. *Facebook*. https://about.fb.com/news/2017/04/working-to-stop-misinformation-and-false-news

Mourão, R. R., & Robertson, C. T. (2019). Fake news as discursive integration: An analysis of sites that publish false, misleading, hyperpartisan and sensational information. *Journalism Studies, 20*(14), 2077–2095. https://doi.org/10.1080/1461670X.2019.1566871

Mühle, A., Grüner, A., Gayvoronskaya, T., & Meinel, C. (2018). A survey on essential components of a self-sovereign identity. *Computer Science Review, 30*, 80–86. https://doi.org/10.1016/j.cosrev.2018.10.002

Muller, M., Lange, I., Wang, D., Piorkowski, D., Tsay, J., Liao, Q. V., Dugan, C., & Erickson, T. (2019). *How data science workers work with data: Discovery, capture, curation, design, creation*. In *CHI '19: Proceedings of the 2019 CHI Conference on Human Factors in Computing Systems, Glasgow, Scotland, May 4–9, 2019* (Paper 126). Association for Computing Machinery. https://doi.org/10.1145/3290605.3300356

Muller, S., Feith, J. A., & Fruin, R. (2003). *Manual for the arrangement and description of archives* (A. H. Leavitt, Trans.) (2nd ed.). Society of American Archivists. Original work published in 1920.

Müller, S. M., & Tworek, H. J. (2016). Imagined use as a category of analysis: New approaches to the history of technology. *History and Technology, 32*(2), 105–119. https://doi.org/10.1080/07341512.2016.1218957

Murray, T. (2021, January 16). A man who says he threw away a hard drive loaded with 7,500 bitcoins in 2013 is offering his city $70 million to dig it up from the dump. *Business Insider*. www.businessinsider.com/man-offers-council-70-million-dig-up-bitcoin-hard-drive-2021-1

Myers West, S. (2018). Censored, suspended, shadowbanned: User interpretations of content moderation on social media platforms. *New Media and Society, 20*(11), 4366–4383. https://doi.org/10.1177/1461444818773059

Naab, T. K., Kalch, A., & Meitz, T. G. K. (2018). Flagging uncivil user comments: Effects of intervention information, type of victim, and response comments on bystander behavior. *New Media and Society, 20*(2), 777–795. https://doi.org/10.1177/1461444816670923

Nadeau, M. (2020, July 9). What is cryptojacking? How to prevent, detect, and recover from it. *CSO Online*. www.csoonline.com/article/3253572/what-is-cryptojacking-how-to-prevent-detect-and-recover-from-it.html

Nakamoto, S. (2008a). A peer-to-peer electronic cash system. *Bitcoin.org*. https://bitcoin.org/bitcoin.pdf

Nakamoto, S. (2008b, October 31). Bitcoin P2P e-cash paper. *Cryptography Mailing List*. www.metzdowd.com/pipermail/cryptography/2008-October/014810.html

Nakamoto, S. (2008c, November 17). Bitcoin P2P e-cash paper. *Cryptography Mailing List*. www.metzdowd.com/pipermail/cryptography/2008-November/014863.html

Nakamoto, S. (2009a, January 9). Bitcoin v.0.1 released. *Cryptography Mailing List*. www.mail-archive.com/cryptography@metzdowd.com/msg10142.html

Nakamoto, S. (2009b, February 11). Bitcoin open source implementation of P2P currency. *P2P Foundation Forum.* http://p2pfoundation.ning.com/forum/topics/bit coin-open-source

Narayanan, A., Bonneau, J., Felton, E., Miller, A., & Goldfeder, S. (2016). *Bitcoin and cryptocurrency technologies: A comprehensive introduction.* Princeton University Press.

Naqvi, S. (2018). Challenges of cryptocurrencies forensics – A case study of investigating, evidencing and prosecuting organised cybercriminals. In *ARES 2018: Proceedings of the 13th International Conference on Availability, Reliability and Security, Hamburg, Germany, August 27–30, 2018* (Article 63). Association for Computing Machinery. https://doi.org/10.1145/3230833.3233290

Newman, N., Fletcher, R., Kalogeropoulos, A., Levy, D. A. L., & Nielsen, R. K. (2018). *Reuters institute digital news report 2018.* Reuters Institute for the Study of Journalism. media.digitalnewsreport.org/wp-content/uploads/2018/06/digital-news-report-2018.pdf?x89475

Newton, K., & Norris, P. (2000). Confidence in public institutions: Faith, culture, or performance? In S. J. Pharr & R. D. Putnam. *Disaffected democracies. What's troubling the trilateral countries* (pp. 52–73). Princeton University Press.

Nickel, P. (2007). Trust and obligation-ascription. *Ethical Theory and Moral Practice, 10*(3), 309–319. https://doi.org/10.1007/s10677-007-9069-3

Nickel, P. J. (2012). Trust and testimony. *Pacific Philosophical Quarterly, 93*(3), 301–316. https://doi.org/10.1111/j.1468-0114.2012.01427.x

Nickel, P. J., Franssen, M., & Kroes, P. (2010). Can we make sense of the notion of trustworthy technology? *Knowledge, Technology & Policy, 23*(3–4), 429–444. https://doi.org/10.1007/s12130-010-9124-6

Nickerson, R. S. (1998). Confirmation bias: A ubiquitous phenomenon in many guises. *Review of General Psychology 2*(2), 175–220. https://doi.org/10.1037/1089-2680.2.2.175

Nikolić, I., Kolluri, A., Sergey, I., Saxena, P., & Hobor, A. (2018). Finding the greedy, prodigal, and suicidal contracts at scale. In *ASAC '18: Proceedings of the 34th Annual Computer Security Applications Conference, San Juan, Puerto Rico, USA, December 3–7, 2018* (pp. 653–663). Association for Computing Machinery. https://doi.org/10.1145/3274694.3274743

Nirkin, Y., Keller, Y., & Hassner, T. (2019). FSGAN: Subject agnostic face swapping and reenactment. In *Proceedings: 2019 International Conference on Computer Vision (ICCV), Seoul, South Korea, October 27–November 2, 2019* (pp. 7183–7192). IEEE. https://doi.org/10.1109/ICCV.2019.00728

Nissenbaum, H. (2001). Securing trust online: Wisdom or oxymoron? *Boston University Law Review, 81*(30), 635–664. https://papers.ssrn.com/sol3/papers.cfm?abstract_id=2573181

North, D. C. (1990). A transaction cost theory of politics. *Journal of Theoretical Politics, 2*(4), 355–367. https://doi.org/10.1177/0951692890002004001

North, D. C., & Thomas, R. P. (1973). *The rise of the western world: A new economic history.* Cambridge University Press.

Nunziato, D. C. (2020). Misinformation mayhem: Social media platforms' efforts to combat medical and political misinformation. *George Washington University Law*

School (GW Law) Faculty Publications and Other Works. https://scholarship
.law.gwu.edu/cgi/viewcontent.cgi?article=2758&context=faculty_publications

Nguyen, C. T. (in press). Trust as an unquestioning attitude. In T. S. Gendler, &
J. Hawthorne (Eds.), *Oxford studies in epistemology*, vol. 7. Oxford University Press.

Nye, J. S. (1997). Introduction: The decline of confidence in government. In J. S. Nye,
Jr., P. D. Zelikow, & D. C. King (Eds.), *Why people don't trust government* (pp. 1–19).
Harvard University Press.

Object Management Group. (2020). Home. Unified Modelling Language. www.uml.org
/index.htm

Occeñola, P. (2018, December 15). Fake news, real women: Disinformation gone
macho. *Rappler.* https://specials.rappler.com/newsbreak/in-depth/217563-
disinformation-gone-macho/index.html

Oclarino, R. (2020, September 15). Blockchain's technology of trust. *ISO News.* www
.iso.org/news/isofocus_142–5.html

O'Connor, T. (2020). Emergent properties. In E. N. Zalta (Ed.), *Stanford encyclopedia
of philosophy* (Fall 2020 ed.) https://plato.stanford.edu/entries/properties-emergent

OECD [Organisation for Economic Co-operation and Development]. (2013).
Government at a glance 2013. https://doi.org/10.1787/gov_glance-2013-en

O'Neal, S. (2019, January 3). From Dorian Nakamoto to Elon Musk: The incomplete list of
people speculated to be Satoshi Nakamoto. *CoinTelegraph.* https://cointelegraph.com
/news/from-dorian-nakamoto-to-elon-musk-the-incomplete-list-of-people-speculated-to
-be-satoshi-nakamoto

O'Neil, C., & Schutt, R. (2013). *Doing data science: Straight talk from the frontline.*
O'Reilly Media.

O'Neill, O. (2020). Questioning trust. In J. Simon (Ed.), *The Routledge handbook of
trust and philosophy* (pp. 17–27). Taylor & Francis.

Origgi, G. (2004). Is trust an epistemological notion? *Episteme, 1*(1), 61–72. https://doi
.org/10.3366/epi.2004.1.1.61

Origgi, G. (2019). Trust and reputation as filtering mechanism for knowledge. In
M. Fricker, P. J. Graham, D. Henderson, & N. J. L. L. Pedersen (Eds.), *The
Routledge handbook of social epistemology* (pp.78–86). Routledge.

Origgi, G. (2020). Trust and reputation. In J. Simon (Ed.), *The Routledge handbook of
trust and philosophy* (pp. 88–96). Taylor & Francis.

Orphan block. (2019, May 16). In *Bitcoin Wiki.* https://en.bitcoin.it/wiki/Orphan_Block

OSCE [Organization for Security and Co-operation in Europe]. (2017, March 3). *Joint
declaration on freedom of expression and "fake news", disinformation and propaganda.* Organization for Security and Co-operation in Europe. www.osce.org/fom/
302796

Owens, T. (2018). *The theory and craft of digital preservation.* Johns Hopkins
University Press.

Oxford University Press (2016, November). Word of the year 2016. Oxford University
Press. https://languages.oup.com/word-of-the-year/2016

Oxford University Press. (2021a) Cartulary, n. In *Oxford English dictionary.* www
.oed.com/view/Entry/28326

Oxford University Press. (2021b). Data, n.1. In *Oxford English dictionary.* www
.oed.com/view/Entry/159867

Oxford University Press. (2021c). Document, n. In *Oxford English dictionary*. www .oed.com/view/Entry/56328

Oxford University Press. (2021d). Record, n.1 and adj. In *Oxford English dictionary*. www.oed.com/view/Entry/159867

Oxford University Press. (2021e). Testimony, n. In *Oxford English dictionary*. www .oed.com/view/Entry/199748

Palmer, C. K., Rowell, C., & Lemieux, V. L. (2021). Multidisciplinary blockchain research and design: A case study in moving from theory to pedagogy to practice. In K. Toeppe, H. Yan, & S. K. W. Chu (Eds.), *Lecture notes in computer science*, vol. 12645: *Diversity, Divergence, Dialogue, 16th International Conference, iConference 2021, Beijing, China, March 17–31, 2021, Proceedings*, Part I (pp. 587–602). Springer. https://doi.org/10.1007/978-3-030-71292-1_46

Parsons, T. (1954). Psychology and sociology. In J. Gillin (Ed.), *For a science of social man: Convergences in anthropology, psychology, and sociology* (pp. 67–101). MacMillan Co.

Pattenden-Fail, J., Ballaux, B., Sørensen, A. B., Kruse, F., & Thøgersen, J. (2008). *Report on usage models for libraries, archives, and data centres, results of the second iteration*. Deliverable PP/3-D2v1.3. Preservation and Long-term Access through NETworked Services (PLANETS) Project. www.planets-project.eu/docs/reports/ Planets_PP3-D2ReportOnUsageModels.pdf

Pearce-Moses, R. (2005). *A glossary of archival and records terminology*. Society of American Archivists. https://files.archivists.org/pubs/free/SAA-Glossary-2005.pdf

Pearce-Moses, R. (2018). Record. In *InterPARES trust terminology*. https://interpares trust.org/terminology/term/record/en

Peng, R. D. (2011). Reproducible research in computational science. *Science, 334* (6060), 1226–1227. https://doi.org/10.1126/science.1213847

Pennycook, G., & Rand, D. G. (2021). Research note: Examining false beliefs about voter fraud in the wake of the 2020 presidential election. *Harvard Kennedy School (HKS) Misinformation Review*. https://doi.org/10.37016/mr-2020-51

Pérez-Rosas, V., Kleinberg, B., Lefevre, A., & Mihalcea, R. (2018). Automatic detection of fake news. In E. M. Bender, L. Derczynski, P. Isabelle (Eds.), *Proceedings of the 27th International Conference on Computational Linguistics (COLING 2018), Santa Fe, New Mexico, USA, August 20–26, 2018* (pp. 3391–3401). Association for Computational Linguistics. www.aclweb.org/anthol ogy/C18-1287

Pettit, P. (1995). The cunning of trust. *Philosophy & Public Affairs, 24*(3), 202–225. https://doi.org/10.1111/j.1088-4963.1995.tb00029.x

Phillips, R., & Wilder, H. (2020). Tracing cryptocurrency scams: Clustering replicated advance-fee and phishing websites. In *Proceedings: 2020 IEEE International Conference on Blockchain and Cryptocurrency (ICBC), Toronto, ON, Canada, May 2–6, 2020* (pp. 159–166). IEEE. https://doi.org/10.1109/ICBC48266 .2020.9169433

Piore, A. (2018, November 19). New internet: Blockchain technology could help us take back our data from Facebook, Google and Amazon. *Newsweek*. www.newsweek.com /2018/11/16/new-internet-blockchain-technology-could-help-us-take-back-our-data -facebook-1222860.html

Pitropakis, N., Panaousis, E., Giannetsos, T., Anastasiadis, E., & Loukas, G. (2019). A taxonomy and survey of attacks against machine learning. *Computer Science Review, 34.* https://doi.org/10.1016/j.cosrev.2019.100199

Plutchak, S. T. (2018). Op ed: Epistemology – A matter of trust. *Against the Grain, 30* (6). https://doi.org/10.7771/2380-176X.8207

Pogue, D. (2017, February 1). The ultimate cure for the fake news epidemic will be more skeptical readers. *Scientific American, 316*(2), 24. https://doi.org/10.1038/scientifica merican0217-24

Pollitt, M. (2010). A history of digital forensics. In K. P. Chow & S Shenoi (Eds). *IFIP advances in information and communication technology,* vol. 337: *Advances in Digital Forensics VI. DigitalForensics 2010, Hong Kong, China, January 4–6, 2010.* (pp. 3–15). Springer. https://doi.org/10.1007/978-3-642-15506-2_1

Pomerantsev, P. (2015, January 4). Inside Putin's information war. *Politico.* www .politico.com/magazine/story/2015/01/putin-russia-tv-113960

Pomerantsev, P. (2019, July 27). The disinformation age: A revolution in propaganda. *Guardian.* www.theguardian.com/books/2019/jul/27/the-disinformation-age-a-revo lution-in-propaganda

Poole, A. H. (2020). An ethical quandary that dare not speak its name: Archival privacy and access to queer erotica. *Library & Information Science Research, 42*(2). https:// doi.org/10.1016/j.lisr.2020.101020

Poon, J., & Dryja, T. (2016). *The bitcoin lightning network: Scalable off-chain instant payments* [White paper]. Lightning Network. www.bitcoinlightning.com/wp-content /uploads/2018/03/lightning-network-paper.pdf

Poovey, M. (1998). *A history of the modern fact: Problems of knowledge in the sciences of wealth and society.* University of Chicago Press.

Popovski V. (2010). Conclusion: Trust is a must in government. In G. S. Cheema & V. Popovski (Eds.), *Building trust in government: Innovations in governance reform in Asia* (pp. 234–239). United Nations University Press. https://collections.unu.edu /eserv/UNU:2502/ebrary9789280811896.pdf

Popper, N. (2016a). *Digital gold: Bitcoin and the inside story of the misfits and millionaires trying to reinvent money.* Harper Paperbacks.

Popper, N. (2016b, January 14). A Bitcoin believer's crisis of faith. *New York Times.* www.nytimes.com/2016/01/17/business/dealbook/the-bitcoin-believer-who-gave-up.html

Popper, N., & Lattman, P. (2013, April 11). Never mind Facebook; Winklevoss twins rule in digital money. *New York Times.* https://dealbook.nytimes.com/2013/04/11/as-big-investors-emerge-bitcoin-gets-ready-for-its-close-up/

Posetti, J. (2018). Combatting online abuse: When journalists and their sources are targeted. In C. Ireton & J. Posetti (Eds.) *Journalism, fake news and disinformation: Handbook for journalism education and training* (pp. 109–120). UNESCO. https://en .unesco.org/sites/default/files/journalism_fake_news_disinformation_print_ friendly_0.pdf

Posetti, J., & Matthews, A. (2018). *A short guide to the history of "fake news" and disinformation.* International Center for Journalists. www.icfj.org/sites/default/ files/2018–07/A%20Short%20Guide%20to%20History%20of%20Fake%20News% 20and%20Disinformation_ICFJ%20Final.pdf

Prasajo, E. C. D. (2015, April 21). *Strengthening innovation, prioritization, informed decision-making and the integration of policy development processes for enhanced impact* (E/C.16/2015/4) [Report presentation]. 14th Session of the United Nations Committee of Experts on Public Administration, New York. https://undocs.org/E/C .16/2015/4

Prat, N. & Madnick, S. (2007). *Evaluating and aggregating data believability across quality sub-dimensions and data lineage* (ESD Working Paper 2008–05). Massachusetts Institute of Technology: Engineering Systems Division. http://hdl .handle.net/1721.1/102858

Prat, N., & Madnick, S. (2008). Measuring data believability: A provenance approach. In *Proceedings of the 41st Annual Hawaii International Conference on System Sciences (HICSS 2008), Waikoloa, HI, USA, January 7–10, 2008* (pp. 393–393). IEEE. https://doi.org/10.1109/HICSS.2008.243

Proctor, R. N., & Schiebinger, L. (Eds.) (2008). *Agnotology: The making & unmaking of ignorance*. Stanford University Press.

Putnam, R. D. (2000). *Bowling alone: The collapse and revival of American community*. Simon & Schuster.

Rabinowitz, M., Latella, L., Stern, C., & Jost, J. T. (2016). Beliefs about childhood vaccination in the United States: Political ideology, false consensus, and the illusion of uniqueness. *PLoS ONE, 11*(7). https://doi.org/10.1371/journal.pone.0158382

Raj, J., & Owen, M. (2003). *BPMN and business process management: Introduction to the new business process modeling standard*. Popkin Software. Available at: www .omg.org/bpmn/Documents/6AD5D16960.BPMN_and_BPM.pdf

Ram, S., & Liu, J. (2006). Understanding the semantics of data provenance to support active conceptual modeling. In P. P. Chen, & L. Y. Wong (Eds.), *Lecture notes in computer science*, vol. 4512: *Active conceptual modeling of learning: Next generation learning-base system development, Proceedings of Active Conceptual Modeling-Learning (ACM-L) Workshop, Tucson, AZ, USA, November 8, 2006* (pp. 17–29). Springer. https://doi.org/10.1007/978-3-540-77503-4_3

Rampton, S. (2005, March 26). Fake news? We told you so, ten years ago. *PR Watch*. www.prwatch.org/news/2005/03/3518/fake-news-we-told-you-so-ten-years-ago

Rashidian, N. (2020, December 17). Platforms and publishers: The great pandemic funding push. *Columbia Journalism Review*. www.cjr.org/tow_center_reports/plat forms-publishers-pandemic-funding-news.php

Ratzan, L. (2004). *Understanding information systems: What they do and why we need them*. American Library Association.

Recker, J., Indulska, M., Green, P., Burton-Jones, A., & Weber, R. (2019). Information systems as representations: A review of the theory and evidence. *Journal of the Association for Information Systems, 20*(6), 735–786. https://doi.org/10.17705/1jais .00550

Reynolds, L. D., & Wilson, N. G. (1991). *Scribes and scholars: A guide to the transmission of Greek and Latin literature* (3rd ed.). Oxford University Press.

Ridge, M. [@mia_out], Scheltjens, S. [@saschel], Barnes, G. [@barnaclebarnes], @thesherrin, Clancy, E. [@clancynewyork], Ryan, T. R. [@TinaRiversRyan], Rodley, E. [@erodley], Houben, R. [@shadur], Lih, A. [@fuzheado], & @WAHa_06x36. (2021, March 13–14).The point of open access for digitised collections was to let a thousand flowers bloom . . . [Twitter thread]. *Twitter.* https://twitter.com/mia_out/status/1370728396599230464?s=21

Riedl, M. J., Whipple, K. N, & Wallace, R. (2021). Antecedents of support for social media content moderation and platform regulation: The role of presumed effects on self and others. *Information, Communication & Society.* https://doi.org/10.1080/1369118X.2021.1874040

Rochefort, A. (2020). Regulating social media platforms: A comparative policy analysis. *Communication Law and Policy,* *25*(2), 225–260. https://doi.org/10.1080/10811680.2020.1735194

Roeder, J., Eppard, P., Underwood, W., & Lauriault, T. P. (2008). Part three: Authenticity, reliability and accuracy of digital records in the artistic, scientific and governmental sectors. Domain 2 task force report. In L. Duranti & R. Preston (Eds.), *International research on permanent authentic records in electronic systems (InterPARES) 2: Experiential, interactive and dynamic records* (pp. 120–159). Associazione Nazionale Archivistica Italiana. www.interpares.org/ip2/display_file.cfm?doc=ip2_book_part_3_domain2_task_force.pdf

Rogers, C. (2015). *Virtual authenticity: Authenticity of digital records from theory to practice.* [Doctoral dissertation, University of British Columbia]. http://hdl.handle.net/2429/52722

Roon, M. (2016, June 2). Blockchains – A new source of truth. *LinkedIn.* www.linkedin.com/pulse/blockchains-new-source-truth-micha-roon/

Rorty, R. M. (Ed.). (1992). *The linguistic turn: Essays in philosophical method.* University of Chicago Press.

Rosenfeld, M. (2012). Overview of colored coins. *Bitcoil.* https://bitcoil.co.il/BitcoinX.pdf

Rosenthol, L., Parsons, A., Scouten, E., Aythora, J., MacCormack, B., England, P., Levallee, M., Dotan, J., Hanna, S., Farid, H., & Gregory, S. (2020, August). *The content authenticity initiative: Setting the standard for digital content attribution.* Coalition for Content Provenance and Authenticity. https://c2pa.org/about/resources

Rosling, H. (2018). *Factfulness: Ten reasons we're wrong about the world – and why things are better than you think.* Flatiron Books.

Rouhani, S., & Deters, R. (2019). Security, performance, and applications of smart contracts: A systematic survey. *IEEE Access,* *7,* 50759–50779. https://doi.org/10.1109/ACCESS.2019.2911031

Rousseau, D. M., Sitkin, S. B., Burt, R. S., & Camerer, C. (1998). Not so different after all: A cross-discipline view of trust. *Academy of Management Review,* *23*(3), 393–404. https://doi.org/10.5465/amr.1998.926617

Rubbi, L. N. (2018). The age of disinformation. *Fundacion UADE.* https://repositorio.uade.edu.ar/xmlui/bitstream/handle/123456789/7798/A17S28%20-%20Divulgaci%C3%B3n.pdf

Ruchansky, N., Seo, S., & Liu, Y. (2017). CSI: A hybrid deep model for fake news detection. In *CIKM '17: Proceedings of the 2017 ACM on Conference on Information and Knowledge Management, Singapore, November 6–10, 2017* (pp. 797–806). Association for Computing Machinery. https://doi.org/10.1145/3132847.3132877

Saberi, S., Kouhizadeh, M., Sarkis, J., & Shen, L. (2019). Blockchain technology and its relationships to sustainable supply chain management. *International Journal of*

Production Research, *57*(7), 2117–2135. https://doi.org/10.1080/00207543
.2018.1533261

Saha, B., & Srivastava, D. (2014). Data quality: The other face of big data. In *2014 IEEE 30th International Conference on Data Engineering (ICDE), Chicago, IL, USA, March 31–April 4, 2014, conference proceedings* (pp. 1294–1297). IEEE.

Sanitt, A. (2021, February). What sort of property is a cryptoasset? *Norton Rose Fulbright*. www.nortonrosefulbright.com/en/knowledge/publications/26ade77a/what-sort-of-property-is-a-cryptoasset#1

Saracevic, T. (2017). Information Science. In J. D. MacDonald & M. Levine-Clark (Eds.), *Encyclopedia of library and information science* (4th ed.) (pp. 2216–2231). CRC Press.

Sas, C., & Khairuddin, I. E. (2017). Design for trust: An exploration of the challenges and opportunities of bitcoin users. In *Proceedings of the 2017 ACM SIGCHI conference on Human Factors in Computing Systems, CHI'17, Denver, CO, USA, May 6 – 11, 2017* (pp. 6499–6510). Association for Computing Machinery.

Scaling Bitcoin. (n.d.). *Scaling Bitcoin workshops for the engineering and academic community*. Scaling Bitcoin. https://scalingbitcoin.org

Schellenberg, T. R. (1956). *Modern archives*. University of Chicago Press.

Schick, N. (2020). *Deepfakes: The coming infocalypse*. Twelve.

Searle, J. R. (1985). *Expression and meaning: Studies in the theory of speech acts*. Cambridge University Press.

Searle, J. R. (1999). *Mind, language and society: Philosophy in the real world*. Basic Books.

Searle, J. R. (2010). *Making the social world: The structure of human civilization*. Oxford University Press.

Segregated Witness. (2021, March 14). *Bitcoin Wiki*. https://en.bitcoin.it/wiki/Segregated_Witness

Seligman, A. B. (1997). *The problem of trust*. Princeton University Press.

Shankaranarayanan, G., & Blake, R. (2017). From content to context: The evolution and growth of data quality research. *Journal of Data and Information Quality*, *8*(2), Article 9. https://doi.org/10.1145/2996198

Shankaranarayanan, G., Iyer, B., & Stoddard, D. (2012). Quality of social media data and implications of social media for data quality. In *Proceedings of the 17th International Conference on Information Quality, IQ 2012, Paris, France, November 16–17, 2012* (pp. 311–325). MIT.

Shapin, S. (1994). *A social history of truth*. Chicago University Press.

Shera, J. H. (1961). What is librarianship? *Louisiana Library Association*, *24*(3), 95–97.

Shera, J. H. (1968). An epistemological foundation for library science. In E. B. Montgomery (Ed.), *The foundations of access to knowledge: A symposium*. Syracuse University Press.

Shera, J. H. (1972). *The foundations of education for librarianship*. Becker and Hayes.

Shrestha, A. K., & Vassileva, A. (2019) User acceptance of usable blockchain-based research data sharing system: An extended TAM-based study. In *2019 First IEEE International Conference on Trust, Privacy and Security in Intelligent Systems and Applications (TPS-ISA), Los Angeles, CA, USA, December 12–14, 2019* (pp. 203–208). IEEE.

Siegel, D. (2016, June 19). Understanding the DAO hack for journalists. *Medium.* https://pullnews.medium.com/understanding-the-dao-hack-for-journalists-2312dd43e993

Silverman, C. (2016, November 16). This analysis shows how viral fake election news stories outperformed real news on Facebook. *BuzzFeed News.* www.buzzfeednews.com/article/craigsilverman/viral-fake-election-news-outperformed-real-news-on-facebook

Simmhan, Y. L., Plale, B., & Gannon, D. (2005). A survey of data provenance in e-science. *ACM SIGMOD Record, 34*(3), 31–36. https://doi.org/10.1145/1084805.1084812

Simon, H. A. (2013). *Administrative behavior* (4th ed.). Simon and Schuster.

Singh, A., & Chatterjee, K. (2017). Cloud security issues and challenges: A survey. *Journal of Network and Computer Applications, 79*, 88–115. https://doi.org/10.1016/j.jnca.2016.11.027

Skarpelis, A. (2019). Life on file: archival epistemology as theory. *Comparative and Historical Sociology.* http://chs.asa-comparative-historical.org/life-on-file-archival-epistemology-as-theory

Skarpelis, A. K. M. (2020). Life on file: Archival epistemology and theory. *Qualitative Sociology, 43*, 385–405. https://doi.org/10.1007/s11133-020-09460-1

Smart, P. R., & Shadbolt, N. R. (2015). Social machines. In *Encyclopedia of information science and technology* (3rd ed.) (pp. 6855–6862). IGI Global.

Smit, F., Glaudemans, A., & Jonker, R. (Eds.). (2017). *Archives in liquid times.* Stichting Archiefpublicaties.

Smith, A. (1776). *The wealth of nations.* W. Strahan & T. Cadell.

Smith, D. E. (1990). *Texts, facts and femininity: Exploring the relations of ruling.* Routledge.

Sozeri, E. K. (2020, February 28). How the alt-right's PizzaGate conspiracy hid real scandal in Turkey. *daily dot.* www.dailydot.com/debug/pizzagate-alt-right-turkey-trolls-child-abuse

Spinney, L. (2017). How Facebook, fake news and friends are warping your memory. *Nature, 543* (7644). www.nature.com/news/how-facebook-fake-news-and-friends-are-warping-your-memory-1.21596

Stančić, H. (Ed.). (2020). *Trust and records in an open digital environment.* Routledge.

State of Arizona. (2017). Signatures; Electronic Transactions; Blockchain Technology, HB 2417, 53rd Legislature, 1st Regular Session (AZ 2017). https://legiscan.com/AZ/text/HB2417/id/1588180/Arizona-2017-HB2417-Chaptered.html

State of Vermont. (2016). An Act Relating to Miscellaneous Economic Development Provisions, (Act 157), 2015/2016 Session (VT 2016). https://legislature.vermont.gov/Documents/2016/Docs/ACTS/ACT157/ACT157%20As%20Enacted.pdf

Steele, C. W. J., Hannigan, T. R., Glaser, V. L., Toubiana, M., & Gehman, J. (2020). Macrofoundations: Exploring the institutionally situated nature of activity. In C. W. J. Steele, T. R. Hannigan. V. L. Glaser, M. Toubiana, & J. Gehman (Eds.), *Macrofoundations: Exploring the institutionally situated nature of activity* (Research in the sociology of organizations, vol. 68) (pp. 3–16). Emerald Publishing.

Stenberg, G. (2006). Conceptual and perceptual factors in the picture superiority effect. *European Journal of Cognitive Psychology, 18*(6), 813–847. https://doi.org/10.1080/09541440500412361

Stoler, A. (2002). Colonial archives and the arts of governance. *Archival Science, 2*(1/2), 87–109. https://doi.org/10.1007/BF02435632

Stoler, A. L. (2010). *Along the archival grain: Epistemic anxieties and colonial common sense.* Princeton University Press.

Storch, S. (1998). Diplomatics: Modern archival method or medieval artifact. *American Archivist, 61*(2), 365–383. https://doi.org/10.17723/aarc.61.2.h0358316qn85p2lm

Straits Times. (2017, January 6). Indonesia to set up agency to combat fake news. *Straits Times.* www.straitstimes.com/asia/se-asia/indonesia-to-set-up-agency-to-combat-fake-news-0

Straub, D. W. (2012). Editor's comments: Does MIS have native theories? *MIS Quarterly, 36*(2), iii–xii. https://doi.org/10.2307/41703457

Suisani, A., Clifford, A., Stone, A., Beijnoff, E., Rizun, P., Tschipper, P., Federova, A., Feng, C., Lemieux, V., & Matthews, S. (2017). *Measuring maximum sustained transaction throughput on a global network of Bitcoin nodes.* Paper presented at Scaling Bitcoin 2017 "Scaling the Edge," November 4–5, 2017, Stanford, CA, USA.

Sullivan, H. (2015, February 9). What can governments and leaders do when trust evaporates? *The Conversation.* http://theconversation.com/what-can-governments-and-leaders-do-when-trust-evaporates-37333

Sunarya, P. A., Henderi, Sulistiawati, Khoirunisa, A., & Nursaputri, P. (2020). Blockchain family deed certificate for privacy and data security. In *ICIC '20: Proceeding of the 5th International Conference on Informatics and Computing, Gorontalo, Indonesia, November 3–4, 2020* (pp. 361–365). IEEE. https://doi.org/10.1109/ICIC50835.2020.9288528

Sundar, S. S. (2008). The MAIN model: A heuristic approach to understanding technology effects on credibility. In M. J. Metzger & A. J. Flanagin (Eds.), *Digital media, youth, and credibility* (pp. 73–100). John D. MacArthur Foundation Series on Digital Media and Learning. MIT Press. https://doi.org/10.1162/dmal.9780262562324.073

Swan, M. (2015). *Blockchain: Blueprint for a new economy.* O'Reilly.

Sward, A., Vecna, I., & Stonedahl, F. (2018). Data insertion in bitcoin's blockchain. *Ledger, 3.* https://doi.org/10.5195/ledger.2018.101

Szabo, N. (1994). Smart contract. *PiPiWiki.* https://pipiwiki.com/wiki/Agoric_computing

Szabo, N. (1997). Formalizing and securing relationships on public networks. *First Monday.* https://firstmonday.org/ojs/index.php/fm/article/download/548/469

Szabo, N. (2017, February 9). Money, blockchains, and social scalability. *Unenumerated.* http://unenumerated.blogspot.com/2017/02/money-blockchains-and-social-scalability.html

Szalachowski, P. (2019). PADVA: A blockchain-based TLS notary service. In *Proceedings of the 2019 IEEE 25th International Conference on Parallel and Distributed Systems (ICPADS 2019), Tianjin, China, December 4–6, 2019* (pp. 836–843). IEEE. https://doi.org/10.1109/ICPADS47876.2019.00124

Tandoc Jr, E. C., Lim, Z. W., & Ling, R. (2018). Defining "fake news": A typology of scholarly definitions. *Digital Journalism, 6*(2), 137–153. https://doi.org/10.1080/21670811.2017.1360143

Tapscott, D., & Tapscott, A. (2016). *Blockchain revolution: How the technology behind bitcoin is changing money, business, and the world.* Penguin.

Taylor, C. (2004). What is a "social imaginary"? In C. Taylor, *Modern social imaginaries* (pp. 23–30). Duke University Press.

Theiss-Morse, E., & Hibbing, J. R. (2005). Citizenship and civic engagement. *Annual Review of Political Science, 8,* 227–249. https://doi.org/10.1146/annurev.polisci.8.082103.104829

Thielman, S. (2016, August 22). Same Russian hackers likely breached the Olympic drug-testing agency and DNC. *Guardian.* www.theguardian.com/technology/2016/aug/22/russian-hackers-world-anti-doping-agency-dnc-hack-fancy-bear

Thomassen, T. (2015). Archival science. In L. Duranti & P. C. Franks, *Encyclopedia of archival science* (pp. 84–86). Rowman & Littlefield.

Tobin, A., & Reed, D. (2016). Inevitable rise of self-sovereign identity. *Sovrin Foundation.* https://sovrin.org/library/inevitable-rise-of-self-sovereign-identity/

Tout, T. F. (1919). Mediaeval forgers and forgeries. *Bulletin of the John Rylands Library, 5*(3–4), 208–234. www.jstor.org/stable/10.2307/community.28210958

Treat, D. (2016, September 20/21). Accenture: Absolute immutability will slow blockchain progress. *Coindesk.* www.coindesk.com/absolute-immutability-will-slow-permissioned-blockchain-progress

Treisman, A. (1985). Preattentive processing in vision. *Computer Vision, Graphics, and Image Processing, 31*(2), 156–177. https://doi.org/10.1016/S0734-189X(85)80004-9

Truby, J. (2018). Decarbonizing Bitcoin: Law and policy choices for reducing the energy consumption of blockchain technologies and digital currencies. *Energy Research & Social Science, 44,* 399–410. https://doi.org/10.1016/j.erss.2018.06.009

Turner, F. C., & Martz, J. D. (1997). Institutional confidence and democratic consolidation in Latin America. *Studies in Comparative International Development, 32*(3), 65–84. https://doi.org/10.1007/BF02687331

Turner, S. (2019). The philosophical origins of classical sociology of knowledge. In M. Fricker, P. J. Graham, D. Henderson, & N .J. L. L. Pedersen (Eds.), *The Routledge handbook of social epistemology* (pp. 31–39). Routledge.

Tworek, H., & Leerssen, P. (2019). *An analysis of Germany's NetxDG law.* Transatlantic High Level Working Group on Content Moderation Online and Freedom of Expression. www.ivir.nl/publicaties/download/NetzDG_Tworek_Leerssen_April_2019.pdf

Uscinski, J. E. (2015). The epistemology of fact checking (is still naïve): Rejoinder to Amazeen. *Critical Review, 27*(2), 243–252. https://doi.org/10.1080/08913811.2015.1055892

Uscinski, J. E., & Butler, R. W. (2013). The epistemology of fact checking. *Critical Review, 25*(2), 162–180. https://doi.org/10.1080/08913811.2013.843872

Vaccari, C., & Chadwick, A. (2020). Deepfakes and disinformation: Exploring the impact of synthetic political video on deception, uncertainty, and trust in news. *Social Media + Society, 6*(1). https://doi.org/10.1177/2056305120903408

Vaidhyanathan, S. (2012). *The Googlization of everything (and why we should worry).* University of California Press.

van Bussel, G .J. (2017). The theoretical framework of the "archive-as-is." An organization oriented view on archives. Part I. Setting the stage: Enterprise information management and archival theories. In F. Smit, A. Glaudemans, & R. Jonker (Eds.), *Archives in liquid times* (pp. 17–41). Stichting Archiefpublicaties.

Van der Linden, C. (2020, August 12). Canada is not immune to the politics of coronavirus masks. *The Conversation.* https://theconversation.com/canada-is-not-immune-to-the-politics-of-coronavirus-masks-144110

Van de Walle, S., Van Roosbroek, S., & Bouckaert, G. (2008). Trust in the public sector: Is there any evidence for a long-term decline? *International Review of Administrative Sciences, 74*(1), 47–64. https://doi.org/10.1177/0020852307085733

van Elswyk, P. (2019). Testimony and grammatical evidentials. In M. Fricker, P. J. Graham, D. Henderson, & N. J. L. L. Pedersen (Eds.), *The Routledge handbook of social epistemology* (pp. 135–144). Routledge.

van Ruth, S. M., Luning, P. A., Silvis, I. C. J., Yang, Y., & Huisman, W. (2018). Differences in fraud vulnerability in various food supply chains and their tiers. *Food Control, 84*, 375–381. https://doi.org/10.1016/j.foodcont.2017.08.020

van Wirdum, A. (2017, August 23). The long road to SegWit: How Bitcoin's biggest protocol upgrade became reality. *Bitcoin Magazine.* https://bitcoinmagazine.com/articles/long-road-segwit-how-bitcoins-biggest-protocol-upgrade-became-reality

Varol, O., Ferrara, E., Menczer, F., & Flammini, A. (2017). Early detection of promoted campaigns on social media. *EPJ Data Science, 6*(1). https://doi.org/10.1140/epjds/s13688-017-0111-y

Vigna, P., & Casey, M. J. (2018). *The truth machine: The blockchain and the future of everything.* Picador.

Vincent, J. (2018, August 23). Browser plug-ins that spot fake news show the difficulty of tackling the "information apocalypse." *The Verge.* www.theverge.com/2018/8/23/17383912/fake-news-browser-plug-ins-ai-information-apocalypse

Vivek, S. K., Yashank, R. S., Prashanth, Y., Yashas, N., & Namratha, M. (2020). E-voting System using Hyperledger Sawtooth. In *2020 International Conference on Advances in Computing, Communication & Materials (ICACCM), Dehradun, India, August 21–22, 2020* (pp. 29–35). IEEE. https://doi.org/10.1109/ICACCM50413.2020.9212945

Vogels, E. A., Perrin, A., & Anderson, M. (2020, August 19). *Most Americans think social media sites censor political viewpoints.* Pew Research Center. www.pewresearch.org/internet/2020/08/19/most-americans-think-social-media-sites-censor-political-viewpoints

Von Bertalanffy, L. (1950). An outline of general system theory. *British Journal for the Philosophy of Science, 1*(2), 134–165. https://doi.org/10.1093/bjps/I.2.134

Von Bertalanffy, L. (1968). *General system theory: Foundations, development, applications.* Braziller.

von Ranke L. (1824) *Die Geschichten der romanischen und germanischen Völker von 1494 bis 1535* [The history of the Latin and Teutonic nations, 1494–1535]. G. Reimer.

Voskobojnikov, A., Obada-Obieh, B., Huang, Y., & Beznosov, K. (2020). Surviving the cryptojungle: Perception and management of risk among North American cryptocurrency (non) users. In J. Bonneau & N. Heninger (Eds.), *Lecture notes in computer science*, vol. 12059: *Financial Cryptography and Data Security, 24th International Conference, FC 2020, Koto Kinabalu, Malaysia, February 10–14, 2020, revised selected papers* (pp. 595–614). Springer.

Vosoughi, S., Roy, D., & Aral, S. (2018). The spread of true and false news online. *Science, 359*(6380), 1146–1151. https://doi.org/10.1126/science.aap9559

WADA [World Anti-Doping Agency]. (2016, September 23). Cyber hack update: Data leak concerning 41 athletes from 13 countries and 17 sports. World Anti-Doping Agency. www.wada-ama.org/en/media/news/2016–09/cyber-hack-update-data-leak-concerning-41-athletes-from-13-countries-and-17

Walch, A. (2015). The bitcoin blockchain as financial market infrastructure: A consideration of operational risk. *New York University Journal of Legislation & Public Policy*, *18*, 837–893. Available at SSRN: https://ssrn.com/abstract=2579482

Walch, A. (2017a). The path of the blockchain lexicon (and the law). *Review of Banking & Financial Law*, *36*(2), 713–765. www.bu.edu/rbfl/files/2017/09/p729.pdf

Walch, A. (2017b). Blockchain's treacherous vocabulary: One more challenge for regulators. *Journal of Internet Law*, *21*(2),1, 9–16. Available at SSRN: https://ssrn .com/abstract=3019328

Walch, A. (2018). Open-source operational risk: should public blockchains serve as financial market infrastructures? In D. L. K. Chuen & R. Deng (Eds.), *Handbook of blockchain, digital finance, and inclusion*, vol. 2: *ChinaTech, Mobile Security, and Distributed Ledger* (pp. 243–269). Academic Press.

Walter, N., Cohen, J., Holbert, R. L., & Morag, Y. (2020). Fact-checking: A meta-analysis of what works and for whom. *Political Communication*, *37*(3), 350–375. https://doi.org/10.1080/10584609.2019.1668894

Wand, Y., & Weber, R. (1995). On the deep structure of information systems. *Information Systems Journal*, *5*(3), 203–223. https://doi.org/10.1111/j.1365-2575 .1995.tb00108.x

Wang, C-C. (2020). Fake news and related concepts: Definitions and recent research development. *Contemporary Management Research*, *16*(3), 145–174. https://doi.org /10.7903/cmr.20677

Wang, S., Zhang, D., & Zhang, Y. (2019). Blockchain-based personal health records sharing scheme with data integrity verifiable. *IEEE Access*, *7*, 102887–102901. 10.1109/ACCESS.2019.2931531

Wang, X., Li, J., Kuang, X., Tan, Y-A., & Li, J. (2019). The security of machine learning in an adversarial setting: A survey. *Journal of Parallel and Distributed Computing*, *130*, 12–23. https://doi.org/10.1016/j.jpdc.2019.03.003

Warburton, N. (Ed.) (2018, March 14). Say goodbye to the information age: It's all about reputation now. *Aeon*. https://aeon.co/ideas/say-goodbye-to-the-information-age-its-all-about-reputation-now

Ward, M., Grinstein, G., & Keim, D. (2010), *Interactive data visualization: Foundations, techniques, and applications*. A K Peters.

Wardle, C. (2018). The need for smarter definitions and practical, timely empirical research on information disorder. *Digital Journalism*, *6*(8), 951–963. https://doi.org /10.1080/21670811.2018.1502047

Wardle, C. (2019). Misinformation has created a new world disorder. *Scientific American*, September, 88–91. www.scientificamerican.com/article/misinformation-has-created-a-new-world-disorder

Wardle, C., & Derakhshan, H. (2017). *Information disorder: Toward an interdisciplinary framework for research and policy making* (Report No. DGI (2017) 09). Council of Europe. https://tverezo.info/wp-content/uploads/2017/11/PREMS-162317-GBR -2018-Report-desinformation-A4-BAT.pdf

Warner, M. (2012). Cybersecurity: A pre-history. *Intelligence and National Security, 27* (5), 781–799. https://doi.org/10.1080/02684527.2012.708530

Warren, M. E. (2006). Democracy and deceit: Regulating appearances of corruption. *American Journal of Political Science, 50*(1), 160–174. www.jstor.org/stable/3694263

Weeks, B. E. (2015) Emotions, partisanship, and misperceptions: How anger and anxiety moderate the effect of partisan bias on susceptibility to political misinformation. *Journal of Communication, 65*(4), 699–719. https://doi.org/10.1111/jcom.12164

Weinberger, D. (2007). *Everything is miscellaneous: The power of the new digital disorder.* Macmillan.

Wempen, F. (2014). *Computing fundamentals*: IC3 edition. Wiley.

Wendling, M. (2016, December 22). The saga of "Pizzagate": The fake story that shows how conspiracy theories spread. *BBC News.* www.bbc.com/news/blogs-trending-38156985

Werbach, K. (2018). Trust, but verify: Why the blockchain needs the law. *Berkeley Technology Law Journal, 33*(2), 487–550. http://dx.doi.org/10.15779/Z38H41JM9 N

Werbach, K. (2019). *Summary: Blockchain, the rise of trustless trust?* Wharton PPI B-School for Public Policy Seminar Summaries. https://repository.upenn.edu/cgi/viewcontent.cgi?article=1002&context=pennwhartonppi_bschool

West, D. M. (2017, December 18). *Report: How to combat fake news and disinformation.* Brookings Institute. www.brookings.edu/research/how-to-combat-fake-news-and-disinformation

Wiggers, K. (2019, December 11). Facebook, Microsoft, and others launch deepfake detection challenge. *Venture Beat, The Machine.* https://venturebeat.com/2019/12/11/facebook-microsoft-and-others-launch-deepfake-detection-challenge

Williams, A. (2018, February 9). 2004: When fake news was cool. *New York Times.* www.nytimes.com/2018/02/09/style/2004-when-fake-news-was-cool.html

Williams, C. (2005). Diplomatic attitudes: From Mabillon to metadata. *Journal of the Society of Archivists, 26*(1), 1–24. http://dx.doi.org/10.1080/00039810500047417

Williamson, O. E. (1993). Calculativeness, trust, and economic organization. *Journal of Law and Economics, 36*(1), 453–486. https://doi.org/10.1086/467284

Wilson, M. I., Kellerman, A., & Corey, K. E. (2013). *Global information society: Technology, knowledge, and mobility.* Rowman & Littlefield.

Winner, L. (1978). *Autonomous technology: Technics-out-of-control as a theme in political thought.* MIT Press.

Winner, L. (1985). Do artifacts have politics? In D. Mackenzie & J. Wajcman (Eds.), *The social shaping of technology.* Open University Press.

Witkowski, T. H. (1991). Promise them anything: A cultural history of cigarette advertising health claims. *Current Issues and Research in Advertising, 13*(1–2), 393–409. https://doi.org/10.1080/01633392.1991.10504973

Witten, I. B., & Knudsen, E. I. (2005). Why seeing is believing: Merging auditory and visual worlds. *Neuron, 48*(3), 489–496. https://doi.org/10.1016/j.neuron.2005.10.020

Wolfson, R. (2020, June 25). From sea to table: Norway's seafood industry hooks into IBM blockchain. *CoinTelegraph.* https://cointelegraph.com/news/from-sea-to-table-norways-seafood-industry-hooks-into-ibm-blockchain

Wood, G. (2016). *Polkadot: Vision for a heterogeneous multi-chain framework* [White Paper]. Polkadot. https://polkadot.network/PolkaDotPaper.pdf

Woodall, A., & Ringel, S. (2020). Blockchain archival discourse: Trust and the imaginaries of digital preservation. *New Media & Society, 22*(12), 2200–2217. https://doi.org/10.1177/1461444819888756

Woolley, S. C., & Guilbeault, D. R. (2017). *Computational propaganda in the United States of America: Manufacturing consensus online.* (Computational Propaganda Research Project Working Paper No. 2017.5). University of Oxford. https://blogs.oii.ox.ac.uk/politicalbots/wp-content/uploads/sites/89/2017/06/Comprop-USA.pdf

Wu, T. (2017). *The attention merchants: The epic scramble to get inside our heads.* Vintage.

Wüst, K., & Gervais, A. (2018). Do you need a blockchain? In *2018 Crypto Valley Conference on Blockchain Technology (CVCBT), Zug, Switzerland, June 20–22, 2018* (pp. 45–54). IEEE.

Xiao, L., & Chen, S. (2020). Misinformation in the Chinese Weibo. In G. Meiselwitz (Ed.), *Lecture notes in computer science,* vol. 12194: *12th International Conference on Social Computing and Social Media (SCSM 2020), held as part of the 22nd International Conference on Human-Computer Interaction (HCII 2020), Copenhagen, Denmark, July 19–24, 2020* (pp. 407–418). Springer. https://doi.org/10.1007/978-3-030-49570-1_28

Xie, R., Wang, Y., Tan, M., Zhu, W., Yang, Z., Wu, J., & Jeon, G. (2020). Ethereum-blockchain-based technology of decentralized smart contract certificate system. *IEEE Internet of Things Magazine, 3*(2), 44–50. https://doi.org/10.1109/IOTM.0001.1900094

Yang, W., Aghasian, E., Garg, S., Herbert, D., Disiuta, L., & Kang, B. (2019). A survey on blockchain-based internet service architecture: Requirements, challenges, trends, and future. *IEEE Access, 7,* 75845–75872. https://doi.org/10.1109/ACCESS.2019.2917562

Yang, X., & Li, W. (2020). A zero-knowledge-proof-based digital identity management scheme in blockchain. *Computers & Security, 99.* https://doi.org/10.1016/j.cose.2020.102050

Yang, X., Pei, X., Wang, M., Li, T., & Wang, C. (2020). Multi-replica and multi-cloud data public audit scheme based on blockchain. *IEEE Access, 8,* 144809–144822. https://doi.org/10.1109/ACCESS.2020.3014510

Yeo, G. (2007). Concepts of record (1): Evidence, information, and persistent representations. *American Archivist, 70*(2), 315–343. www.jstor.org/stable/40294573

Yeo, G. (2008). Concepts of record (2): Prototypes and boundary objects. *American Archivist, 71*(1), 118–143. www.jstor.org/stable/40294496

Yeo, G. (2012). Bringing things together: Aggregate records in a digital age. *Archivaria, 74,* 43–91. https://archivaria.ca/index.php/archivaria/article/view/13407

Yeo, G. (2013). Trust and context in cyberspace. *Archives and Records, 34*(2), 214–234. https://doi.org/10.1080/23257962.2013.825207

Yeo, G. (2015). Record(s). In L. Duranti & P. C. Franks (Eds.), *Encyclopedia of archival science* (pp. 315–319). Rowman & Littlefield.

Yeo, G. (2017). Information, records, and the philosophy of speech acts. In F. Smit, A. Glaudemans, & R. Jonker (Eds.), *Archives in liquid times* (pp. 92–118). Stichting Archiefpublicaties.

Yeo, G. (2018). *Records, information and data: Exploring the role of record-keeping in an information culture.* Facet Publishing.

Yeung, K. (2019). Regulation by blockchain: The emerging battle for supremacy between the code of law and code as law. *Modern Law Review, 82*(2), 207–239. www.modernlawreview.co.uk/march-2019/regulation-blockchain-emerging-battle-supremacy-code-law-code-law/

Yocom-Piatt, J. (2015, December 15). Decred: Rethink digital currency. *Company Zero.* https://blog.companyzero.com/2015/12/decred-rethink-digital-currency/

Yutia, S. N., & Rahardjo, B. (2019). Design of a blockchain-based e-tendering system: A case study in LPSE. In *Proceedings: ICISS 2019: International Conference on ICT for Smart Society 2019: Innovation and Transformation Toward Smart Region, Bandung, Indonesia, November 19–20, 2019.* IEEE. https://doi.org/10.1109/ICISS48059.2019.8969824

Zhang, L., & Clark, C. (Eds.). (2018). *Affect, emotion, and rhetorical persuasion in mass communication.* Routledge.

Zhang, X., & Ghorbani, A. A. (2020). An overview of online fake news: Characterization, detection and discussion. *Information Processing & Management, 57*(2). https://doi.org/10.1016/j.ipm.2019.03.004

Zhou, X., & Zafarani, R. (2020). A survey of fake news: Fundamental theories, detection methods, and opportunities. *ACM Computing Surveys, 53*(5), 1–40. https://doi.org/10.1145/3395046

Zhou, X., Zafarani, R., Shu, K., & Liu, H. (2019). Fake news: Fundamental theories, detection strategies and challenges. In *WDSM'19: Proceedings of the Twelfth ACM international Conference on Web Search and Data Mining, Melbourne, VIC, Australia, February 11–15, 2019* (pp. 836–837). Association for Computing Machinery.

Index

Printed in the United States
by Baker & Taylor Publisher Services